RUSSIA AND THE
USSR, 1855–1991

Russia and the USSR, 1855–1991 explores all the key aspects of this extremely important period in Russian history. Stephen J. Lee examines and compares the ideologies of Tsarist autocracy and Soviet Communism and the opposition to these regimes. The 1917 Revolution, the use of repression and terror by these regimes and the impact of the First and Second World Wars on Russia are also analysed. A major feature of the book is the guidance provided for students preparing for the synoptic module of A2 exams.

Stephen J. Lee is Head of History at Bromsgrove School. His many publications include *European Dictatorships* (2nd edition, 2000) and, in this series, *Gladstone and Disraeli* (2005) and *Lenin and Revolutionary Russia* (2003).

QUESTIONS AND ANALYSIS IN HISTORY

Edited by Stephen J. Lee, Sean Lang and Jocelyn Hunt

Other titles in this series:

WITHDRAWN

RUSSIA AND THE USSR, 1855–1991

Autocracy and Dictatorship

STEPHEN J. LEE

Routledge
Taylor & Francis Group

LONDON AND NEW YORK

First published 2006
by Routledge
2–4 Park Square, Milton Park, Abingdon, Oxon OX14 4RN

Simultaneously published in the USA and Canada
by Routledge
270 Madison Ave, New York, NY 10016

Routledge is an imprint of the Taylor & Francis Group

© 2006 Stephen J. Lee

Typeset in Akzidenz Grotesk and Perpetua by
Florence Production Ltd, Stoodleigh, Devon
Printed and bound in Great Britain by
TJ International Ltd, Padstow, Cornwall

British Library Cataloguing in Publication Data
A catalogue record for this book is available from the British Library

Library of Congress Cataloging in Publication Data
Lee, Stephen J., 1945–
    Russia and the USSR, 1855–1991: autocracy and dictatorship/
    Stephen J. Lee.
        p. cm. – (Questions and analysis in history)
    Includes bibliographical references.
    1. Russia – Politics and government – 1801–1917.   2. Soviet Union –
    Politics and government.   3. Despotism – Russia.   4. Dictatorship – Soviet
    Union.   5. Authoritarianism – Soviet Union.   6. Totalitarianism – History –
    20th century.   I. Title.   II. Series.
    DK61.L42 2005
    947.08 – dc22   2005020925

ISBN10: 0–415–33576–0   ISBN13: 978–0–415–33576–8 (hbk)
ISBN10: 0–415–33577–9   ISBN13: 978–0–415–33577–5 (pbk)

CONTENTS

3   Political parties   51

4   Repression and terror   71

ILLUSTRATIONS

ACKNOWLEDGEMENTS

Russia: The Tsarist and Soviet Legacy, 2nd edition, Edward Acton, Pearson Education Ltd © Edward Acton, 1995.

The publisher will be glad to make suitable arrangements with any copyright holders whom it has not been possible to contact.

INTRODUCTION

The *Questions and Analysis* series was established as a series based on interpretation. Most of the titles cover a brief period in detail, each chapter with a *Background*, two *Analyses* and two sets of *Sources*. These meet the needs of students for A-Level and some undergraduate courses; they are also intended to interest the general reader.

This volume covers a much longer timescale, but in linear strands rather than in more broadly based topics. This is intended to fit the 'synoptic' approach, which has become an increasingly common element in more advanced history courses. *Russia and the USSR, 1855–1991: Autocracy and Dictatorship* therefore overlaps other volumes on Russia, such as *Lenin and Revolutionary Russia* and *Stalin and the Soviet Union*, but provides a different perspective. It focuses on issues across a period of 150 years, in each case indicating examples of overall continuity and change between Tsarist Russia and the Soviet Union. These issues comprise ideology, constitutions, political parties, terror, nationalities, war, the economy and social classes.

There is a common pattern throughout this volume:

Analysis 1 replaces the introductory factual background of the other titles in the series. Instead, it defines the scope of the issue (for example, ideology) and summarises the main developments from the beginning of the period to the end.

continued

Analysis 2 provides, within the broader timescale of 1855–1991, a more detailed analysis of the issue within two periods; an example would be Nicholas II (1894–1917) and Stalin (1929–53). These can be seen as separate from each other or, alternatively, as *end-on* comparisons.

Analysis 3 builds on the approaches of the other two to provide a fully integrated synoptic survey of the whole issue. The emphasis, however, is on *comparative* analysis between regimes (Tsarist Russia and the Soviet Union) and individuals (Alexander II and Alexander III, Alexander III and Stalin, Khrushchev and Alexander II, etc.) rather than on the more chronological approach shown in Analyses 1 and 2. This should provide for the needs of synoptic analysis at the highest level.

Sources 1 and *Sources 2* are based on more specific periods, some with the focus on historical developments and based mainly on primary sources, others exploring historiographical controversy through secondary works. It is also intended to provide references to key historiographical issues in some of the Analyses – although these are intentionally less detailed than in the previously mentioned books in the series on Lenin and Stalin.

This approach is based on practical experience of teaching students the ever-changing techniques of historical analysis – and also on a belief that the most interesting perspectives on historical issues result from frequent changes in the vantage points from which they are surveyed.

OUTLINE CHRONOLOGY

(Explanations of terms and initials can be found in the Glossary starting on p. 190.)

REGIMES

To 1917	Tsarist or Imperial Russia
1917 (March to October)	Provisional Government
1917 (October) to 1991 (December)	Soviet Russia and USSR (from 1924)

RULERS AND LEADERS

Tsars

1825–55	Nicholas I
1855–81	Alexander II
1881–94	Alexander III
1894–1917 (March)	Nicholas II

Provisional Government

1917
  (March to July)   Lvov

1917
  (July to October) Kerensky

Soviet leaders

1917 (October) to 1924	Lenin
1924–29	Succession struggle involving Stalin, Trotsky, Kamenev, Zinoviev, Bukharin, Rykov, Tomsky
1929–53	Stalin
1953–5	Succession involving Khrushchev, Bulganin, Malenkov
1955–64	Khrushchev
1964–82	Brezhnev
1982–4	Andropov
1984–5	Chernenko
1985–91	Gorbachev

Presidents of post-Soviet Russian Federation

1992–2000	Yeltsin
2000–	Putin

REVOLUTIONS, CONSTITUTIONS AND LEGISLATURES

1864	Provincial *zemstva* established
1870	Urban *dumas* established
1881	Alexander II about to sign documents for Consultative Assembly
1905	Revolution and formation of St Petersburg Soviet

1905	October Manifesto issued by Nicholas II
1906	Fundamental Laws establishing a new constitution.
1906–7	First and Second Dumas dissolved
1907	Electoral Law restricting the franchise
1907–12	Third Duma
1912–17	Fourth Duma
1917	March Revolution overthrew Tsarist regime
1917 (March)	Formation of Provisional Committee of the Duma; Provisional Committee formed Provisional Government
1917 (March)	Establishment of Petrograd Soviet
1917 (October)	Overthrow of Provisional Government by Bolsheviks
1917 (November)	Bolsheviks announced elections for Constituent Assembly after seizing power in October
1918	Constituent Assembly elected. Immediately dissolved by Lenin
1918	Constitution of the Russian Soviet Federated Socialist Republic (RSFSR)
1922	Treaty signed for new federal constitution
1924	Constitution of the Union of Soviet Socialist Republics (USSR)
1936	Constitution (Stalin)
1977	Constitution (Brezhnev)
1989	Constitution (Gorbachev)
1989	Sakharov's amendment
1991 (August)	Failure of attempted coup against Gorbachev
1991 (31 January)	End of Soviet Union
1992	Post-Soviet constitutions established in successor states
1992	Establishment of Commonwealth of Independent States (CIS)

POLITICAL PARTIES

1876	Land and Liberty (Populist movement) split Black Partition and People's Will (*Narodnaya Volya*)
1898	Formation of Russian Social Democratic Labour Party
1900	Formation of Socialist Revolutionaries (SRs)
1903	Split between Bolsheviks and Mensheviks at Brussels and London Congresses.
1905	October Manifesto: acceptance of political parties by Nicholas II
1906	Fundamental Laws
1906	Parties legalised: *Revolutionary left*: Social Democrats (Bolsheviks and Mensheviks), SRs *Constitutionalists*: Constitutional Democrats (Kadets) and Octobrists *Reactionary right*: Union of Russian Men and Union of Russian People *Sectional groups*: representing nationalities, business
1906	Kadets and SRs confronted government in First Duma
1907	Kadets and Social Democrats in conflict with government in Second Duma
1907	Change in electoral system reduced size of left in Duma
1907–12	Parties more compliant in Third Duma
1912–17	Parties more active in Fourth Duma
1915	All left-wing parties (SRs, Mensheviks, Bolsheviks) opposed involvement in First World War
1915	Formation of Progressive Bloc by Kadets and Octobrists

1917 (March)	Influence of SRs and Mensheviks on Revolution; Kadets and Octobrists behind formation of Provisional Committee of the Duma
1917 (March)	Formation of Petrograd Soviet (SRs, Mensheviks and other moderate socialists)
1917 (April)	Return of Lenin to Petrograd
1917 (July)	Failure of Bolshevik-inspired uprising against Provisional Government
1917 (August to October)	Growing strength of Bolsheviks
1917 (October)	Bolshevik majorities in Petrograd and Moscow Soviets
1917 (October)	Bolsheviks seized power, assisted by Left SRs and Menshevik Internationalists
1918 (January)	Lenin's dissolution of Constituent Assembly
1918	Constitution of the RSFSR establishing a one-party state
1918	Bolshevik action against SR governments in the Urals
1921	*Cheka* and show trials against Kadet, SR, Menshevik leaders
1924	Constitution – unofficially dominated by the Communist Party of the Soviet Union (CPSU)
1917–24	Stalin's rise within CPSU
1925–9	Factions within CPSU between strategies ('Socialism in One Country' vs 'Permanent Revolution') and groups (Stalinists, Left Opposition, Rightists)
1929–41	Stalin established personal control over CPSU; purges of former Bolsheviks
1945–53	Politburo and Central Committee rarely met
1956	Khrushchev's destalinisation campaign
1957	Official history: removal of references to Stalin; gaps filled by reference to 'the Party'

1989	Divisions within CPSU: moderates (Gorbachev), radicals (Yeltsin), conservatives (Ligachev)
1991 (August)	Failed coup by conservative neo-Stalinists
1991 (August)	CPSU banned from operating in RSFSR. Other republics followed suit
1991 (31 December)	End of USSR
1992	Return of multi-party systems in some former members of USSR

SECRET POLICE AND TERROR

1547–84	Reign of Ivan the Terrible (introduced *Oprichnina* and *Oprichniki*)
1682–1725	Reign of Peter the Great (introduced *Preobrazhensky Prikaz*)
1825–55	Reign of Nicholas I (introduced Third Section of Imperial Chancellery)
1880	Alexander II replaced Third Section with Department of State Police
1881–1917	Reigns of Alexander III and Nicholas II (Department of State Police became the *Okhrana*)
1917 (February/ March)	*Okhrana* terminated by Provisional Government
1918–22	*Cheka* active under Dzerzhinsky
1922	*Cheka* replaced by State Political Administration (GPU)
1924	GPU expanded into Unified State Political Administration (OGPU)
1934	Establishment of the People's Commissariat for Internal Affairs (NKVD)
1934–1940	Stalin's purges and show trials. Expansion of the *Gulag* system

1943	NKVD replaced by the People's Commissariat for State Security (NKGB)
1946	NKGB replaced by the Ministry for State Security (MGB), which coexisted with the Ministry for Internal Affairs (MVD)
After 1953	MGB replaced by Committee for State Security (KGB), which was separated from MVD
1989	Gorbachev made KGB accountable to Supreme Soviet of USSR
1991	End of Soviet Union. From 1991 KGB replaced in successor states

NATIONALITIES

1815	Polish Constitution granted by Alexander I
1863	Polish Revolt. Constitution suspended
1881–94	Reign of Alexander III
1894–1905	Early reign of Nicholas II
1906	Fundamental Laws allowing political parties (including parties for national minorities)
1918	Independence to Finland, Baltic states, Poland, Ukraine – by Treaty of Brest-Litovsk
1918–21	Russian Civil War: reconquest of Ukraine; other areas prevented from seceding
1918	Constitution: establishment of RSFSR to unite nationalities within Russia
1920–1	Loss of western Ukraine to Poland in Russo-Polish War
1924	Constitution: establishment of the USSR, comprising RSFSR, Ukraine, Belorussia and Transcaucasia (Georgia, Armenia and Azerbaijan)
1936	Constitution: expansion of USSR to include 11 Republics – reconstituted from the 4 of 1924:

	RSFSR, Ukraine, Belorussia, Azerbaijan, Georgia, Armenia, Kazakhstan, Uzbekistan, Turkmenia, Kirghizia and Tajikistan
1939	Recovery of western Ukraine from Poland as a result of the Nazi-Soviet Non-Aggression Pact
1939	Annexation of western Ukraine from Poland – added to Ukrainian SSR. Annexation of Estonia, Latvia and Lithuania – each eventually given SSR status
1940	Annexation of Moldova from Romania
1941–6	Stalin accused some of the national minorities of disloyalty and treason during the 'Great Patriotic War'. Purges applied through the NKVD and NKGB
From 1947	Soviet control over Communist regimes in eastern European states outside USSR (Poland, East Germany, Czechoslovakia, Hungary, Romania, Bulgaria)
1989	'People's revolutions' removing Communist regimes in Poland, East Germany, Czechoslovakia, Hungary, Romania, Bulgaria. Beginning of disturbances with USSR (Estonia, Latvia, Lithuania, Ukraine, Moldova)
1991 (31 December)	End of USSR. Independence for Russian Federation, Estonia, Latvia, Lithuania, Belarus, Ukraine, Moldova, Georgia, Azerbaijan, Armenia, Kazakhstan, Turkmenistan, Kirgistan, Tajikistan and Uzbekistan

WARS INVOLVING RUSSIA AND THE SOVIET UNION 1854–1991

1854–6	Crimean War (ended by Treaty of Paris)
1877–8	Russo-Turkish War (ended by Treaty of San Stefano)

1904–5	Russo-Japanese War (ended by Treaty of Portsmouth)
1914–18	First World War (ended by Treaty of Brest-Litovsk)
1918–21	Russian Civil War
1920–1	Russo-Polish War (ended by Treaty of Riga)
1939–40	Russo-Finnish War
1941–5	Great Patriotic War (within the Second World War)
1945–89	Cold War (declared over at Malta Summit 1989)
1979–88	War in Afghanistan

ECONOMIC AND SOCIAL DEVELOPMENTS

1855	Alexander II's Manifesto on emancipating the serfs
1860	Introduction of state bank
1861	Alexander II's Edict of Emancipation
1881	End of 'temporary obligation'
1881	State peasant bank
1887	Abolition of poll tax
1887–92	Vyshnegradskii Finance Minister
1892–1903	Witte Finance Minister
1903	End of responsibility of communes for land tenure
1905	Bloody Sunday
1905	End of redemption payments
1906	Law on Associations
1906–11	Stolypin's agricultural reforms
1912	Scheme for national insurance

1917	Decree on land
1918	Introduction of War Communism
1921	Introduction of New Economic Policy (NEP)
1921–2	Famine
1922	Financial crisis
1926–7	Procurement crisis
1929	Introduction of collectivisation
1928	First Five-Year Plan
1932–3	Famine
1933	Second Five-Year Plan
1938	Third Five-Year Plan (interrupted by Hitler's invasion of the Soviet Union 1941)
1946	Fourth Five-Year Plan
1949	Establishment of Council for Mutual Economic Assistance (Comecon)
1951	Fifth Five-Year Plan
1954	Launch of virgin-lands scheme
1956	Sixth Five-Year Plan (interrupted by Seven-Year Plan 1959)
1957	Decentralisation of industry and construction
1960	Reform of wage structure
1963	Harvest failure
1966	Seventh Five-Year Plan
1966	Eight Five-Year Plan
1971	Nine Five-Year Plan
1976	Tenth Five-Year Plan
1981	Eleventh Five-Year Plan
1986	Twelfth Five-Year Plan
1985	Introduction of *perestroika* by Gorbachev

ABBREVIATIONS

ASSR	Autonomous Soviet Socialist Republic
CIS	Commonwealth of Independent States
Comecon/CMEA	Council for Mutual Economic Assistance
CPSU	Communist Party of the Soviet Union
GOKO	State Committee for Defence
GPU	State Political Administration
GTU	Main Prison Administration
KGB	Committee for State Security
MGB	Ministry for State Security
MVD	Ministry of Internal Affairs
NEP	New Economic Policy
NKGB	People's Commissariat for State Security
NKVD	People's Commissariat for Internal Affairs
OGPU	Unified State Political Administration
RSDLP	Russian Social Democratic Labour Party
RSFSR	Russian Soviet Federated Socialist Republic
SRs	Socialist Revolutionaries
SSR	Soviet Socialist Republic
TO	provincial prison branches
TsIK	Central Executive Committee
USSR	Union of Soviet Socialist Republics

hierarchy and ensure the welfare of the people. The autocrat had the support of the Russian Orthodox Church, which established a special relationship with the Romanovs and a vital place within the political and social hierarchy.

The exercise of the autocratic power varied from Tsar to Tsar. The general pattern of Russian history was either dominance by strong rulers (such as Ivan III, Ivan the Terrible, Michael Romanov, Peter the Great, Catherine the Great and Alexander I) or by political vacuums and weak rulers (such as Peter II, Peter III and Paul). There was very little between the two extremes and the last three Tsars, Alexander II (1855–81), Alexander III (1881–94) and Nicholas II (1894–1914), were particularly conscious of this. They all emphasised their auto-cratic powers and had others, whether official mentors or strong-willed consorts, to provide constant reminders of their responsibilities.

Although Russian autocracy has not had any great political philosopher as such, there have been theorists who tried to elevate it to something more than merely the exercise of unrestrained power. The most important of these was Konstantin Pobedonostsev, a professor of civil law and, between 1880 and 1905, Procurator General of the Holy Synod. The latter post gave him control over the affairs of the Russian Orthodox Church, to add to his secular powers to appoint ministers of state and to prepare imperial edicts concern-ing education, censorship and the protection of morals. He also had a strong personal influence as tutor and mentor to two future Tsars – Alexander III and Nicholas II. Pobedonostsev based his political thought on the supposition that man is by nature bad, lazy, vicious, selfish and ignorant. Russians he considered particularly flawed, as 'inertness and laziness are generally characteristic of the Slavonic nature'. The vast majority of humanity is unable to reason, apart from a small proportion who were the 'aristocracy of the intellect'.[1] The rest are influenced by three forces: the unconscious, land and history. Any attempt to understand these beyond an instinctive feeling threatens the social equilibrium and leads to the idolising of reason. In his *Reflections of a Russian Statesman*, he made clear his objec-tions to all progressive trends. Among the falsest of political prin-ciples was that 'all power issues from the people, and is based upon the national will – a principle which has unhappily become more firmly established since the time of the French Revolution'.[2] From this came 'Parliamentarism', which was 'one of the greatest illustra-tions of human delusion'.[3] Similarly pernicious were political parties, 'the formation of ministries on parliamentary or party principles', and the press – 'one of the falsest institutions of our time'.[4] These all combined to produce what Pobedonostsev considered the great evil of the nineteenth century – liberal democracy. Russia had to be protected from this trend by the maintenance of autocracy as the only valid form of government. To ensure this, Pobedonostsev exerted all the influence at his disposal on the last three Romanovs.

Of these, the least autocratic by inclination was Alexander II (1855–81), who sought to introduce changes to Russia's economic and social structure; he was also prepared to make some modifications to local government. His view was very much that reform should be handed down from above – before it was seized from below. During the second half of his reign, however, he retreated into more reactionary policies, partly in response to the growth of Populist revolutionary movements. He was eventually assassinated in 1881 by People's Will, an event that shaped the whole approach of Alexander III (1881–94) and made him particularly receptive to Pobedonostsev's ideas and counsel. The reign saw the end of concessions and reform, and a significant increase in the use of police powers. Nicholas II (1894–1917) continued where Alexander III had left off, his inclination to autocracy under the triple influence of Pobedonostsev, his father's memory and his wife's determination. Nicholas articulated Pobedonostsev's ideas and resisted demands for constitutional reform – at least until 1905.

By then, Russia had been through a recession and lost a war with Japan. The military base had been shaken, although not yet smashed. The result was an impossible compromise. A constitution was granted in 1905 that allowed for political parties and a legislature in the form of the Duma – but the Tsar was determined to reimpose the 'autocratic power'. This time there was no Pobedonostsev to give autocracy a theoretical rationale. Instead, royal authority was irretrievably damaged by a combination of military defeat in the First World War and, in the absence of Nicholas at the front, the arbitrary use of autocratic power by Alexandra and Rasputin. The result was the alienation even of those sectors that had once supported the system – the bureaucracy and the nobility.

As both an ideology and an institution, autocracy died with the Revolution of March 1917. The Tsar was forced to abdicate and autocracy replaced by a brief experiment with liberal democracy and moderate socialism by the Provisional Government. These alternatives lasted only a few months until, in October 1917, they were replaced by the ideology of Marxism-Leninism, or Communism.

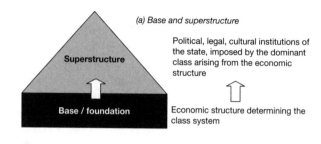

(a) Base and superstructure

Superstructure

Base / foundation

Political, legal, cultural institutions of the state, imposed by the dominant class arising from the economic structure

Economic structure determining the class system

(b) The Hegelian dialectic

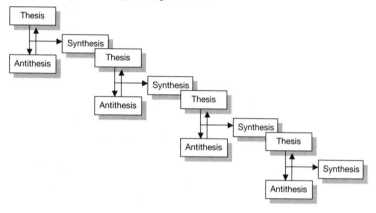

(c) Application of the dialectic to the theory of class conflict

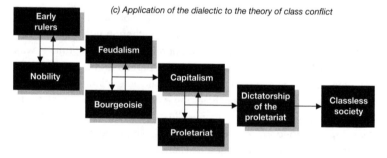

BASE, SUPERSTRUCTURE, THE DIALECTIC AND CLASS CONFLICT

Figure 1.

Soviet Communism

Marxism entered Russia during the 1880s, promoted by revolutionaries seeking an alternative to the Russian-based Populist groups. It was officially represented by the Russian Social Democratic Labour Party (RSDLP) from 1898, although this divided into moderate and radical approaches – Menshevism and Bolshevism respectively. The latter, Marxism-Leninism or Communism, became the official ideology of Russia and the Soviet Union between 1918 and 1991. Communism has remained in Russia since the collapse of the Soviet state, but as one of a number of ideologies competing for power through a new multi-party process.

Marxism in whatever form derives ultimately from the writings of Karl Marx and Friedrich Engels. Despite the quantity and complexity of their writings, it is possible to identify three main constituents in their thought.

The first was a determinist conception of society and of the relationship between economic circumstances and political power. They maintained that the *foundation*, or base, of society was always the state of economic development reached by the ruling class. The *superstructure* consisted of the political, juridical and religious institutions by which the ruling class maintained its grip. Any meaningful change to these institutions could be achieved only by removing the economic base from which they sprang. This immediately invalidated the sort of piecemeal reform to the superstructure that was often proposed by regimes attempting to maintain their base intact.

The second component of Marxist theory was value and profit. The proletariat, Marx and Engels believed, were created and used by the bourgeoisie as wage labourers but were always paid far less than the real value of what they produced. The balance of the value therefore constituted profit, which was used as capital to exploit more wage labour. The proletariat, as a result, became 'concentrated in greater masses' and would seek to overcome their 'misery, oppression, slavery, degradation, exploitation'.[5]

The way in which this change was expected to occur was the third main element of Marxist thought. This was the theory of class struggle, operating through a dialectical process. In their *Communist Manifesto* (1848), Marx and Engels argued: 'The history of all human society, past and present, has been the history of class struggles.' The basic pattern was dialectical: each thesis developed an antithesis and the resulting interaction produced a synthesis, which, as a new thesis, generated a further antithesis and hence revived conflict.

Each economic system and class had created its own antithesis, which would inevitably interact with the thesis to form a new system. According to Engels, 'from its origin the bourgeoisie has been saddled with its antithesis: that capitalists cannot exist without wage workers'.[6] Thus, as the *Communist Manifesto* asserted: 'What the bourgeoisie, therefore, produces, above all, is its own gravediggers. Its fall and the victory of the proletariat are equally inevitable.'[7]

In order to effect this change it might well be necessary to resort to violence, since 'force is the midwife of every old society pregnant with a new one'. The alternative to bourgeois rule would initially be the 'dictatorship of the proletariat', which would dismantle the capitalist superstructure and extend the powers of the state to cover credit, communication, education, land and the instruments of production. Eventually society and the economy would become fully collective and cooperative in the spirit of communism. This would mean that the coercive elements of the state could disappear, followed by political institutions themselves. Engels believed that: 'The interference of the state power in social relations becomes superfluous in one sphere after another, and then dies away of itself. ... The state is not "abolished", it withers away.'[8] What would be left is the Marxist ideal – the 'classless society'.

The actual method of bringing about the 'dictatorship of the proletariat' in the mid-nineteenth century was never clearly stated. Although, in the words of the *Communist Manifesto*, a 'spectre haunted Europe', it was still mainly a theoretical one. Marx and Engels assumed that the dialectical process, by which capitalism would be destroyed, would operate more rapidly in those countries that had already reached an advanced stage of capitalism than in those that were predominantly feudal. After all, the most developed countries would possess the largest and most discontented proletariats, who would be able to seize the initiative as the economic system entered its period of crisis. As Marx had predicted, Marxism developed most rapidly in Germany. What had not been foreseen was that there would be a major dispute over the interpretation of Marxist principles – between the radicals, who aimed for revolution sooner rather than later, and the moderates, who considered it necessary to work properly through the dialectic. This eventually produced in Germany a split between the revolutionary socialists (Communists, or KPD) and the evolutionary socialists (Social Democrats, or SPD). A similar pattern happened elsewhere in Europe.

While it was becoming apparent that western and central Europe would not, after all, be the centre of radical Marxism, a revolutionary impetus was growing in Russia. This was in the form of a new move-ment, Marxism-Leninism, or Bolshevism, the radical wing of the RSDLP formed in 1900. The split between the Bolsheviks and the more moderate Mensheviks in 1903 produced two contrasting interpreta-tions of Marxism, of which Lenin's ultimately proved the longer-lasting for the Russian situation. A prolific writer, Lenin's works amount to over 20 volumes and seem to cover all the different aspects of revolutionary activity. These brought some major shifts to Marxist inter-pretation. Whereas Marx and Engels had looked to Germany as the most likely source of future change, Lenin believed that the first revolution could occur in a more backward country like Russia. He added the significant twist that capitalism was most immediately vulnerable at the weakest link in its chain, rather than where it was most highly developed. The war, he maintained, revealed capitalism in decline everywhere, but the process of overthrowing old regimes would actually begin in Russia.

To achieve this, the whole process of the dialectic would have to be speeded up. In his preparation for revolution in Russia, Lenin disagreed profoundly with the Mensheviks, who argued for a sub-stantial period of parliamentary rule, which, in the long term, could be expected to evolve into a socialist system. Lenin, by contrast, argued that:

> The peculiarity of the current moment in Russia consists in the transition from the first stage of the revolution, which gave power to the bourgeoisie as a result of the insufficient consciousness and organization of the proletariat, to the second stage, which should give the power into the hands of the proletariat.

Forcing the pace like this necessitated a tightly organised Party Central Committee, which consisted of dedicated professional revo-lutionaries. After all, 'in its struggle for power the proletariat has no other weapon but organisation'.[9] The Party adopted conspiratorial methods and the October Revolution, which overthrew the Provisional Government, was a vindication of Lenin's concentration of 'a great superiority of forces at the decisive point, at the decisive moment'.

The aftermath of the Revolution saw the establishment of Lenin's own version of the 'dictatorship of the proletariat' and the adop-tion of his interpretation of socialism as the first step towards the ultimate ideal of communism. Considerable coercion was used to accomplish this, although the roles were now reversed: the 'majority' now suppressed the 'minority'. Possession of power also brought a divergence of views as to the future priorities of Marxism-Leninism. A profound ideological and tactical split developed between Trotsky and Stalin, resulting in the eventual expulsion and assassination of Trotsky.

Trotsky's main contribution was the theory of 'Permanent Revolution' (or 'uninterrupted revolution'), although this had already been partially incorporated into Marxism-Leninism during Lenin's lifetime. Revolution, Trotsky argued, would not end with the overthrow of bourgeois rule by the proletariat. It must continue, as 'Permanent Revolution', on both a national and worldwide scale. Nationally, it could end only 'in the complete liquidation of all class society'. Internationally it could attain completion only in 'the final victory of the new society on our entire planet'.[10] Although this fitted in logically with the theory of the dialectic, in practice the worldwide emphasis seemed inappropriate in the 1920s because of a growing disillusionment with the prospect of Western revolutions. The Bolsheviks had been confronted by extensive Western intervention on the side of counter-revolution during the Civil War (1918–21) and the spontaneous revolutions in Germany and Hungary in 1919 had been crushed. A sharp reaction therefore occurred; the priority was now to develop 'Socialism in One Country', to make Russia self-sufficient and invulnerable in a hostile ideological environment. This was the principal aim of Stalin.

On assuming supreme power by 1927, Stalin restructured Marxist-Leninism in a number of ways. For example, he elevated the role of leadership to a new pinnacle by redefining the Marxist concepts of 'base' and 'superstructure'. He argued that the superstructure could actually reshape the base to help in the development of 'the new order'. The superstructure redesigned the base in a series of Five-Year Plans, which forcibly collectivised agriculture and converted the Soviet Union into an industrial and military power. He also personalised the superstructure in the form of dictatorship. This applied during the 1930s and 1940s, converting Marxism-Leninism into a Stalinist personality cult, one of the most extreme of the twentieth century. It also justified the use of coercion and the development of repressive organs and the interference of the leadership in all political decisions.

Stalin's successor, Khrushchev, found the hero cult and extremes of coercion equally unacceptable and proceeded to redress the balance by launching a destalinisation campaign. Khrushchev stated in 1956 that 'Stalin abandoned the Leninist method of convincing and educating for one of administrative violence, mass repression and terror.' Hence it was necessary 'to eradicate the cult of the individual as alien to Marxism-Leninism'.[11] Khrushchev did much to remove the terror from the Soviet system; yet the superstructure of totalitarianism remained intact during his regime – and that of his successors, Brezhnev, Andropov and Chernenko. It was not until the reforms of Gorbachev from 1985 that the superstructure, which had become so firmly embedded in Soviet Communism, collapsed, taking with it Communism itself.

Questions

1. How did the Tsars and Soviet leaders justify their authority over their subjects?
2. How did the Tsars and Soviet leaders see the role of the 'change'?

ANALYSIS 2: 'THEIR RULE WAS CONDITIONED BY A FUNDAMENTAL IDEOLOGY ON WHICH THEIR POWER DEPENDED'. TO WHAT EXTENT WOULD YOU AGREE WITH THIS ASSESSMENT OF *EITHER* NICHOLAS II *OR* STALIN?

Both Nicholas II and Stalin claimed to base their power on ideological precepts and precedents. To an extent this was true. At the same time, we must also allow for a considerable degree of pragmatism and opportunism. The key issue, in each case, is whether pragmatism controlled ideology or the ideology pragmatism. The basic answer differs between the two practitioners of power in ways that are rather surprising.

Nicholas II (1894–1917)

Nicholas II was always conscious of the autocratic heritage of Tsarist Russia, which expressed itself through the family line, and through the personal preference of his advisers. His father, Alexander III (1881–94), had systematically instituted a political reaction following the assassination of Alexander II in 1881, while his consort, Alexandra, exerted a constant influence throughout his reign to exert his authority to the full. Behind these influences was the assumption that the Tsar's power was unchallengeable.

Whether or not the Tsar's attachment to autocracy was anything more than a convenient personal heritage is open to question. One view is that there was a systematic underlying theory. This was codified by Pobedonostsev, who articulated centuries of practice. The alternative is that Tsarist absolutism was more random, based on the personality of individual rulers in relation to their court and ministers: that what really mattered was a tough pragmatism. What Pobedonostsev tried to do was not so much codify existing theory as to construct one that would guarantee consistency between reigns and provide guidelines for dealing with 'modern' problems such as 'Parliamentarism'.

Both views are applicable to Nicholas II – at least, before 1905. There was certainly an underlying continuity in the basic principle of autocracy. Nicholas II expressed his intention, in 1895, to 'uphold the principle of autocracy as firmly and unflinchingly as did my ever-lamented father'.[12] This 'senseless dreams' speech, delivered to representatives of the *zemstva* (the elected councils), may well have been drafted by Pobedonostsev. It did, however, echo influences that preceded Pobedonostsev, including the Fundamental Laws issued in 1832 by Nicholas I: 'The Emperor of all the Russias is an autocratic and unlimited monarch. God himself ordains that all must bow to his supreme power, not only out of fear but also out of conscience.' The tradition of autocracy, as redefined by Pobedonostsev, was more frequently and publicly stated under Nicholas II, which meant that any major changes in Russia had to be justified in its name. The most important forward-looking developments before 1905 were the economic and industrial reforms of Witte (Finance Minister 1892–1903), which greatly expanded Russia's railway network. This was, however, justified as a means of modernising Russia through a systematic strengthening of the autocratic infrastructure.

What about the period after the 1905 Revolution? Again, there are two possible ways of seeing the relative importance of ideology and pragmatism in the exercise of Tsarist autocracy.

One is that Nicholas II was so shaken by the experience that he adopted a more realistic approach as a means of political survival. This would be in line with the view of 'Optimist' historians, who consider that the period 1906–14 saw major changes in Russia that would have ensured the permanence of the Tsarist regime had it not been for Russia's defeat in the First World War. Autocracy was downgraded by the guarantees given in the 1905 October Manifesto, by the establishment in 1906 of the State Council and State Duma, and by a remarkable range of social reforms, especially related to trade union rights and agricultural reform. Indeed, Stolypin's intention to create a peasant elite was blurring that distinction between social classes that had so long been one of the key pillars of autocracy. It is true that autocracy did at times reassert itself, but this was usually as either a corrective or as an aberration. The corrective was shown, for example, in 1907 when the Electoral Law narrowed the electoral franchise after the rapid closure of the First and Second Dumas. The aberration occurred under the pressure of war when, from 1915 onwards, the Tsar's absence at the front meant that a more capricious form of autocracy emerged in Petrograd, exercised by Alexandra through Rasputin. In each case, what was happening was a departure from the new pragmatic norm, not the revival of an old ideology.

The argument for the 'Pessimists' is based on the assumption that there was no real change in the intentions of the Tsar. The Fundamental Laws of 1906, for example, reasserted the place of autocracy in the new constitution and the failure of the constitutional experiment between 1906 and 1916 was due, above all, to the refusal of Nicholas to cooperate with the new system. He was directly involved in the closure of the Duma in 1906 and 1907 and did all in his power to restrict the range of parties. It is significant that the only parties that met his approval were those on the far right – the Monarchists – whose aim was to end the Duma altogether. As for the social reforms, they were intended as a precaution against the further spread of radicalism. Stolypin was attempting to secure the autocratic base by creating a new peasant elite with a vested interest in the status quo. As for the more ridiculous element of autocracy after 1915, all that changed was the removal of whatever common sense Tsarism still had. Alexandra and Rasputin were not responsible for the collapse of autocracy: the damage had already been done by 1907.

A more recent emphasis by revisionist historians adds further weight to this view. As the Tsarist system of power tried to reclaim the autocratic base, the rest of Russia became increasingly involved in a major social upheaval. This applied especially to the majority of the peasantry and the rapidly expanding urban proletariat, both of which became more politicised and revolutionary. Tsarism fell, not because of the untimely intervention of war, but through the polarisation of social pressures – expressed through heightened ideologies.

Stalin (1924–53)

Like Nicholas II, Stalin claimed ideological legitimacy as the base of his political power. As with late-Tsarist Russia, this has been controversial. Stalin's claim was upheld by the official Soviet view of the time, as expressed through the *Short History of the Communist Party of the Soviet Union*, but has since been challenged from a number of directions.

The case for the ideological base to Stalin's power consists of three main arguments. First, Stalin claimed that 'Socialism in One Country' was more in line with Marxism-Leninism as it had been developing up to 1924 than was Trotsky's variant – 'Permanent Revolution'. He used this to justify a strong domestic focus to socialist construction, as opposed to the internationalist approach of many other 'old Bolsheviks'. Second, in this construction, he placed particular emphasis on the 'dictatorship of the proletariat'. This enabled him to intensify measures against any form of political opposition and, more importantly, against whole sectors of the population. Third, he explained the considerable increase in his own authority by reference to the original Marxist relationship between 'base' and 'superstructure'. He claimed to be updating an ideological adaptation already started by Lenin. Marx and Engels had argued that the economic 'base' gave rise to the political and social 'superstructure', the assumption being that economic transformation would come first. Stalin used the same metaphors but reversed their relationship. He argued that the superstructure needed to become 'the greatest active force' to 'assist its basis to take shape and acquire strength' and 'to help the new order to finish off and liquidate the old basis and the old classes'.[13] This directly justified the introduction of a centralised bureaucracy, and the reshaping of the economy through collectivisation and industrial planning.

Stalin therefore placed himself directly in line with a Marxist-Leninist legacy, making certain refinements to justify what he saw as an acceleration of socialist construction in the same way that Lenin had adapted Marxism to accelerate the revolution. Few continued after his death in 1953 to believe that Stalin made any genuine contributions to Marxist theory or that he was really the 'great educator' claimed as part of his personality cult. Instead, he was seen increasingly as the 'great opportunist', merely using ideological arguments to support policies he was making through other motives. Here, however, there are two further possible explanations.

One is that Stalin was not only opportunist and pragmatic, but that he actually distorted a genuine ideological legacy for his own purposes. This is evident in the development of his dictatorship. First, his decision to implement a command economy had less to do with a change in ideological emphasis than with the consolidation of his own political position. The essential background to the introduction of collectivisation and the Five-Year Plans was his determination to outmanoeuvre first Trotsky, then the Left Opposition of Trotsky, Kamenev and Zinoviev, and finally the Rightists comprising Bukharin, Rykov and Tomsky. Stalin did this by adhering to the New Economic Policy (NEP) against Trotsky's proposals for radical economic change – until the latter had been removed from political contention by 1927. He was then able to adopt his own version of the command economy by 1929 in order to dispose of the NEP – largely to remove the base of the moderates, like Bukharin, who were no longer needed as political allies. Once firmly in control he was able to weaken the role of the Communist Party by the systematic removal of all the Bolsheviks originally identified with the Leninist revolution. Although presented at the time as an ideological struggle against opposition to further economic and social change, the purges were actually a blatant example of the construction of a personal dictatorship devoid of any ideology at all. The same applies to the development of Stalin's personality cult, which Khrushchev saw as nothing more than the gratification of a 'psychotic' personality. Even Stalin's contributions to Soviet culture consisted of bogus theory as a veil for personal preferences. 'Socialist Realism' amounted to the revival of Russian nationalism, now in service to the totalitarian state, and the rehabilitation of Stalinesque surrogates, such as Ivan the Terrible, pulled out of the Tsarist past.

This approach emphasises the distortion of Leninist ideology by Stalin's opportunism. An alternative view, now increasingly popular among historians, is that Stalin's opportunism had already been foreshadowed by Lenin's. The real difference between the two leaders is that Lenin was more effective than Stalin at developing a new interpretation of original Marxist theories to justify policies that were actually quite unmarxist; Stalin was rather better than Lenin at getting these policies implemented in practice. From the occasion of the split with the Mensheviks in 1903, Lenin's interpretation of Marxism had been exclusive rather than inclusive, emphasising power and organisation at the expense of debate or representation. Bolshevism therefore gave to Soviet Communism a monolithic structure that eliminated all political alternatives, promoted centralism and effected economic change through a political bureaucracy. Lenin's method, rooted as it was in the 'dictatorship of the proletariat', lacked the potential for any future 'withering away' of coercive institutions or for the evolution of a 'classless society'. The course was already set for his successor and, although Stalin's changes went much further than Lenin could ever have envisaged, they were not so much a deviation as over-fulfilment. The reversal of the Marxist roles of 'base' and 'superstructure' was not a Stalinist distortion of Marxism-Leninism. It was actually the means by which Marxism-Leninism had reshaped Marxism in the first place – into an instrument of power. The process was criticised by other Marxists, such as the Mensheviks, between 1903 and 1921, and by western European Communist parties in the 1970s and 1980s. The latter argued that the left needed to bypass not only Stalin but also Lenin, a view that gained ground in the Soviet Union itself during the era of *glasnost* under Gorbachev (1985–91).

Conclusion

Nicholas II was reared in the autocratic tradition and Stalin in the new spirit of revolution. Stalin probably made more cynical use of his ideological background than did Nicholas II. But he also possessed a huge advantage in that the momentum of change was with him, whereas it was against Nicholas II. Stalin was moving a system into the next stage. Nicholas was trying to prevent the disintegration of the previous stage. Stalin mobilised ideology for measures he wanted to take for other reasons. Nicholas II sought comfort from ideology in his attempts to neutralise measures that had been forced upon him for other reasons.

Questions

1. How seriously did either Nicholas II or Stalin take the ideologies that underlay their political power?
2. How heavily influenced were Nicholas II or Stalin by their immediate predecessors?

ANALYSIS 3: COMPARE AUTOCRACY AND MARXISM-LENINISM AS IDEOLOGIES WITHIN THE CONTEXT OF TSARIST AND SOVIET RUSSIA.

Both 'autocracy' and 'Marxism' have variations in meaning, depending on which particular type or period is being referred to. Autocracy in its strictest form was that advocated by Pobedonostsev (Procurator

General of the Holy Synod 1880–1905) and applied with varying degrees of consistency up to 1905; between 1905 and 1917, the theory of autocracy remained, but became increasingly mixed with pragmatic action. Similarly, the theoretical basis of Marxism was established between 1848 and 1900, with the Russian variant being more and more influenced by other factors, especially after 1924. Comparisons therefore need to be based on the original theories and the subsequent adaptations.

In their more theoretical form, autocracy and Marxism had fundamental differences – at least as they were *officially* propounded in Russia. There are several examples of this. One is the contrast in their understanding of history and change. Pobedonostsev saw history as the organic development of an authoritarian tradition, justifying a social hierarchy with a narrow political apex. Marx and Engels, by contrast, viewed history as a process of class conflict, operating dialectically and leading inevitably to the removal of hierarchies and a broadening of the power base. This was based, in turn, on different conceptions of human nature. Pobedonostsev based his political thought on the supposition that man is by nature bad, lazy, vicious, selfish and ignorant. Marx and Engels viewed human nature in a more neutral way, maintaining that it was the product of its environment – especially of its social class. For Pobedonostsev, the corollary was that the few should dominate the many; this, of course, was what Marxism aimed to reverse.

Autocracy and Marxism therefore had differing perceptions of threats, enemies and origins of exploitation. For Pobedonostsev the threat came from aspirations to universal suffrage – a 'fatal error', since political power would be 'shattered into a number of infinitesimal bits, of which each citizen acquires a single one'. This meant that the whole notion of 'Parliamentarism' was a delusion. Marxism showed a similar contempt for the institutions of liberal democracy, but from a different perspective. Parliamentary representation was essentially a class-based concept, enabling the bourgeoisie to legitimise its permanent exploitation of the proletariat. In their alternatives to liberal democracy, Pobedonostsev and Marxism showed their greatest contrast. The former saw no alternative to restoring the narrowest possible base of political authority, through which the Tsar would display his 'God-given' right to rule. Reform was a dangerous aberration: Pobedonostsev later accused Alexander II (1855–81) of distorting autocracy through his reforming programme, under which 'all our institutions were systematically remade according to false principles'.[14] It was an experiment that should not be repeated. Marxism similarly distrusted reform – not because it *threatened* the system but because it *perpetuated* it. The only solution was to overthrow the system and to institute a new one, the 'dictatorship of the proletariat'. This was a necessary preliminary stage to remove the control of the bourgeoisie. In the longer term, however, the aim would be to achieve the 'classless society' where, 'in place of the old bourgeois society, with its classes and class antagonisms, we shall have an association, in which the free development of each is the condition for the free development of all'. In this situation the natural outcome was that the state, 'as a coercive institution', would no longer be needed and would therefore 'wither away'. This was at the opposite end of the theoretical scale to autocracy.

The main contrasts between autocracy and Marxism are therefore a conservative versus a radical concept of society and a determination to tighten the status quo versus one to destroy it. Yet once Marxism had been adapted to Russian conditions – in the form of Marxism-Leninism – a number of similarities began to emerge. One reason for this was the grafting of a western European theory on to a Russian revolutionary base that had its own organisational tendencies to autocratic leadership and conspiratorial strategy. Another was the chaotic situation in Russia during and after the First World War that seemed to demand impromptu measures of the type never considered by Marx and Engels. The most extreme case was the emergence of the Stalinist dictatorship, which was considered in Analysis 2.

There are four main examples of similarities in practice between late-Tsarist autocracy and Marxism-Leninism. The first was the insistence on absolute control by the political apex: if anything, Marxism-Leninism was more successful that late Tsarism could ever be. Nicholas II (1894–1917) always claimed the 'supreme autocratic power', even after he had been forced to concede the October Manifesto in 1905 and the Fundamental Laws in 1906. In 1903, meanwhile, Lenin forced a split within the RSDLP between his own (arguably distorted) version of Marxism and the more orthodox and moderate line taken by Martov. The origins of Bolshevism show Lenin's intention to institute personalised leadership and decision-making, together with a limited membership and a tight organisation. This became a key feature of Soviet Communism from 1918 onwards. It remained democratic in theory, professing to be broadening the base of power through the 'dictatorship of the proletariat' and the adoption of representative soviets. Yet in practice the Bolsheviks, or

Communists, acted as a controlling force at all levels. The contradiction was explained under the formula of democratic centralism. This was almost as paradoxical as the 'limited autocracy' that the Fundamental Laws seemed to set up in 1906. Article 4 stated that 'the All-Russian Emperor possesses the supreme autocratic power', while, according to Articles 42 and 44, 'the Russian Empire is governed by firmly established laws that have been properly enacted' with 'the approval of the State Council and the State Duma'.

A second similarity between the two systems was the emergence of a structure that neither ideology seemed to justify. Late-Tsarist Russia and the Soviet Union are both closely associated with an elaborate bureaucracy. Alexander II's reforms in local government, education and the army generated a major increase in officialdom, to which Alexander III added an upgraded security service, which was further expanded by Nicholas II. The intention was to ensure effective Tsarist control through the delegation of certain functions: in this way, bureaucracy and autocracy were logically connected. The place of bureaucracy in a Marxist system is rather more problematic, since the theory is that the 'dictatorship of the proletariat' will move towards the 'classless society' and the 'withering away' of formal structures. The experience of the Soviet Union was, in fact, the opposite. Under Stalin it developed a command economy that was administered through a planning system that became increasingly complex. Predictably – at least in retrospect – the very rigidity of the Stalinist structure prevented any genuine modernisation, let alone the emergence of the 'classless society'.

Third, Tsarist autocracy and Marxism-Leninism shared an aversion to open societies, freedom of expression and power-sharing. Both imposed their authority, claiming legitimacy on behalf of the people rather than seeking it from them. For autocracy, this was simply a matter of consistency. The population had to be kept insulated from the forces of sedition, including the greatest of all disseminators of lies – the press. According to Pobedonostsev: 'From the day that man first fell falsehood has ruled the world; ... the Press is one of the falsest institutions of our time.' Under Alexander III the same principle applied to political parties, although this had to be modified by Nicholas II as a consequence of the 1905 Revolution. Marxism-Leninism proved even more intolerant to alternative views. Shortly after coming to power in October 1917, the Bolsheviks closed down all of Russia's other parties. These included not only the Constitutional Democrats and Octobrists, but also fellow radicals such as the Mensheviks and the Socialist Revolutionaries (SRs). Lenin and his successors claimed exclusivity in the correct interpretation of the original doctrine of Marxism. In so doing, they established a monolithic and closed society that had all the constraints to which autocracy could only aspire.

Fourth, both systems were based on the personification of power. Pobedonostsev saw this as a natural expression of autocracy and advised Alexander III that: 'The whole secret of Russian order and prosperity is in the top, in the person of the supreme authority' and in the use of 'that power which was destined to you from God'. In this sense the person of the autocrat was less important than the office he filled, since the office was inseparable from the ideology. Marxism in its original form attached no significance to personal leadership: the emphasis was all on the mass application of impersonal forces through the dialectical process. In reinterpreting Marxism for Russian conditions, however, Lenin added the 'leadership' factor and made this absolute when he excluded other approaches to Marxism. Stalin went further, adding the trappings of 'personality cult' and justifying all his changes through his ideological inversion of the relationship between the Marxist concepts of 'base' and 'superstructure' (see Analysis 2). Although Khrushchev removed the cult of Stalin after 1953, the iconic influence of Lenin remained. When that, in turn, came to be questioned in the late 1980s, the Soviet system was already in decline.

Finally, once established, both systems proved resistant to meaningful reform. But both had to dictate any change, not to accept change as an impartial agent. As a result, both distrusted the idea of reform as applied to change – autocracy because it might damage the structure; Marxism-Leninism because it was applying the wrong approach. Both ideologies therefore became stuck within a time-mould. Tsarist autocracy, accustomed to instituting changes as reform from above, failed to adapt to growing pressures from below. Soviet Communism, used to dictating change through democratic centralism and Stalin's planning system, could not compete with economic pressures from outside. Hence the Tsarist regime was overthrown in March 1917, while the Soviet Union folded at the end of 1991.

Questions

1. Which was the more absolute form of power: 'Tsarist autocracy' or 'Soviet Communism'?
2. How far did Tsarist autocracy and Soviet Communism differ in their theoretical and practical interpretation of 'human nature'?

SOURCES

1. THE THEORY AND PRACTICE OF AUTOCRACY IN LATE-TSARIST RUSSIA

Source 1: Pobedonostsev's advice to Crown Prince Alexander (the future Alexander III) in 1876.

The whole secret of Russian order and prosperity is in the top, in the person of the supreme authority. Do not believe that the subordinates to your authority themselves will limit and regulate things, if you yourself do not limit and regulate. ... Your work advances all things, your indulgence inundates all the land with indulgence – here is the meaning of that union with the land, to which you were born, and that power which was destined to you from God.

Source 2: From Alexandr Blok's poem *Revenge*.

Pobedonostsev had unfurled
His owlish wings over Russia.
There was neither day nor night,
Only the shadow of giant wings.

Source 3: Extracts from the 1906 Fundamental Laws.

Article 4: The All-Russian Emperor possesses the supreme autocratic power. Not only fear and conscience, but God himself, commands obedience to his authority.

Article 5: The person of the Sovereign Emperor is sacred and inviolable.

Article 42: The Russian Empire is governed by firmly established laws that have been properly enacted.

Article 44: No new law can be enacted without the approval of the State Council and the State Duma, and it shall not be legally binding without the approval of the Sovereign Emperor.

Source 4: Extracts from correspondence of Empress Alexandra to Tsar Nicholas II on the subject of Rasputin.

And guided by him we shall get through this heavy time. It will be hard fighting, but a Man of God is near to guard your boat safely through the reefs. ...

7 September 1916
Do listen to Rasputin, who only wants your good and whom God has given more insight, wisdom and enlightenment than all the military put together. His love for you and Russia is so intense and God has sent him to be your help and guide. ...

4 December 1916
Why do people hate me? Because they know I have a strong will and when I am convinced of a thing being right (when besides blessed by Gregory) do not change my mind and that they can't bear. . . .

Source 5: From a speech by Miliukov, leader of the Constitutional Democrats and of the Progressive Bloc, to the Duma (1916).

We now see and know that we can no longer legislate with this government than we can lead Russia to victory with it. . . . We have many different reasons for being discontented with this government . . . but all these reasons boil down to one general one: the incompetence and evil intentions of the present government.

Questions

1. Explain the view given in Source 2 of the role of Pobedonostsev in late-Tsarist autocracy. (10)
2. Compare Sources 1 and 3 as evidence of official attitudes to the scope of Tsarist authority. (20)
3. 'Tsarist autocracy had no consistent theory behind it; it was therefore open to individual abuse in practice.' Do Sources 1 to 5, and your own knowledge, support this view? (30)

Total (60)

Worked answers

[Sources 1 to 5 are primary only. The technique needed for second-ary sources is explained in Chapter 2, Sources 1, pp. 45–8.]

1. [Advice: Use the wording in the source and supplement it with your own knowledge to explain each specific reference.]

As Procurator General of the Holy Synod, Pobedonostsev was government minister responsible for the Russian Orthodox Church. He also used his position to control the moral and intellectual life of Russia – which he did with some rigour. Each of the metaphors in Blok's poem illustrate this. The brooding presence of Pobedonostsev is clear from his 'wings', which are 'unfurled' and casting a 'shadow' over the people, their ideas and their institutions; this could relate to the different types of control and repression through censorship and controls on freedom of expression and thought. 'Owlish' adds the sharp-sightedness of a bird of prey, also associated with his office and his particular commitment to carrying it out effectively. Pobedonostsev exercised a powerful influence on Alexander III and Nicholas II, both of whom fully supported his uncompromising approach. In such conditions there would be no variation in policy and hence no distinction between 'day' and 'night'.

2. [Advice: 'Compare' as 'evidence' means the identification of similarities and differences in an integrated analysis, bearing in mind that the provenance and purpose of the sources will also have some bearing on these.]

The content of Sources 1 and 3 contain obvious similarities and rather more subtle differences. Both stem from the provenance and purpose of the sources.

The similarities are clear from the wording itself. Both sources refer to the importance of the Tsar's personal power, whether as the 'person of the supreme authority' (Source 1) or 'supreme autocratic power' (Source 3); this authority is delegated or 'destined to you by God' (Source 1) and demands obedience 'as God himself commands' (Source 3). The underlying difference appears in the extent to which this authority might be shared. Source 1 assumes that full power must be imposed by the Tsar himself rather than by 'subordinates' who should not be delegated authority to 'limit and regulate'. Source 3, by contrast, implies a degree of shared power in government by 'properly enacted' laws, which would require the 'approval of the State Council and the State Duma' as well as that of 'the Sovereign Emperor'.

The context in which these documents were produced provides substance for the comparisons. Both assume that autocracy is the natural political process. But the ultra-conservative slant on autocracy was bound to emerge more clearly in the privately stated view of Pobedonostsev than in an official state document produced 30 years later in an attempt to re-establish an agreed base of authority after a disruptive if unsuccessful revolution. Nicholas II, also influenced by Pobedonostsev, certainly inclined towards the more uncompromising expressions of autocracy. Source 1 would therefore have expressed his true feeling just as it had that of Alexander III. On the other hand, the slight concessions allowed in Source 3 to shared power would have been a concession made from a position of disadvantage. The continued use of the word 'autocratic' in Source 3 shows that Nicholas intended such power sharing to be diluted as much as possible.

3. *[Advice: The question needs to be covered fully, i.e. (1) whether there was a consistent theory behind autocracy and (2) the extent to which its absence (or presence) allowed practical abuse of power. The material for this should come partly from the sources (allowing for the way in which their veracity might be affected by their provenance) and partly from 'own knowledge'. The latter could be used in two ways: (1) to deal with issues raised in the sources and (2) to consider what can be added to rectify omissions from the sources. It is better to adopt an integrated approach based on an overall argument than to approach each source in sequence.]*

Autocracy was based partly on the long-term development of Tsarist power and partly on a belief in 'divine right' as refined by official theorists like Pobedonostsev (Procurator General of the Holy Synod between 1880 and 1905). Whether it was an inconsistent theory allowing for individual abuse depends on how the five sources are interpreted.

Two of them make explicit reference to a 'theory'. In Source 1 autocracy is given perhaps the ultimate sanction of divine ordination; the Tsar's power is 'destined to you from God', which therefore defines the real 'meaning' of his 'union with the land, to which you were born'. A theory is certainly apparent, although one which excludes all others. An attempt is made in Source 3 to provide for a more updated theory, by referring to a sharing of authority between the 'Emperor', 'State Duma' and 'State Council'. Yet here there is an apparent contradiction that is not present in Source 1: the Emperor still 'possesses the supreme autocratic power', with 'God himself' commanding 'obedience to his authority'. This inconsistency is largely because the Fundamental Laws were a concession made on the advice of Witte (Finance Minister 1892–1903) by the Tsar, who tried to leave open the possibility of a future retraction. Two of the sources, 2 and 5, make no reference to theory, while Source 4 has an implicit belief in the divine sanction of autocracy – more consistent with Source 1 than with Source 3. This could be because it shows the frankness that characterises private correspondence; in any case, Alexandra had no liking for shared power through the Duma.

There was, therefore, theory behind autocracy, but, by the last decade of Nicholas II's reign, it had indeed become inconsistent. Whether it was the inconsistency or the theory itself that led to individual abuse of power is debatable. On the one hand, it could be argued that autocracy was at its greatest when it was unchallenged. During the reign of Alexander III, for example, Pobedonostsev was able to exercise arbitrary influence with the 'shadow of giant wings' (Source 2). It is also clear that the period 1881–94 saw the dilution of many of the reforms of Alexander II (1855–81), including powers given to the *zemstva*, and cancellation of the proposal to call a consultative assembly. On the other hand, the actions most clearly identified at the time as 'abuse' of power occurred after 1905, probably because they were seen as a step backward from shared power to the original form of autocracy. It is clear from Source 5 that Miliukov considered that the Tsar's abuse of power had been extreme, resulting from 'evil intentions'. The result of this is apparent in Source 4, where the Empress acknowledges that the 'people hate me' because 'they know I have a strong will', used in this instance to follow the dictates of Rasputin.

Several areas are not actually covered by the sources but would add weight to Miliukov's accusation. The Tsar dissolved the First and Second Dumas in 1906 and 1907 – largely because they questioned some of the policies of his government; he also issued an edict that considerably reduced the franchise granted in 1906. The Fourth Duma recognised the increasingly arbitrary nature of the Tsar's autocracy, forming a Progressive Bloc in 1915. It seems therefore that 'the individual abuse in practice' was partly connected with the inconsistency in the theory from 1905 onwards but was actually motivated by an attempt to return to the unambiguous autocracy of the past.

2. MARXISM, MARXISM-LENINISM AND STALINISM

Source 6: Extracts from the *Communist Manifesto*, written by Marx and Engels and published in 1848.

... Not only has the bourgeoisie forged the weapons that bring death to itself; it has also called into existence the men who are to wield those weapons – the modern working class – the proletarians. ... The development of Modern Industry, therefore, cuts from under its feet the very foundation on which the bourgeoisie produces and appropriates products. What the bourgeoisie, therefore, produces, above all, is its own gravediggers. Its fall and the victory of the proletariat are equally inevitable. ...

When, in the course of development, class distinctions have disappeared, and all production has been concentrated in the hands of a vast association of the whole nation, the public power will lose its political character. Political power, properly so called, is merely the organised power of one class for oppressing another. If the proletariat during its contest with the bourgeoisie is compelled, by the force of circumstances, to organise itself as a class, if, by means of a revolution, it makes itself the ruling class, and, as such, sweeps away by force the old conditions of production, then it will, along with these conditions, have swept away the conditions for the existence of class antagonisms and all classes generally, and will thereby have abolished its own supremacy as a class.

In place of the old bourgeois society, with its classes and class antagonisms, we shall have an association, in which the free development of each is the condition for the free development of all.

Source 7: From an official Soviet biography of Lenin (prepared by the Institute of Marxism-Leninism, Moscow 1959), explaining Lenin's adaptation of Marxism to Russian conditions.

In the shape of the Bolshevik Party there appeared a powerful force capable of rallying the working class and all the working people of Russia for the overthrow of the power of the landowners and capitalists and for the building of socialism. The Bolshevik Party, organised by Lenin and his supporters, became a model for all communist and workers' parties.

The success of Lenin's plan for creating a revolutionary Marxist party showed that in Lenin the Russian and international proletariat had an outstanding theoretician, who carried on the work and teaching of Marx and Engels and was endowed with a clear insight into the prospects of developing the working-class movement.

Source 8: Stalin's redefinition of the Marxist relationship between 'base' and 'superstructure', 1950.

The base gives rise to the superstructure, but this does not at all mean that it merely reflects the basis, that it is passive, neutral, is indifferent to the fate of its basis, to the fates of classes, to the character of the system. On the contrary ... it becomes the greatest active force, actively assists its basis to take shape and acquire strength, and makes every effort to help the new order to finish off and liquidate the old basis and the old classes.

Source 9: Extracts from Khrushchev's speech to the Twentieth Congress of the Soviet Communist Party (February 1956). Khrushchev was denouncing Stalin's record.

He discarded the Leninist method of convincing and educating; he abandoned the method of ideological struggle for that of administrative violence, mass repressions and terror....

Comrades! The cult of the individual acquired such monstrous size chiefly because Stalin himself, using all conceivable methods, supported the glorification of his own person.

Questions

1. Using Source 6, and your own knowledge, explain the following reference in Source 6: 'What the bourgeoisie, therefore, produces, above all, is its own gravediggers.' (10)
2. Compare Sources 8 and 9 as evidence for Stalin's contributions to Marxism-Leninism. (20)
3. 'The ideology of Communism in Russia and the Soviet Union, was a distortion, not a fulfilment of Marxism.' Do Sources 5 to 8, and your own knowledge, support this view? (30)

Total (60)

2

CONSTITUTIONAL DEVELOPMENT

ANALYSIS 1: OUTLINE THE DEVELOPMENT OF RUSSIA'S CONSTITUTIONAL STRUCTURE BETWEEN 1855 AND 1991.

Russia's constitutional development encompassed two main trends. One was evolution, within the broader periods of 1855–1917 and 1918–91. The other was revolution, covering the more specific periods of 1905-6, 1917–18 and 1991–2. Within this overall time-scale, major constitutional changes were made in 1906, 1918, 1924, 1936, 1977, 1989 and 1992.

The Tsarist period saw very few constitutional reforms until the reign of Alexander II (1855–81). Even then, these were confined to local government, with the introduction of the *zemstva* in 1864 and the urban councils (*dumas*) in 1870. Alexander II was more reluctant to temper Tsarist autocracy with a central legislature, although there is evidence that he was eventually persuaded to take the first step in that direction by his Minister of the Interior, Loris Melikov. Indeed, he was on his way to sign the document that would have established Russia's first Consultative Assembly when he was assassinated by a bomb thrown by a member of *Narodnaya Volya*. His successor, Alexander III (1881–94), under the influence of Konstantin Pobedonostsev, was determined to backtrack on any such guarantees and also to reduce the powers of the local government institutions that had already been established.

Nicholas II (1894–1917) was similarly committed to the maintenance of autocracy and to resisting any trend towards a parliamentary

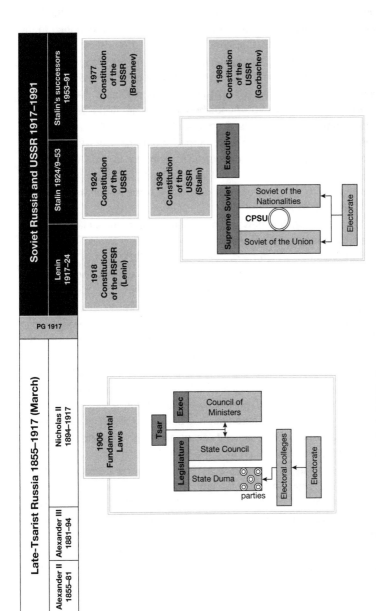

THE MAIN CONSTITUTIONAL CHANGES 1855–1991

Figure 2.

system. All political parties were considered subversive, whether they aimed for the constitutional limitation of Tsarist power or for the revolutionary removal of that power altogether. The Tsar's response to the 1905 Revolution was therefore tactical and defensive. Threatened with the overthrow of his regime, but possessing the means to prevent it, Nicholas bought off the constitutionalist opposition in order to deal with the revolutionaries. The result was a concession that he meant to water down. The 1906 Fundamental Laws granted a legislature of two chambers, the State Duma and the State Council. It also permitted political parties that ranged from the Social Democrats and the Socialist Revolutionaries (SRs) on the far left, through the Constitutional Democrats and the Octobrists, on the moderate left and moderate right, to far right nationalist parties such as the Union of Russian People.

Unfortunately, the new constitutional experiment lacked any real basis for success. The Tsar was still able to veto legislation and dissolve the Duma, which he did in 1906 and 1907, on the latter occasion also changing the electoral system to restrict the franchise. Frustration with the reassertion of autocracy led to the formation of a Progressive Bloc within the Duma during the First World War, which played a crucial part in the establishment of a new regime. Following the spontaneous eruption of revolution in March 1917, the moderate parties in the Duma established a Provisional Committee, which rapidly became the Provisional Government. Two factors influenced this acceptance of a change to the regime. First, the concessions of 1905–6 had been systematically undermined by the attempted reassertion of autocracy. And, second, this autocracy had been discredited as never before by a combination of ridicule for its association with Rasputin and military defeat by German armies during the First World War.

Between March and October 1917 there was a real opportunity to install a more meaningful legislature. Unfortunately, there was confusion from the outset as to what this should comprise. Should it be a Western-style parliament – an extension of the former Duma, 'elected by universal, equal, direct and secret suffrage'? This is certainly what the Provisional Government promised for the future, but only after the successful conclusion of the war. Or should it be an enlarged version of the Petrograd Soviet, which would give priority to the needs of workers, peasants and soldiers? The Bolsheviks, who had seized the political initiative by August – and power by October – started by promising the former and ended by delivering the latter. When elections were called by the Bolshevik regime they produced an anti-Bolshevik majority, with the result that the new Constituent Assembly was closed immediately in January 1918, ending the prospect of any Western-style constitution being established. Instead, Lenin announced that the legislative powers would be given to the soviets. He claimed that the Assembly had been 'an expression of the old relation of political forces' and that 'a republic of soviets is a higher form of democratic principle than the bourgeois republic with its Constituent Assembly'.[1]

The establishment of the Communist regime therefore saw the rapid transition to the principle of popular sovereignty based on centralism. The 1918 Constitution established a new federal system for Russia, now renamed the Russian Soviet Federated Socialist Republic (RSFSR). It declared the All-Russian Congress of Soviets to be the supreme power of the state and in control of the Central Executive Committee (TsIK) and the government (*Sovnarkom*). The 1924 Constitution, which set up the Union of Soviet Socialist Republics (USSR), extended the principle of national self-determination to five other republics. In theory, this was the most advanced system the country had ever possessed. But in practice it was democracy without the element of choice: soviets at all levels were dominated by the one party that was allowed to exist – the Communist Party of the Soviet Union (CPSU) – which quickly controlled all the executive organs as well.

The next half-century produced refinements of the Soviet system rather than substantive change. The principle of democratic centralism, exercised through the CPSU, remained intact in Stalin's 1936 Constitution, even though this refined the representative process by removing separate electoral rolls and introducing a new central legislature based on the Soviet of the Union and the Soviet of the Nationalities. The number of republics was also increased to 16, each possessing the right to secede from the Soviet Union. Khrushchev (1953–64) launched a campaign for further changes to recognise the end of the phase of the 'dictatorship of the proletariat', but these were toned down by the time that they eventually translated into Brezhnev's 1977 Constitution. Although intended to herald a new era of 'Developed Socialism', the Brezhnev constitution closely resembled that of Stalin. This was sustained under Brezhnev's immediate successors, Andropov (1982–4) and Chernenko (1984–5), but under Gorbachev (1985–91) major changes were instituted. The initial focus was economic, through the policy of *perestroika*, followed by greater freedom of expression through *glasnost*. The logical next step was a constitutional adjustment, which Gorbachev made in 1988.

A new Congress of People's Deputies was set up, along with a reformed Supreme Soviet and an executive presidency. It was even suggested that other parties should be allowed. Before this experiment could be extended, however, the 1991 crisis brought the collapse of the Soviet Union and the secession of its member states, each of which adopted its own constitution.

The Russian Federation, established as the RSFSR in 1918, remained in existence, under the presidency of Yeltsin. The Communist Party had, however, been banned in August 1991. The entire system of soviets, established in 1918 and subsequently refined by Stalin and Brezhnev, was abolished. The decision was made to replace the 'soviet democracy' and 'democratic centralism' with a multi-party Western-style assembly and a directly elected president. Continuity was claimed with the late-Tsarist period as the new legislature was officially named the Duma.

Questions

1. Why were more constitutions introduced during the Soviet era (1918–91) than under the last three Tsars (1855–1917)?
2. Were there more constitutional changes during the Tsarist period than there were during the Soviet period?

ANALYSIS 2: EXPLAIN WHY, AND WITH WHAT DEGREE OF SUCCESS, NEW CONSTITUTIONAL STRUCTURES WERE INTRODUCED IN *EITHER* THE LATE-TSARIST *OR* SOVIET PERIODS.

The main constitutions established during the period 1894–1953 were those of 1906, 1918, 1924 and 1936. The reasons for their introduction come down largely to whether they were extracted from the regime of the time as a concession, or whether they were a more controlled method of advancing the regime's power. The degree of success might, therefore, be measured from the proper functioning of the constitution once introduced or, alternatively, from constraints imposed to prevent the constitution from working properly.

The late-Tsarist period (1855–1917)

The establishment of a constitution in 1906 in theory went against the traditional autocratic base of Tsarist authority: both Nicholas II and

Alexander III had issued manifestos and edicts refusing any such concession (see Chapter 1). The sudden change of direction must therefore have been the result of a major trauma.

This was the combination of military defeat in the Russo-Japanese War (1904–5) and the outbreak of the 1905 Revolution. The former undermined Russia's reputation as a major naval and military power, especially in the Battles of Tsushima and Mukden. It also reduced the effectiveness of the armed forces as the first line of internal security, as waves of strikes, protests and revolution affected the provinces and the streets of the major cities, especially St Petersburg and Moscow. His throne threatened, the Tsar was forced to act on the advice of Witte to grant immediate concessions to split the revolutionaries. Hence the peasantry were pacified by the undertaking to cancel redemption payments and the middle classes by the October Manifesto, which promised constitutional amendments. This was followed by the establishment of a State Duma and Council, together with the legalising of political parties, by the 1906 Fundamental Laws. Hence the first real constitution that Russia had ever possessed was the result of a strategy used by the regime to divide and rule. It succeeded in ending the revolution, since the urban workers were left isolated and were no match for an army that, although shaken and discredited, was still intact.

The 1906 constitutional changes can therefore be seen as the price paid for the survival of Tsarism beyond 1905. There is, however, another perspective. They were also a logical outcome of pre-1905 initiatives of the Tsars themselves. Alexander I had sometimes shown progressive sympathies, while Alexander II (1855–81) had established some of Russia's first representative institutions in local government. These had included the *zemstva* (1864) and the city *dumas* (1870), each of which had electoral rolls representing the different classes. In 1881 Alexander had been on the point of signing an edict to establish a consultative assembly. The 1906 changes were not, therefore, entirely unheralded. They transferred to central government some of the practices in representation already tried in local government and extended the principle of consultation already recognised by Alexander II. Although there is no evidence that Nicholas II would have made these changes had he not been under pressure, there was a certain sense of long-term continuity that made the 1906 constitutional changes seem feasible to liberal and conservative parties, such as the Kadets and the Octobrists. The same applied even to some of the ministers of the Tsarist bureaucracy, including premiers Kokovtsev (1911–14) and Goremykin (1914–16 and 1916 to March 1917).

This constitutional succession contained much potential for success – at least that is the argument of the 'Optimist' school of historians. Any representative system takes time to become embedded and it was inevitable that there should have been a period of intense competition between a newly empowered legislature and a traditional executive standing on its traditional dignity: hence the conflict between the first two Dumas and Stolypin's government between 1906 and 1907, leading to the restriction of the franchise by the 1907 Electoral Law. Yet it is also reasonable to presuppose a gradual osmosis by which the new legislature becomes more aware of its capacity to change through persuasion, and the executive is more likely to seek stability through cautious reform. This was already beginning to happen during the period of the Third Duma (1907–12), in which the Duma put the government under less intense pressure and the government introduced a series of reforms concerning agriculture and education. By 1914 there was therefore the real prospect that, given time, the constitutional experiment might eventually work. This interpretation seems to have been reflected by the President of the Duma, Rodzianko, who said at the time: 'Give us ten years and we are safe.'[2] What, of course, made the difference was the destabilising impact of the First World War, which interrupted the constitutional experiment during its transitional and most vulnerable phase. Without its sudden incursion, there is every likelihood that autocracy would have been controlled by constitutional influences and that revolutionary influences would have been neutralised. Without a 1914 there would have been no 1917; 1906 could therefore have been a more permanent solution for the problems thrown up in 1905.

Yet the fact is that the whole system *had* folded up in 1917. For this reason the new constitution has to be seen as a long-term failure. Several strands come together in the approach of the historians known as the 'Pessimists'. The first is the blatant unwillingness of Nicholas II to come to terms with the implications of the new constitution and his unalterable determination to interpret literally any residual references to the 'autocratic power' contained within the 1906 Fundamental Laws. Quite simply, the underlying mentality that regarded political parties as subversive – and that took any opportunity to narrow their electoral base – meant that the concessions were not genuine and were therefore bound to fail. The descent from 1915 onwards into the arbitrary autocracy of Alexandra and Rasputin showed that any idea of responsible government was entirely absent. With or without the impact of the war, personalised government contrived during this period not only to provoke a broad Progressive Bloc within the Duma but also to alienate its more traditional base of support – the bureaucracy of state officials right up to prime-ministerial level. Why else would the Duma and much of the bureaucracy have acted in support of the revolutionaries of March 1917? On 13 March, for example, Rodzianko replied to the Tsar's offer to share power with the Duma with the words: 'The measures you propose are too late. The time for them is gone. There is no return.'[3] The 'Pessimist' interpretation also considers that the constitutional experiment could not have saved the regime since the hostility of the revolutionary groups was too deeply embedded. Hence the problems that led to the eruption in 1905 were only temporarily contained by the constitutional experiment initiated in 1906. Therefore 1917 was inevitable, with or without the trauma of 1914.

Any conclusion on whether the 1906 changes succeeded is paradoxical. They failed to save the Tsarist regime because the Duma was increasingly alienated by the Tsar's attitude and by his deliberate attempts to prevent its effective operation. If anything, the Duma contributed to his demise by stepping into the March Revolution with the intention of preventing a descent into the anarchy that the early stages seemed to portend. From the Provisional Committee of the Duma emerged the Provisional Government and Russia's continuing experiment with constitutionalism. Yet there was a backlash. The revolutionaries of March 1917 were largely moderate socialists, whether Mensheviks, SRs or non-party. In terms of popular support, they were the natural successors to the Tsarist regime in March, especially with the establishment of the Petrograd Soviet. But when their leaders, especially Kerensky, collaborated with the Provisional Government, they provided an opportunity for the Bolsheviks. Unable to overthrow the Tsarist system, the latter succeeded with relative ease in removing the Tsar's constitutional successor in October.

The Soviet period (1918–91)

The new regime established by the Bolsheviks in 1918 was intended as an improved form of representative government in line both with Marxist principles and with revolutionary precedent. Stalin's subsequent additions in 1924 and 1936 were seen as progressive refinements that, with a few minor adjustments by Brezhnev and Gorbachev, lasted until the collapse of the Soviet Union in 1991.

The 1918 Constitution, which set up the RSFSR, was based on the premise that the industrial proletariat and rural peasantry would be more effectively represented through an institution already tried in 1905 and 1917 than on a Western-style constituent assembly. In theory, at least, this explains why the latter was dissolved in January 1918 and replaced by the All-Russian Congress of Soviets, which, in turn, presided over a hierarchy of soviets at regional and local levels. Democracy would be guaranteed by the control by the Congress of Soviets over the executive government, *Sovnarkom* and the Central Executive Committee, while the 'dictatorship of the proletariat' would be ensured through the operation of 'democratic centralism' by the dominant Communist Party. Once the formative period of the Bolshevik state had been completed, further refinements could be added to show that 'dictatorship of the proletariat' was beginning to move towards the 'classless society'. Hence the 1924 Constitution added a second federal structure – the USSR – to the existing RSFSR, while Stalin's 1936 Constitution extended the vote to all at the age of 18, removed any remaining discriminatory or weighted franchise, and rebalanced the representation of constituencies and nationalities through the Soviet of the Union and the Soviet of the Nationalities.

By this interpretation – typical of the official Soviet view embodied in works such as *A Short History of the CPSU* – the Soviet constitutional structure was the practical fulfilment of Marxist theory as interpreted by Lenin and promised in the latter's 1917 *April Theses*. There is, however, an alternative explanation for the constitutions of 1918, 1924 and 1936 – that the regime was adjusted more by necessity and convenience than through any ideological considerations. The Constituent Assembly, which contained a majority hostile to the Bolsheviks, was replaced by a system of soviets from which the Bolsheviks had been able to squeeze out other parties like the SRs and Mensheviks. Similarly, the establishment of a federal structure was impelled on Lenin by the attempted secession of many of the nationalities during the Civil War period (1918–21). Thus the changes made by Lenin were motivated by the need to end competition. Those of Stalin were intended to improve efficiency while, at the same time, giving the illusion of progressive evolution. From 1929 Stalin established a complex and unwieldy bureaucracy to operate a newly implemented command economy based on state planning. The front to this structure was a modern and streamlined legislature in which the workers and peasants, whether as Russians, Ukrainians or Kazakhs, held the leadership accountable. Its actual purpose, however, was to provide a facade behind which the regime could exercise coercion and terror, whether through Gosplan or the NKVD, to achieve economic or political objectives. By this analysis, the

1936 Constitution saw the intensification of dictatorship rather than its dilution.

Again, there are two dimensions on whether the political system established by Lenin and Stalin worked in practice. The answer depends very much on whether their changes are seen at their original face value or in a more sceptical way. Similarly, the break-up of the Soviet Union in 1991 will itself have helped shape more recent views.

It might be argued that both Lenin and Stalin did succeed in advancing the representative structure of the Soviet Union, whatever individual leaders did behind the scenes to distort the power allowed by the structure. The franchise provided in 1918 was the first genuine provision of universal suffrage in Russian history, while the 1936 Constitution reduced the voting age to 18 – the lowest in Europe. Provision for the nationalities, enshrined in the 1924 and 1936 Constitutions, was based on the principle of voluntary membership – and hence on the right to secession. All three constitutions subordinated the executive to the legislature. Some degree of success is shown by the limited changes made by Khrushchev and Brezhnev. Even allowing for the excesses of Stalin, the 1977 Constitution acknowledged the progress made by its three predecessors in moving the country into the phase of 'Developed Socialism', a halfway point between the 'dictatorship of the proletariat' and the 'classless society'. Even Gorbachev found it possible to adapt the system to one based on more openness (*glasnost*) and competition. Finally, could the 15 successor states have emerged so peacefully after 1991 had it not been for the nationalities clauses within the constitutions?

Of course, an alternative approach would be to show that the main clauses of the constitutions were a fiction. This could, in turn, indicate either their success or their failure, depending on the criteria used.

On the one hand, it could be said that the constitutions succeeded in their purpose precisely *because* they were a fiction. Lenin and Stalin were able to perpetuate their authoritarian leadership within an apparently broadly based Soviet regime through the ideological contradiction of democratic centralism, while ending the multi-party Constituent Assembly could be justified by the need to impose the 'dictatorship of the proletariat' to remove residual 'bourgeois-Western' influences. Other appearances could be more positive – but equally unrealistic. Conceding the executive power to legislative control – both in 1918 and in 1936 – meant little change in practice since the legislature was dominated by the Party, which, in turn, provided the leadership of the executive. Similarly, the right of the nationalities to autonomy and even secession was cancelled out by their political subordination to republic and regional branches of the CPSU, which, of course, was the key agent for centralisation and Russification within the Soviet Union. The ultimate paradox was that the most advanced constitution of the whole period – that of 1936 – emerged during the transition of Stalin's regime into personal dictatorship and terror. The explanation is that the former had no impact on the latter apart from providing brutal efficiency with a veneer of legitimacy. If this is what Lenin and Stalin actually wanted, then it may be considered successful.

But there is another possibility. What if the constitutional fiction, created to provide a veneer of legitimacy for the reality of power, actually served to *undermine* that power? This notion would have been considered preposterous before 1990. Yet the collapse of the Soviet Union in 1991 has caused a major rethink about whether the constitutions were in practice neutralised by 'democratic centralism'. There are two examples of where apparently suppressed democracy seems to have the last laugh. First, the broadly based franchise was a key factor in Gorbachev's decision to open the country to political debate, directly challenging the notion that the Communist Party had to be a tightknit and homogeneous group. Second, and more spectacularly, the Soviet Union fell apart on the fault-line of national self-determination. Once the Communist Party had ceased to count, all the Soviet republics were entitled to exercise the legal right to secession allowed to them in the constitutions of 1924, 1936 and 1977. This can hardly have been what Lenin and Stalin had in mind.

Questions

1. Did the Tsarist constitution of 1906 work?
2. Did democracy triumph in the Soviet constitutional structure?

ANALYSIS 3: DISCUSS THE SIMILARITIES AND DIFFERENCES BETWEEN THE CONSTITUTIONS INTRODUCED DURING THE LATE-TSARIST AND SOVIET PERIODS.

All constitutions are introduced to define institutional power, as well as the accountability and representation upon which it is based. But the motive for doing this differed fundamentally between the Tsarist and Soviet regimes.

The Tsarist constitutional system tended to be reactive, in that it responded to a situation that demanded change; it therefore included defensive mechanisms to prevent the changes from becoming too effective – and therefore intrusive. This was evident in two ways. The first example was the measures used by Alexander III (1881–94) to limit the impact of the constitutional reforms introduced by Alexander II (1855–81). In 1890 he insisted on separate electoral rolls for elections to the *zemstva* (established in 1864), while in 1892 he narrowed the electorate for the municipal *dumas* (1870) to property owners. More seriously, he resolutely refused to revive plans for a Consultative Assembly, shelved after Alexander II's assassination in 1881. The second example of limitations was the desperate attempt made by Nicholas II to restrict the scope of the constitution he had been forced to grant after the 1905 Revolution. The Fundamental Laws (1906) were really intended to weaken any such concessions and to salvage as much of autocracy as possible. The 23 articles of Chapter 1 of the Fundamental Laws therefore defined the 'essence of the supreme autocratic power'; the overriding impression is that the whole constitution was an unsought imposition that had to be carefully controlled.

The origins of the Soviet constitutions were somewhat different. It might, of course, be argued that the 1918 Constitution establishing the RSFSR had to be rushed into existence to replace the Constituent Assembly and its anti-Bolshevik majority. But this could be put down to timing rather than to a decision forced by events. Lenin's *April Theses* (1917) had undertaken to hold elections for a Constituent Assembly merely to gain support for a Bolshevik Revolution; his ultimate intention was to abandon the liberal-democratic approach and, instead, to use a system of soviets. This would be easier to reconcile with the ideological roots of his movement. Whereas the 1906 constitutional changes were gradually undermined by subsequent manipulation by a resentful Tsar, the constitutions of the Soviet period were refined and adapted in a way that was reflective rather than reactive. Each was seen as a milestone. Lenin's 1918 Constitution set up the system of soviets for Russia itself; the 1924 Constitution extended this to the principle of a broader federation in the form of the USSR; Stalin's 1936 Constitution broadened the democratic base in acknowledgement that the 'dictatorship of the proletariat' was nearing an end; and Brezhnev's 1977 Constitution was intended for an era of 'Developed Socialism', an intermediate phase between the 'dictatorship of the proletariat' and the 'classless society'. Even the constitution introduced by Gorbachev in 1989 was designed to shape the future, this time under the guiding principles of *glasnost* and *perestroika*.

The contrasts between 'reactive' and 'reflective' influences are apparent in the way in which the various constitutions describe the functions of the institutions. By and large, the 1906 Fundamental Laws expressed these negatively. Although two chambers were set up, the purpose of the largely appointed State Council was to limit the initiative of the elected Duma. The Tsar retained a strong watching brief over them both. Article 8, for example, stated that: 'The Sovereign Emperor enjoys the legislative initiative in all legislative matters. The State Council and the State Duma may examine the Fundamental State Laws only on his initiative.'[4] There was also no acknowledgement of legislative control over the executive: according to Article 18: 'As supreme administrator the Sovereign Emperor determines the scope of activity of all state officials in accordance with the needs of the state.'[5] As for the various ethnic groups, it was made clear in Article 1 that there to be no special concessions: 'The Russian State is unified and indivisible.'[6] The Soviet constitutions were different in all three respects. For example, the bicameral structure established in 1936 seemed to enhance legislative power rather than to restrict it. The Soviet of the Union represented the country as a whole and the Soviet of the Nationalities the constituent Republics; there was therefore a balance between 'unitary' and 'federal' rather than a dominance of 'upper' over 'lower'. Unlike that of 1906, the Soviet constitutions all emphasised the subordination of the executive to the legislature. In the 1918 Constitution, for example, 'sovereign power' was 'vested in the All-Russian Congress of Soviets',[7] which elected the Central Executive Committee (TsIK). The 1936 Constitution similarly allowed for the election of the Council of People's Commissars (changed in 1946 to the Council of Ministers) by the Supreme Soviet. In contrast to the lack of any such provisions in the 1906 Fundamental Laws, the 1924, 1936 and 1977 Constitutions all upheld the rights of the various ethnic groups. According to the 1936 Constitution: 'The Union of Soviet Socialist Republics is a federal state, formed on the basis of the voluntary union of . . . Soviet Socialist Republics equal in rights' (Article 13).[8]

So far it may appear that there is a straightforward difference between 'undemocratic' and 'democratic' regimes. From one angle this may be true. The 1906 Fundamental Laws were never intended to introduce Tsarist Russia to democracy of any kind; Nicholas II was always reluctant to describe his concession as an actual 'constitution'. By contrast, the entire Soviet system claimed legitimacy through the actual achievement of democracy. The transition in Russia's history was therefore obvious: from a 'pre-democratic' to a 'democratic' phase. This would, however, be to ignore a great deal below the surface. If democracy is interpreted in the sense of 'liberal democracy', then a different perspective emerges. The 'pre-democratic' constitution of Tsarist Russia, with its constrained legislature but multi-party system, was prevented from achieving the type of 'democracy' that existed at the time in the United States, Britain, France, Italy and – arguably – Germany. The opportunity to do so was missed in 1917 by the Provisional Government, which deferred any constitutional change until after the conclusion of war. The nearest that Russia came to a 'democratic' constitution was there-fore the Constituent Assembly elected in November 1917. This, however, was dissolved by the Bolsheviks in January 1918, on the grounds that it was 'an expression of the old relation of political forces which existed when power was held by the compromisers'.[9] Instead, Lenin settled on 'a higher form of democratic principle than the customary bourgeois republic with its Constituent Assembly'.[10] The short-lived Assembly was therefore the point at which a possible transition from 'pre-democracy' to 'democracy' became, instead, a slide from 'pre-' to 'post-democracy'.

Although underpinning different systems, the parallels between 'pre-' and 'post-democracy' are striking. Both, for example, were subordinated to a centralising system: the Tsarist regime to bureaucratic absolutism and the Soviet state to democratic centralism. Within each the legislature had little chance of sustaining 'democracy' in practice; instead, it was controlled by a much more powerful executive. The Dumas were supposedly elected for five-year terms; the first two, however, came into conflict with the Tsar's ministers and were dissolved in 1906 and 1907, while the third and fourth lasted their full term by being largely bypassed or ignored. The USSR had a more effective form of control. It established the fiction that the legislature, in the form of soviets, controlled the Central Executive Committee or Council of Ministers. Yet the Soviets met periodically rather than continuously and, according to the 1918 Constitution, 'sovereign power' was 'vested, ... in the interim between congresses, in the All-Russian Central Executive Committee'.[11] The Tsarist constitution never entrusted power to its elected delegates, while the Soviet system ensured that such delegates immediately transferred their power as a mandate. In Western 'liberal-democratic' systems, the legislature retains its influence through party politics. Both the Tsarist and Soviet systems managed to remove the 'politics' from 'party' altogether. Under the 1906 Fundamental Laws multiple parties were to be allowed – but were given no access to the institutions of power; their competition was therefore factional rather than political. In the constitutions of 1918, 1924, 1936 and 1977, the Communist Party was the only one permitted, thus transforming party politics into competition between individuals. It was only during the Gorbachev era that the reappearance of other parties became a possibility. Even then, a multi-party assembly was not achieved until 1992 – after the banning of the Communist Party by Yeltsin and the collapse of the Soviet Union itself.

Another parallel between the Tsarist and Soviet constitutional structures was the scope for individual power. In the former this amounted to openly declared 'autocracy', in the latter to unstated 'dictatorship'. Under the Fundamental Laws, Nicholas II retained the 'supreme autocratic power' (Article 4), covering the 'legislative initiative in all legislative matters' (Article 5), 'administrative power in its totality' (Article 10), 'the direction of foreign policy' (Article 12), the declaration of war (Article 13) and the command of the armed forces (Article 14).[12] Although no such authority could be claimed by any individual *from* the Soviet constitutions, it could emerge in practice *through* these constitutions. The method operated as follows. The Supreme Soviet elected the Council of Ministers; both were under the control of the Party, the inner core of which was the Politburo or Presidium. It was from within the Politburo that the succession normally emerged, although this was played to the wider audience of Party Congresses and sessions of the soviets. In this process, the General Secretary of the Party had a natural advantage, which explains the emergence of Stalin after Lenin, of Khrushchev after Stalin and of Brezhnev after Khrushchev. Yet, during the timescale of these three successions (all leading to highly personalised rule), the role of the Party was scarcely mentioned constitutionally. It was only in 1977 that Brezhnev thought to make it more explicit (see Source 7, p. 49). The most telling criticism of the whole process came in the *glasnost* period, when Sakharov articulated the growing view that the role of the legislature should be increased and that of the Party reduced (see Source 8, pp. 49–50).

There is even a parallel in that apparent change was often no change at all. In 1906 the initiatives for reform still came from the top. Stolypin, who might, through his agricultural and financial reforms, have saved the dynasty from revolution, was nevertheless an enemy of the Duma. Foreign policy and the outbreak of the war, which ensured that the regime *did* collapse, were quite deliberately excluded from the Duma's influence. In the Soviet system what was, in theory at least, progressive change could actually be seen as hardening the arteries against change. If the constitutions were reflective, it was in a backward-looking rather than forward-looking sense – justifying current practice rather than allowing for future change. Until Gorbachev's leadership, the actual changes were quite limited. The 1918 Constitution was merely extended to the non-Russian areas by that of 1924, while the 'democratic' principles of both were still constrained in 1936. 'I must admit', observed Stalin, 'that the draft of the new [1936] constitution actually leaves in force the regime of the dictatorship of the proletariat as well as preserving unchanged the present leading position of the Communist Party.'[13] Despite all of Khrushchev's ambitions for a new constitution – and following a decade of consultation and planning – Brezhnev's 1977 version differed from that of 1936 only in its clause on the Communist Party.

In the end, of course, both regimes collapsed unceremoniously and with surprisingly little resistance. There is, however, a final similarity – perhaps the most important of all. In both cases, the constitutions provided a vehicle for focusing opposition, breaking the central authority that had held it in check. In March 1917, the last Tsar was forced to abdicate by representatives of the Provisional Committee, drawn from the Progressive Bloc. These bodies had emerged *within* the constitutional changes – the Provisional Committee inside the State Duma and the Progressive Bloc from the moderate political parties. They brought an orderly transfer of power to what had previously been a series of street demonstrations, strikes and riots. In August 1991, 74 years later, Gorbachev, as the last Soviet President, watched helplessly while Yeltsin used the Russian parliament – successor to the Republic Soviet of the RSFSR – to ban the operation of the Communist Party within Russia. This signalled the collapse of the Soviet Union in the constitutional revolution of 31 December 1991, a paradox that is examined in Chapter 6.

Questions

1. Which regime better represented the Russian people: Tsarist or Soviet?
2. 'Nicholas II grew weaker after the Fundamental Laws of 1906; Stalin grew stronger after the constitution of 1936.' Comment.

SOURCES

1. THE IMPERIAL CONSTITUTION OF 1906

Source 1: Extracts from the Fundamental Laws of 1906.

4. The All-Russian Emperor possesses the supreme autocratic power. Not only fear and conscience, but God himself, commands obedience to his authority.

7. The Sovereign Emperor exercises the legislative authority jointly with the State Council and the State Duma.

8. The Sovereign Emperor enjoys the legislative initiative in all legislative matters. The State Council and the State Duma may examine the Fundamental State Laws only on his initiative.

9. The Sovereign Emperor approves laws; and without his approval no legislative measure can become law.

10. The Sovereign Emperor possesses the administrative power in its totality throughout the entire Russian state. On the highest level of administration his authority is direct; on subordinate levels of administration, in conformity with the law, he determines the degree of authority of subordinate branches and officials who act in his name and in accordance with his orders.

11. As supreme administrator, the Sovereign Emperor, in conformity with the existing laws, issues decrees for the organization and functioning of diverse branches of state administration as well as directives essential for the execution of the laws.

12. The Sovereign Emperor alone is the supreme leader of all foreign relations of the Russian state with foreign countries. He also determines the direction of foreign policy of the Russian state.

13. The Sovereign Emperor alone declares war, concludes peace and negotiates treaties with foreign states.

14. The Sovereign Emperor is the Commander-in-Chief of the Russian Army and of the Fleet. He possesses supreme command over all the land and sea forces of the Russian state. ...

15. The Sovereign Emperor has the power to declare martial law or a state of emergency in localities.

17. The Sovereign Emperor appoints and dismisses the Chairman of the Council of Ministers, Ministers, and Chief Administrators of various departments. ...

42. The Russian Empire is governed by firmly established laws that have been properly enacted.

44. No new law can be enacted without the approval of the State Council and the State Duma, and it shall not be legally binding without the approval of the Sovereign Emperor.

Source 2: Extracts from *A Short History of the Communist Party of the Soviet Union*. These are from the 1970 edition.

Frightened by the growth of the revolution, the government hastily made further concessions to the people in order to save the autocracy. On October 17, 1905, the tsar published a Manifesto containing many false promises about freedom and the setting up of a State Duma with legislative powers. The temporary equilibrium of forces made it possible to issue this Manifesto. The workers and peasants were not strong enough to overthrow tsarism, and tsarism, for its part, could no longer rule in the old way.

The bourgeoisie joyously accepted this sop from the tsar. The big capitalists and the landowners, who ran their estates on capitalist lines, sided with the tsarist government but continued to bargain for a share of power. The bourgeoisie regarded the Manifesto as a means of steering the revolution towards a peaceful, constitutional conclusion and thereby saving the monarchy. . . .

The continuing revolution compelled the tsarist government to convene the promised State Duma, and it endeavoured to sow the illusion among the masses that land and political rights could be won by peaceful means through the Duma. In face of this new piece of deceit, the Bolsheviks did their best to shatter these illusions, to explain to the people that victory could be achieved only through a revolutionary struggle.

Source 3: From Alexander Chubarov, *The Fragile Empire*, published in 2001.

The social upheavals of 1905 had finally forced out of the government the promise to introduce a constitutional system with an elected parliament. However, Nicholas's reluctance to allow any weakening of his autocratic powers ensured that the government's attempt to devise a workable constitutional framework would be half-hearted and incomplete. When drawing up the Fundamental Laws early in 1906, Nicholas did all he could to limit the powers of the Duma. The electoral system discriminated heavily against peasants and workers; elections were to be indirect; and votes were to be cast and counted by separate constituencies (called *curios*), set up for each class or property group.

Moreover, the powers vested in the new legislative forum were severely limited. Ministers remained responsible solely to the tsar and continued to be appointed and dismissed solely by him. The Duma had the power to reject only parts of the state budget. The new constitution transformed the traditional supreme body within the bureaucracy, the State Council, into an upper house, many of whose members were to be appointed by the tsar or nominated by the government. The tsar retained the power to veto all legislation, while Article 87 of the Fundamental Laws enabled him to rule by decree when the Duma was not in session. In addition, Nicholas insisted on referring to his own authority as 'autocratic,' though he agreed to drop the word 'unlimited' from the traditional formula describing the sovereign's power. This now read: 'Supreme autocratic power belongs to the emperor of all Russia' (Article 4). ...

The constitutional reform had failed to bridge the gap between the government and Russia's rapidly changing educated elites. The new upper classes were politically disaffected, antagonised by Nicholas's attempts to stifle the potentially democratic institution of the Duma and his refusal to introduce a Western-style government. Even the backing the regime could expect from its traditional supporters, such as the landed nobility, was hesitant and uncertain. Its power now rested on the bureaucracy and the army alone. The most dangerous aspect of the government's position was the political blindness of the tsar, who still believed in the loyalty of the masses of the peasants, the army, and the nobility. Nicholas simply was unable to see how isolated his government was and how narrow was the base of support for a government about to lead its country into a devastating international war.

Source 4: From Michael T. Florinsky, *The End of the Russian Empire*, originally published in 1931.

In spite of these important handicaps one must admit that the introduction of an elective legislative chamber presented a striking and extremely important departure in the political and social life of the country. The first and most difficult step toward the establishment of a constitutional system of government had been made. Not only were the autocratic powers of the Tsar limited by the legislative control of the two chambers, the Duma and the State Council, but, what seems far more important, the country at large in the person of its chosen representatives was at last called to take a direct part in the conduct of public affairs. It is not denied that the franchise was limited and that the law secured the election of a majority representing the landed gentry. The really significant fact seems to be that the admission of the country to a participation – however slight it was at first – in the work of government offered an extraordinary and novel opportunity for the political education of the masses. Progress along these lines naturally was slow, but it was a forward movement and ended the political stagnation in which the country had been kept for centuries. There was no immediate prospect of an expansion of the franchise; but years or even decades are very short periods in the life of a nation, and it was perhaps not unreasonable to expect that in due course democratic institutions in Russia would develop along the same lines as in other countries. The door for these changes was now open.

Questions

1. Compare Sources 2 and 3 as comments on the constitution conceded by Nicholas II. (20)

2. Using all of Sources 1 to 4, and your own knowledge, consider the view that 'irrespective of the 1906 Constitution, Tsarist Russia was doomed'. (40)

Total (60)

Worked answers

[Apart from the first, the above sources are secondary. The technique for dealing with them is broadly similar to that with primary sources – covered in Chapter 1, Sources 1, pp. 20–3. There are, however, some exceptions, covered below.]

1. [Focus on an integrated comparison – through similarities and differences – of the content and slant of the two sources.]

The main similarities between Sources 2 and 3 concern the way in which Nicholas II conceded the October Manifesto and subsequently tried to retract it. The contrasts are more to do with various attitudes to the Tsar's policy.

There seems to be agreement that the Tsar was obliged to act, since he was 'frightened by the growth of the revolution' (Source 2) or, as Source 3 puts it 'the social upheavals of 1905'. According to Source 2, the government therefore 'hastily made further concessions to the people in order to save the autocracy'; Source 3's version is that the 1905 revolution had forced the government 'to introduce a constitutional system with an elected parliament'. There is also agreement that the concession did not live up to expectations; Source 2 refers to the 'many false promises about freedom', while Source 3 maintains that Nicholas II's attitude meant that the changes 'would be half-hearted and incomplete'.

The differences have to do with the response to the concessions. Source 2 implies that there was broad agreement between the Tsarist system and the bourgeoisie, 'who joyously accepted this sop'; even though the 'big capitalists and the landowners' did continue to 'bargain for a share of power' there was nevertheless a common interest and identity. It was the 'people' who felt betrayed – after, of course, their eyes had been opened by the Bolsheviks. This is hardly surprising since the *Short History of the CPSU* follows a class-based analysis retrospectively imposed by the direct heirs of the Bolsheviks. Source 3 takes an altogether different approach, untrammelled by ideological influences and therefore able to comment more subtly on the response of classes to the concessions. The analysis therefore refers to the unfavourable reaction of Russia's elites. Instead of the Tsar heading a class-based strategic adjustment, he is seen as 'isolated' in the 'political blindness' of his attempts to reverse the constitutional settlement.

2. *[Advice: Much of the technique is similar to that for Question 3 on p. 20. In this case there is, however, an additional dimension since three out of the four sources are secondary rather than primary: the debate therefore needs an historiographical as well as an historical context. Otherwise, as on pp. 22–3, the answer should consider the contribution of the sources partly for content and partly for provenance, and 'own' knowledge should be used partly in such comments on the sources and partly to add further material outside their immediate range. An overall approach might be to consider arguments for and against the quotation in the question, before coming to a considered conclusion. There may be some overlap with Question 1, but it is better to use different extracts if possible.]*

Whether Tsarist Russia was doomed to collapse after 1905 has been widely debated by historians. Opinions of those prepared to commit themselves divide largely between 'pessimists', who believe that the regime was entering its final phase irrespective of subsequent events, and 'optimists', who argue that the regime was pulled down as a direct result of the First World War – without which it might well have survived. Three of these sources directly reflect this debate. Sources 2 and 3 are basically 'pessimistic', although for different reasons, while 4 is more obviously 'optimistic'. Source 1 predates the collapse and the debate but has an underlying expectation of survival.

'Pessimistic' arguments carry a range of different arguments, which can be quite different to each other. Source 2, for example, attributes the subsequent collapse of the regime to the Bolshevik revelation of the 'deceit' of the Tsar and his allies (the 'bourgeoisie', 'big capitalists' and 'landowners'). Source 3, on the other hand, emphasises the growing isolation of a regime that provoked widespread opposition. These are typical of the contrasting approaches of Soviet and Western historical approaches, the former being more ideological, the latter more academic. The official Soviet view embraces the Marxist concept of class warfare and the inevitability of the triumph of the proletariat. This is implicit in the analysis given in Source 2. There is, however, the adaptation of Marxism typical of Lenin – that capitalism would be broken where it was weakest – in Russia. This explains the importance of the Bolsheviks in explaining 'to the people that victory could be achieved only through a revolutionary struggle'. Source 3, on the other hand, stresses the importance of the alienation of 'Russia's rapidly changing educated elites' in weakening the Tsarist regime. The collapse of the regime is not inevitable because of some infrastructural process of class warfare, but gradually becomes the most likely outcome because of the defection of the 'new upper classes', who were 'politically disaffected' by his attempts to 'stifle' the 'Duma', and the 'landed nobility'. The key factor is not the operation of dialectical materialism, but rather of the obstinacy and blindness of the Tsar himself.

Of course, there is an equally valid alternative. The 'optimist' view is strongly represented by Source 4, in which Florinsky argues that the changes after 1905 were full of potential for the future – and 'an extraordinary and novel opportunity for the political education of the masses'. Far from condemning the regime to eventual collapse, 'it was a forward movement' that ended centuries of 'political stagnation'. The Tsar's obstructive attitude need not have been fatal; although there was no 'immediate prospect of an expansion of the franchise', a longer view would indicate a real prospect of more progressive institutions in the future. Florinsky and other 'optimists' have on their side the evidence of social and economic reforms within the same period, legalising trade unions, dealing with issues of land tenure and introducing national insurance. What could not have been anticipated was the catastrophic impact of military defeat in the First World War, which destroyed these constraints on revolution.

Although chronologically outside the debate in the question, Source 1 must be considered at least as evidence for the regime's intended survival. The impression is that at this stage it is possible to operate a constitutional system through the basic understanding in Article 7 that 'The Sovereign Emperor' would exercise legislative authority 'jointly with the State Council and the State Duma'. There is, of course, a major flaw in the Fundamental Laws – that the 'supreme autocratic power' in Article 4 can hardly be reconciled with joint authority, and that Articles 10 and 11 confirmed the Tsar's exclusive control over the administration, 12 to 15 over foreign policy and the declaration of war. But his can be seen either as a 'fatal flaw' that would lead inevitably to failure or as an intermediate weakness that could eventually be remedied.

The argument can be weighted towards the 'pessimist' approach by further evidence that is not included in Sources 1 to 4. Revisionist historians have emphasised the importance of the growing radicalism of the industrial proletariat and rural peasantry both before and after 1905. This is largely independent of the Bolshevik influence claimed in Source 2 but is in addition to the alienation of the elites emphasised in Source 3. In other words opposition to the Tsarist regime had become overwhelming, made all the more serious by the growing experience of the lower classes in *expressing* this opposition. It is therefore difficult to see how Nicholas II could have held out.

2. THE CONSTITUTIONS OF THE USSR

Source 5: Lenin in July 1917.

Positively no steps can be taken towards a correct understanding of our tactical tasks in Russia today unless we concentrate above all on systematically and ruthlessly exposing constitutional illusions, revealing all their roots and re-establishing a proper political perspective.

Source 6: The Dissolution of the Constituent Assembly by the All-Russian Central Executive Committee of the Soviets 19 January 1918.

The Constituent Assembly, elected on the basis of lists drawn up prior to the October revolution, was an expression of the old relation of political forces which existed when power was held by the compromisers and the Kadets. When the people at that time voted for the candidates of the Socialist-Revolutionary Party, they were not in a position to choose between the Right Socialist-Revolutionaries, the supporters of the bourgeoisie, and the Left Socialist-Revolutionaries, the supporters of socialism. Thus the Constituent Assembly, which was to have been the crown of the bourgeois parliamentary republic, could not but become an obstacle in the path of the October revolution and the Soviet power.

The October revolution, by giving power to the Soviets, and through the Soviets to the toiling and exploited classes, aroused the desperate resistance of the exploiters, and in the crushing of this resistance it fully revealed itself as the beginning of the socialist revolution. The toiling classes learnt by experience that the old bourgeois parliamentarism had outlived its purpose and was absolutely incompatible with the aim of achieving socialism, and that not national institutions, but only class institutions (such as the Soviets), were capable of overcoming the resistance of the propertied classes and of laying the foundations of a socialist society. To relinquish the sovereign power of the Soviets, to relinquish the Soviet republic won by the people, for the sake of bourgeois parliamentarism and the Constituent Assembly, would now be a retrograde step and cause the collapse of the October workers' and peasants' revolution. . . .

Accordingly, the Central Executive Committee resolves: The Constituent Assembly is hereby dissolved.

Source 7: The 1977 Brezhnev Constitution.

Article 1. The Union of Soviet Socialist Republics is a socialist state of all the people, expressing the will and interests of the workers, peasants and intelligentsia, the working people of all the nations and nationalities of the country. . . .

Article 3. The Soviet state is organised and functions on the principle of democratic centralism, namely the electiveness of all bodies of state power from the lowest to the highest, their accountability to the people, and the obligation of lower bodies to observe the decisions of higher ones. Democratic centralism combines central leadership with local initiative and creative activity and with the responsibility of each state body and official for the work entrusted to them. . . .

Article 6. The leading and guiding force of Soviet society and the nucleus of its political system, of all state and public organisations, is the Communist Party of the Soviet Union. The CPSU exists for the people and serves the people. The Communist Party, armed with Marxism-Leninism, determines the general perspectives of the development of society and the course of the home and foreign policy of the USSR, directs the great constructive work of the Soviet people, and imparts a planned, systematic and theoretically substantiated character to their struggle for the victory of communism. All party organisations shall function within the framework of the Constitution of the USSR.

Source 8: Extracts from Andrei Sakharov's speech in favour of further constitutional reform, given in the First Congress of People's Deputies on 9 June 1989.

Comrade deputies, on you now – precisely now – lies an enormous historical responsibility. Political decisions are required, without which it will be impossible to strengthen the power of soviet authorities in the localities and to resolve economic, social, ecological and national problems. If the Congress of People's Deputies cannot take power into its own hands here, then there is not the slightest hope that Soviets in the republics, *oblasts, raions* [districts] and villages can do so. But without strong Soviets in the localities agrarian reform will be impossible or any reasonably effective agrarian policy differing from the senseless transfusion of resources into loss-making collective farms. Without a strong Congress and strong Soviets it will be impossible to overcome the diktats of departments, the working out and implementation of laws about enterprises, the struggle against ecological folly. The Congress is called upon to defend democratic principles of popular power and, by the same token, the irreversibility of *perestroika* and the harmonious development of the country. I once again appeal to the Congress to adopt the 'Decree on Power'.

Decree on Power

Proceeding from the principles of democracy, the Congress of People's Deputies declares:

1   Article 6 of the USSR Constitution [of 1977] is annulled.
2   The adoption of USSR laws is the exclusive right of the USSR Congress of People's Deputies. On the territory of a union republic USSR laws gain juridical force only after they have been ratified by the highest legislative body of the union republic.
3   The Supreme Soviet is the working body of the Congress.
4   Commissions and Committees are created by the Congress and Supreme Soviet on principles of parity and are accountable to the Congress. They prepare laws and the state budget, other laws and offer permanent supervision over the activity of state bodies, over the economic, social and ecological situation in the country.
5   The election and recall of the highest USSR officials, namely the chairman of the USSR Supreme Soviet.

Source 9: Yeltsin's resignation from the CPSU, 12 July 1990.

In connection with my election as chairman of the RSFSR Supreme Soviet and the enormous responsibility before the people of Russia, taking into account the transition of society towards a multi-party system, I cannot fulfil only decisions of the CPSU. As head of the highest legislative power of the republic I must subordinate myself to the will of the people and its plenipotentiaries. Therefore, I, in accordance with my promises made in the electoral campaign, declare my departure from the CPSU to be able more effectively to influence the activity of Soviets. I am ready to cooperate with all parties and socio-political organisations in the republic.

Questions

1.   Compare Sources 7 and 8 as comments on the operation of the democratic process in the USSR from 1977. (20)
2.   Using all of Sources 5 to 9, and your own knowledge, consider the view that 'constitutional democracy within the Soviet Union was doomed from 1918'. (40)

Total (60)

3

POLITICAL PARTIES

ANALYSIS 1: EXAMINE THE MEANING AND DEVELOPMENT OF POLITICAL PARTIES BETWEEN 1855 AND 1991.

The concept of 'political party' went through five main phases during this period. First, between 1855 and 1905 parties were illegal and regarded as a subversive form of opposition to the state – irrespective of whether they were revolutionary or reformist. Second, following the 1905 Revolution, Russia experienced a multi-party system that existed within the context of the flawed constitutional experiments of the last Tsarist years. They achieved sudden – but short-lived – power during the third phase, that dominated by the Provisional Government between March and October 1917. Fourth, in 1918 the whole con-cept of party moved away from the multiple base to a single monolithic system. This remained the case until the collapse of the Soviet Union in 1991 and the fifth phase, which saw the return to a multiple-party system along 'Western' lines.

Phase 1: Before 1905 – parties as 'subversive opposition' to the regime

Before 1905 there was no official party system in Russia since there was no central legislature to accommodate the parties. Where parties did appear, therefore, they tended to oppose the regime. This oppos-ition might take the form of revolutionary conspiracy or, alternatively, of reformist pressure. An example of the former was the emergence of Populist groups, based on the ideas of Herzen, and aiming at a political and social republic based on rural socialism. These united to form Land and Liberty in 1876, although this subsequently divided into a propagandist party, Black Partition, and the more violent People's Will, which was responsible for the assassination of Alexander II in 1881. The different wings of Populism came together in 1900 as the Socialist Revolutionary Party, which continued to oppose the Tsarist regime, often with violence and assassinations. Meanwhile, a number of Marxist groups had sprung up during the reign of Alexander III (1881–94). These united in 1898 to form the RSDLP, before splitting in 1903 into moderate and radical wings known respectively as Mensheviks and Bolsheviks. Like the SRs, both were committed to changing the base of the regime, or to removing it altogether. In complete contrast, a more constitutionalist trend was also emerging, rooted in the units of local government established by Alexander II; the main examples were the *Zemstvo* Congress and the Union of Unions (1904). Their ultimate aim was the establishment of a fully representative parliamentary system along Western lines. Alexander III and Nicholas II, however, regarded the revolutionary and constitutionalist opposition with equal hostility and heeded the advice of Pobedonostsev to maintain a total ban on all parties (see Chapter 1).

Phase 2: 1906 to March 1917 – parties legalised but politically marginalised by the regime

The threat from the 1905 Revolution forced the regime to change the legal status of political parties – but its hostility to them remained. This meant that Russia suddenly acquired parties across the full political spectrum, ranging from the reactionary right (Union of the Russian People and Monarchists), the moderate right (Octobrists and Industrialists), the moderate left (Constitutional Democrats or Kadets), the radical left (SRs and Social Democrats), nationalist parties (the Polish League, Lithuanian Circle, Ukrainian Democrats) and religious or ethnic parties (the Muslim Group). Yet none of these had any real opportunity to develop government policy; attempts by the Kadets to do so resulted in the early dissolution of the Duma in 1906 and 1907 and the tightening of the Electoral Law. The 1906 Constitution therefore created a dangerous situation: a parliament with parties – but with no scope for party politics. The outcome was the alienation of virtually all the parties, their role combining in March 1917 to bring down the Tsarist regime. SRs and Mensheviks on the left combined with spontaneous activists to take control of the streets, while the

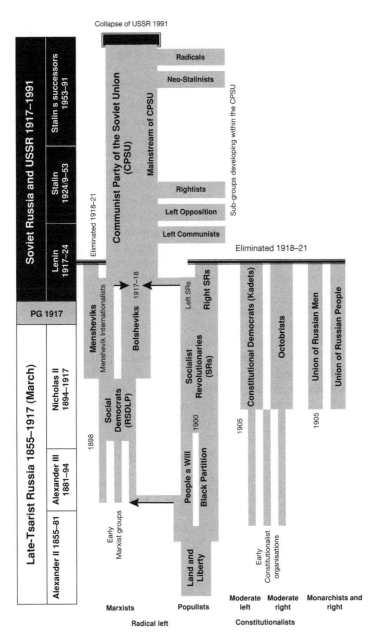

Collapse of USSR 1991

Soviet Russia and USSR 1917–1991

Stalin's successors 1953–91	Stalin 1924/9–53	Lenin 1917–24

PG 1917

Late-Tsarist Russia 1855–1917 (March)

Nicholas II 1894–1917	Alexander III 1881–94	Alexander II 1855–81

Radicals

Neo-Stalinists

Communist Party of the Soviet Union (CPSU)

Mainstream of CPSU

Sub-groups developing within the CPSU

Eliminated 1918–21

Rightists

Left Opposition

Left Communists

Eliminated 1918–21

Mensheviks

Menshevik Internationalists

Bolsheviks 1917–18

Left SRs

Right SRs

Constitutional Democrats (Kadets)

Octobrists

Union of Russian Men

Union of Russian People

Social Democrats (RSDLP)

Socialist Revolutionaries (SRs)

1898

1900

1905

1905

People's Will

Black Partition

Early Marxist groups

Early Constitutionalist organisations

Land and Liberty

Marxists

Populists

Moderate left

Moderate right

Monarchists and right

Radical left

Constitutionalists

THE MAIN POLITICAL PARTIES AND FACTIONS 1855–1991

Figure 3.

Kadets and Octobrists tried to prevent a descent into chaos by setting up the Provisional Committee of the Duma. This, in turn, became the Provisional Government.

Phase 3: March 1917 to January 1918 – multiple parties and power-sharing

After a ten-year exclusion from political decision-making, the parties had created their own system. They now operated through the Petrograd Soviet and the Provisional Government, the Mensheviks and SRs providing members for both organisations. All parties envisaged a permanent constitution based on an elected Constituent Assembly. The Provisional Government, however, made the mistake of postponing elections, and other proposed reforms, until after the end of the war with Germany. More than anything else, this destabilised the whole political structure, bringing about a fundamental party realignment and making possible a second revolution in October. The Bolsheviks (who had contributed very little to the fall of the Tsarist regime) played for popular support after Lenin's return from exile in April. By the beginning of October they had succeeded in gaining a majority in the Petrograd and Moscow Soviets and were identifying the Provisional Government as the new enemy. The Octobrists and Kadets left the Provisional Government in August, while the Mensheviks and SRs developed far-left offshoots (the Menshevik Internationalists and the Left SRs), which formed a coalition with the Bolsheviks. With their broadening support, the latter were able to seize power in October 1917.

Phase 4: 1918–91 – a one-party state based on the CPSU

Lenin's first act was to implement one of the promises in his *April Theses*, the immediate election of the Constituent Assembly. This showed a broad range of support from the new electorate and seemed to indicate that the multi-party system had taken root. But what followed was the most radical change to party politics in the twentieth century. Since the election returned a majority for the SRs rather than for Bolsheviks and their allies, Lenin closed the Constituent Assembly, introducing instead a political structure based on soviets (see Chapter 2). Western-style multi-party systems were seen as socially divisive and class-based; the solution was a one-party state based on the principle of democratic centralism (see Chapter 1). This involved the suppression of all other parties by 1922, including the Mensheviks, SRs and Kadets. The Bolsheviks became the Communist

Party (from 1924 the CPSU), which dominated all the constitutional structures set up in 1918, 1924 and 1936.

After Lenin's death in 1924 two main developments occurred. One was the division of the CPSU into factions, committed to the contrasting strategies of 'Socialism in One Country' on the one hand and 'Permanent Revolution' on the other. These overlapped temporary groups of individual Bolsheviks, such as the Left Opposition (Trotsky, Kamenev, Zinoviev) and the Rightists (Bukharin, Rykov, Tomsky). By 1929 these groups had been outmanoeuvred by Stalin and their leaders expelled from the Politburo and the Party itself. This signalled the beginning of the other development, which lasted until Stalin's death in 1953 – the personalisation of Stalin's dictatorship and the ever-decreasing role played by the CPSU. Stalin also purged the membership of the Party, through a series of show trials in the 1930s, and rarely summoned key organs such as the Central Committee and the Politburo. Having risen to power by pulling Party levers, Stalin managed for most of his period in power to do without them altogether.

The post-Stalinist period saw the return of the formal influence and power of the CPSU. This was the deliberate strategy of Khrushchev, the Party chairman. More was to follow. From 1956, the regime was 'destalinised' and Stalin himself was written out of Soviet history, his achievements attributed instead to 'the Party'. Khrushchev's successors – Brezhnev, Andropov and Chernenko – were all devoted Party men and used it as a centralising and unifying force in a country that was becoming more and more heterogeneous. Under Gorbachev, however, the CPSU became more divided than at any time since the 1920s. Different sections reacted in different ways to Gorbachev's introduction after 1985 of *glasnost* and *perestroika* and the moderate centre supported Gorbachev's initiative as the most effective means of modernising the political and economic structure of the Soviet Union. The neo-Stalinists of the far right (in Western terms, the far left) saw *glasnost* and *perestroika* as a betrayal of everything the CPSU had always stood for. The left (or Western right), under Yeltsin, wanted to go further and to end the CPSU's monopoly of political power altogether. By 1989, therefore, the Party was in deep crisis.

Phase 5: 1991 and after – the collapse of the CPSU and the return to multiple-party politics

The crunch came in August 1991 as the neo-Stalinists, under Yaneyev and Pugo, tried to take over from Gorbachev and end his reforms. Their coup was, however, defied by Yeltsin, and collapsed within the week. Gorbachev returned to power but now had to contend with Yeltsin, who proceeded to ban the Party from operating within the Russian Federation, the largest republic in the Soviet Union. Others followed suit, banning their own branches of the Party and, at the same time, declaring themselves independent sovereign states. Yeltsin introduced a Western parliamentary system, based on a Duma, seats in which were contested by a wide range of political parties. The Communists were legalised as one of these.

Questions

1. Why were there more political parties in late-Tsarist Russia than there were in the Soviet Union?
2. In what ways was the Communist Party of the Soviet Union more influential than the parties in late-Tsarist Russia?

ANALYSIS 2: HOW SUCCESSFUL WERE *EITHER* ALEXANDER III AND NICHOLAS II *OR* LENIN AND STALIN IN CONTROLLING THE POWER OF POLITICAL PARTIES?

The four periods of power between 1881 and 1953, which encompassed the last two Tsars and the first two Soviet leaders, saw an interesting overall trend in the relationship between rulers and parties. This started with parties being denied any constitutional role on the grounds that they were subversive, then moved through reluctant recognition to the reformulation of the role of party and ultimate subjection to the personal control of the leader. Generally speaking, the Soviet regime exerted controls through and *within* the party, while Tsarist action was targeted *against* parties.

Alexander III and Nicholas II (1881–1917)

The approach of Alexander III (1881–94) was based on the assumption that political parties lacked any sort of legitimacy. In this he was strongly influenced by the view of Pobedonostsev (see Chapter 1) that parties were subversive and corrupt. He therefore made no distinction between those groups that wished to be accepted as part of the system and those that sought to overthrow it, between evolutionary constitutionalists on the one hand and revolutionaries on the other. The same attitude continued during the first ten years of Nicholas II's reign; this is hardly surprising since the latter remained firmly committed to the policies of his 'unforgettable dead father' and, like him, had been schooled by Pobedonostsev in the essentials of autocracy.

In one respect Alexander III and Nicholas II were largely successful between 1881 and 1904. They managed to avoid any dilution of the autocratic power and any alternative focus for popular loyalty, which officially sanctioned political parties would have brought to Russia. There was therefore no legal access to any of the executive functions of the state other than by officials appointed by the Tsar himself. Russia did not, therefore, surrender its tradition of bureaucratic autocracy to parliamentary party politics as had happened increasingly in Germany, France, Britain and Italy. The one source from which this might have entered the system was from the local government institutions of the *zemstva* and the municipal *dumas*, set up by Alexander II in 1864 and 1870. Time and again their representatives sought to establish groups of men with like-minded constitutionalist ideas – for example, the union of *zemstva* and the Union of Unions. But the logical next step – the formation of a party – was denied to them by the refusal to set up any central representative system, which meant that nothing could yet grow from the grass roots. At the same time, both Alexander III and Nicholas II took measures to weaken the *zemstva* and *dumas* and, in 1892, to restrict their franchise. Hence there were no equivalents before 1906 to the Liberals and Conservatives in Britain, the National Liberals and Centre in Germany, or the Radicals and Opportunists in France.

Success in this period should not, however, be measured simply by what was not happening above the surface. Underground a very different situation was developing. The period 1881–1904 was one of remarkable growth for revolutionary groups. The Populists, for example, developed into the Socialist Revolutionary Party in 1900, which was to launch a campaign of political activism and targeted assassinations. The RSDLP emerged in 1898 as an amalgam of the various Marxist groups that had started and consolidated during the reign of Alexander II, before going on to divide into Bolsheviks and Mensheviks in 1903. These parties threatened the whole integrity of Tsarist power and authority, even if their full impact was delayed for a while by the efficiency of the *Okhrana* and its agents (see Chapter 4).

This combination of frustrated constitutionalism and repressed radicalism weakened any scope for evolution through constitutionalist parties and strengthened that for more dramatic change at the hands of revolutionary parties. This is the basis of the case for the long-term inevitability of the collapse of Tsarism, examined in Chapters 1 and 2. Yet another chance seemed to appear after 1905 as Nicholas II was forced to accept reality and to make constitutional changes in response to the 1905 Revolution. One of the key changes brought about by the October Manifesto (1905) and the Fundamental Laws (1906) was the legal recognition of political parties and the establishment of a sufficiently broad franchise to give them popular credibility. Given time, the alternative argument claims, this development could have saved Russia from revolution by converting it into a constitutional monarchy. This, however, presupposes that Nicholas II wanted to be part of this transformation. He did not – and did everything within his power to nullify the concessions he had granted. His main target was the political parties, the very monsters against which Pobedonostsev had warned.

In one respect Nicholas II was successful after 1905. He prevented the newly formed parties from exerting any direct role in government and even constrained their influence over legislation in the Duma. This was possible because of the wording of the Fundamental Laws. The Tsar's government was able to survive attacks by the Constitutional Democrats and the radical parties between 1906 and 1907 simply by dissolving the First and Second Dumas, while the restriction of the franchise through the 1907 Electoral Law was successful in reducing the number of subsequent seats won by the Kadets, SRs and Social Democrats and in ensuring that the Third and Fourth Dumas were dominated by parties right of centre. One of these, the Union of Russian People, even aimed to strengthen Tsarist autocracy by destroying the party system altogether. In the drawn-out struggle between autocracy and party politics, Nicholas therefore appeared by 1914 to have won a significant victory.

Yet the very success in constraining Russia's parties was to recoil on the Tsar during the First World War – as they all turned against him and provided the channels by which an alternative regime could be established. The radicals, deprived of any stake in the regime, worked from 1915 for its overthrow from below; the SRs and the Mensheviks were to have at least some influence on the popular uprising in March 1917 and the formation of the Petrograd Soviet in the Tauride Palace. Meanwhile, the Kadets and the Octobrists were so alienated by gratuitous autocracy, exercised by Alexandra and Rasputin on behalf of an absent Tsar, that they formed a Progressive

Bloc within the Duma. By the end of 1916 this had become the main constitutional basis – not just for opposition but also increasingly for resistance to the regime. Ultimately, Nicholas II failed to prevent the Kadets and Octobrists from using the Duma to set up a Provisional Committee with the specific purpose of taking over the revolution through the Provisional Government, which also met in the Tauride.

Alexander III and, at first, Nicholas II drove political parties into introspection and suspicion by making them illegal. Thus it was difficult for autocracy to concede them a meaningful role after this illegality was withdrawn in 1906. A vicious circle was created as radical parties became increasingly revolutionary and constitutionalists sufficiently radicalised to become their accomplices.

Lenin and Stalin (1917–53)

Here a situation existed that was broadly different to that in Tsarist Russia. A one-party system, which was imposed in 1918, would strongly suggest harmony with, and control by, the leadership of the day, especially since the leadership emerged through the Party. Much, however, depends on the *type* of party that Lenin and Stalin actually led. On this there has been a substantial historiographical debate, both in the West and between the West and the former Soviet Union.

As might be expected from a pluralistic society that values academic diversity, there are many Western viewpoints relating to the CPSU and the Soviet leadership. While differing in detail, however, they tend to orbit round two basic approaches that contrast significantly with each other.

The Western Liberal approach, particularly apparent between the 1950s and early 1980s, places the emphasis on the underlying continuity of a disciplined party – under an autocratic leader – first seizing power and then exerting exclusive political authority over the state. It was Lenin who defined the purpose of the Bolsheviks in works such as *What Is To Be Done?*, directed Bolshevik strategy in 1917 through the *April Theses* and dictated the timing of the October Revolution. It was Lenin who ended the brief experiment with Western democracy by closing the Constituent Assembly and substituting for it a system of soviets (see Chapter 2). The Bolshevik Party (subsequently renamed the CPSU) was the means whereby this transition could be made permanent and through which all future leadership would be operated. There was, admittedly, some ambivalence by the end of Lenin's regime as to whether the leadership controlled the Party or the Party the leadership. But this problem was subsequently resolved by Stalin, who used his position within the Party as General Secretary, as well as Head of Orgburo and the Control Commission, to build up support in his leadership contest with Kamenev, Zinoviev and Trotsky. From 1929 onwards, Stalin maintained his grip on the Party by removing all potential opposition and, in the purges of 1937 and 1938, eliminating all the Party members previously associated with Lenin. What Stalin did, in effect, was to downgrade the role of the Party and, through the Stalinist cult, to create a personalised dictatorship that continued until his death in 1953. It was only under Khrushchev (1953–64) and Brezhnev (1964–82) that the Party was allowed to discover its former influence.

A somewhat different perspective is provided by the Western Revisionist approach, which explodes several long-held assumptions. First, the control of the leadership over the Party cannot be taken for granted. Lenin was rarely in full control of the Bolsheviks before 1917 and frequently had to take his cue from the rank and file, which were in turn influenced by local workshop and peasant committees. Even after his return from Russia in April 1917, Lenin had to depend on a broad base of support, including a temporary alliance with the Menshevik Internationalists and Left SRs. This actually meant loosening controls over the Party; as a result, Lenin's personal influence has been questioned and much more credit for the success in October is given to 'imports' like Trotsky. His longer-term success is also very much in doubt. The Civil War (1918–21) showed the greater popularity of the Greens. Even when these and other groups were eliminated by 1921, Lenin experienced opposition to his policies from groups *within* the Party, such as the Left Communists. His adoption of the NEP in 1921 also produced fractious debate on the future of the Soviet economy, which threatened to split the Party permanently.

The second assumption challenged by revisionist historians is that Stalin maintained an effective leadership over the CPSU. He rose to power through his manipulation of the Party and then proceeded to undermine it. That much *is* accepted. But this did not necessarily mean that he was able to *control* it. The crucial problem was meaningful delegation of power in the implementation of economic policies and the conduct of the purges. Far from being the most effective of the totalitarian systems, Stalinist Russia was actually deeply flawed – and the weakest connection was that between the leadership and the Party functionaries. Far from being compliant and subordinate, the latter were actually assertive, self-motivated and ambitious. Either they exceeded orders and had to be reined back; or they resisted change and had to be kicked into action. A Stalinist leadership, served by a lot of 'little Stalins', was a recipe for a loss of control rather than for its fulfilment.

There are already strong indications that the pendulum is swinging back from the more radical revisionist views towards a post-revisionist acceptance of the importance of Lenin and Stalin – although with reservations. An overall synthesis between the two Western approaches might, therefore, be that the Bolshevik Party and CPSU for the most part experienced authoritarian controls by Lenin and Stalin, although this was periodically modified either – in the case of Lenin – by grass-roots influences or – under Stalin – by inefficiency spawned by overzealous officials within an expanding bureaucracy. Ultimately, however, the leadership did have the strength and authority to re-centralise control over the party and to overcome centrifugal tendencies – at least until the next time they occurred.

Views from within the Soviet Union itself are also varied – although for political rather than academic reasons. During the Stalin era, the official interpretation was that all the achievements of the Bolsheviks and the CPSU were due to the inspired leadership of two historic individuals: Lenin and his natural successor, Stalin. This approach justified Stalin's increased control over the Party and confirmed his political and ideological legitimacy – even though it involved a major distortion in emphasising Lenin's approval of the succession. After 1953 the Lenin cult was maintained, while the connection with Stalin was entirely removed. Under Khrushchev (1953–64) and Brezhnev (1964–82) Stalin's place in Soviet history was entirely replaced by the CPSU. According to the *Short History of the CPSU*, it was the 'Party' that held the 'leading position in Soviet society',[1] established the 1936 Constitution, ensured the 'consolidation and development of the socialist system and its material and technical base',[2] promoted 'the collective-farm system' and improved 'the well-being of collective farmers',[3] and took measures to build up the armed forces.[4] Above all, the 'Communist Party rallied and organised the Soviet people to fight the Patriotic War. It worked out a clear programme for mobilising all the country's resources to defeat the enemy'.[5] Undoubtedly motivated by Khrushchev's destalinisation campaign, this involved the greatest historical distortion of the twentieth century, an example of the total subordination of history to political purposes.

It is, of course, ironic that the role of the Party was boosted retrospectively by a totalitarian regime in order to erase any record of that regime's real founder.

Questions

1. Did the political parties achieve anything positive between 1906 and 1917?
2. How strong was the Communist Party between 1924 and 1953?

ANALYSIS 3: 'THE MEANING OF POLITICAL PARTY DIFFERED PROFOUNDLY BETWEEN THE TSARIST AND SOVIET REGIMES'. DO YOU AGREE?

There were substantial differences between the Tsarist and Soviet periods in terms of the range of parties, their relationship to the regime and their place within the constitution – all of which can be explained by fundamentally different ideological approaches. Yet, despite these obvious contrasts, there were also two main similarities. One was that in each case there was a gap between the official status of the parties and the intentions of some of the individual leaders of the regime; the other was the tendency for parties to develop new centres of gravity through fragmentation and regrouping. It is also possible to draw a connection between the alienation of parties and the collapse of the two regimes.

There was certainly a major contrast in the number of parties permitted by each regime. Although it placed a ban on all parties during the nineteenth century, the Tsarist regime tolerated a complete range in the four Dumas between 1906 and 1917. These included the Union of Russian People and the Monarchists on the reactionary right, the Octobrists on the moderate right, the Constitutional Democrats on the moderate left, and the Social Democrats and the SRs on the radical left. There were, in addition, groups representing the various nationalities (the Polish League, Lithuanian Circle and Ukrainian Democrats) as well as industry and business. This was probably the broadest political spectrum there had ever been in any country. It took just three years for Lenin's regime to dismantle the multi-party system and to ensure the complete monopoly of the Bolsheviks, now the CPSU. The intention was to reduce the range of parties, seen as representative of conflicting class interests, instead promoting unity through the CPSU.

This reflected a second difference. From 1918 the political party officially embodied the Soviet regime, whereas in Tsarist Russia political parties were peripheral to it. The leadership of the Soviet Union always came from among top officials within the CPSU, members of the inner-core Politburo or Presidium. Indeed, the succession normally involved direct competition between Party rivals, leading to the rise of Stalin (against Kamenev, Zinoviev, Trotsky and Bukharin), Khrushchev (against Bulganin and Malenkov) and Brezhnev (against Kosygin). By contrast, Nicholas II and his Council of Ministers completely transcended political parties. The same applied to the constitutional structure set up by the Fundamental Laws of 1906, which made no provision for elected members of the Duma, through majority parties, to constitute even part of the executive. By complete contrast, the Soviet constitutions of 1918, 1924, 1936 and 1977 were dependent for their functioning on the role of the CPSU in the formation of any government, although only the 1977 Constitution openly acknowledged this. Ironically, the late-Tsarist system, in playing down the significance of parties, provided a healthier environment for their growth than did the Soviet regime's monolithic approach. The 1906 changes might have eventually evolved into a constitutional monarchy based on a multi-party system, whereas such a development in the Soviet Union would have destroyed the entire structure – as, indeed, it did when Yeltsin, President of the RSFSR, suspended the operation of the Communist Party in Russia pending investigations into its involvement in the 1991 coup.

A fundamental reason for these differences was the ideologies influencing the two regimes. Alexander III (1881–94) had been guided by the advice of Pobedonostsev (see Chaper 1), who had projected an entirely negative view of political parties. The position of Nicholas II was more complex: although inclining towards Pobedonostsev's theories and refusing to concede any portion of executive power to the parties, he had at least to allow their existence and growth after 1905. Autocratic centralism – still the Tsarist theory – was therefore diluted in practice by the growing influence of liberal democracy. Soviet Russia experienced the opposite dynamic. In closing down the Constituent Assembly in January 1918 and banning opposition parties by 1921, Lenin was unpicking the developments that had occurred from 1906 and restoring the central control. This, however, was based in theory on democratic (rather than autocratic) centralism; Marxist-Leninist ideology demanded the end of class divisions, which had only been intensified by a multi-party system, in favour of the CPSU as the class eliminator. The progression from the interim 'dictatorship of the proletariat' to the eventual 'classless society' could be accomplished only by a single party representing only the proletariat.

Any common factors between the parties of the Tsarist and Soviet periods had most to do with perceived threats of subversion.

Here there was much in common between, for example, Nicholas II and Stalin. Even though the purpose of 'party' differed profoundly in the two periods, both worked on the assumption that party power was incompatible with personal authority. Although the Fundamental Laws of 1906 had given parties an official status, Nicholas II sought to strengthen his 'autocratic power' by prematurely dissolving the Duma in 1906 and 1907 and narrowing the electorate in 1907. For his part, Stalin aimed at weakening the role of the CPSU in the formation of policy. Although the Party had been given official sanction by the constitutions of 1918 and 1924, Stalin regarded it as a potential obstacle to the main ingredients of his regime – a command economy based on personal directives and underpinned by terror. The Stalinist equivalent to dissolving the multiple-party Duma was the neglect of the representative organs within the CPSU – especially the Central Committee.

Political parties are organic bodies that experience phases of diversification and regrouping. This certainly applied to both the Tsarist and Soviet periods, although through the contrasting multi-party and single-party systems. In the reign of Nicholas II polarisation occurred at the radical left, the reactionary right, the constitutionalist moderates and the sectional interests; this was especially apparent under the impact of war and arbitrary despotism (characterised by the rule of Alexandra and Rasputin). During the period 1915–16, the constitutionalists (Kadets and Octobrists) developed closer links with some of the sectionalist interest to form the Progressive Bloc within the Duma. In this way, the parties involved actually changed their basic role. A similar development – albeit in reverse – occurred in the post-1917 regime as the groups began to develop within the Bolshevik Party. This applied particularly to the factionalism that accompanied the struggle for the succession to Lenin: the emergence of the Left Opposition was heavily influenced by the radical policies of Trotsky, whereas the Rightists were Bukharinite moderates.

Indeed, such regroupings were to play a major part in the collapse of both the Tsarist and Soviet regimes. Towards the end of their existence, both systems saw the growth of functioning oppositions that became alien to the regime and implicated in its demise. Nicholas II was ultimately overthrown by revolutionaries – some acting spontaneously, others organised by Mensheviks and SRs – and the Provisional Government put in place by the Progressive Bloc within the Duma. There was therefore an extraordinary cooperation between radicals and constitutionalists, against which the regime could not survive in the context of the war. The counterpart to the collaboration of normally diverse parties in the last months of Tsarist Russia was the polarisation of factions within the Communist Party towards the end of the life of the Soviet Union. By 1991 the CPSU had divided into moderates led by Gorbachev, traditionalists such as Ligachev, and radicals such as Yeltsin, who had become increasingly impatient of the whole system. When, therefore, the traditionalists, this time under Yaneyev and Pugo, attempted to constrain Gorbachev's reforms by a coup, Yeltsin seized the opportunity to end Communist rule altogether.

Questions

1. Compare the political groupings that occurred in late-Tsarist Russia and the Soviet Union.
2. 'Political parties brought the collapse of the Tsarist regime and the rise and consolidation of the Soviet Union.' Do you agree?

SOURCES

1. POLITICAL PARTIES IN TSARIST RUSSIA

Source 1: Extracts from the programme of the Bolshevik Party, 1903.

By replacing private with public ownership of the means of production and exchange, by introducing planned organization in the public process of production so that the well being and the many sided development of all members of society may be insured, the social revolution of the proletariat will abolish the division of society into classes and thus emancipate all oppressed humanity, and will terminate all forms of exploitation of one part of society by another.

A necessary condition for this social revolution is the dictatorship of the proletariat; that is, the conquering by the proletariat of such political power as would enable it to crush any resistance offered by the exploiters. In its effort to make the proletariat capable of fulfilling its great historical mission, international social democracy organizes it into an independent political party in opposition to all bourgeois parties, directs all the manifestations of its class struggle, discloses before it the irreconcilable conflict between the interests of the exploiters and those of the exploited, and clarifies for it the historical significance of the imminent social revolution and the conditions necessary for its coming. At the same time, it reveals to the other sections of the toiling and exploited masses the hopelessness of their condition in capitalist society and the need of a social revolution if they wish to be free of the capitalist yoke. The party of the working class, the social democracy, calls upon all strata of the toiling and exploited population to join its ranks insofar as they accept the point of view of the proletariat.

Source 2: Extracts from the programme of the Constitutional Democrats, 1905.

11. The Constitution of the Russian Empire should guarantee all the minorities inhabiting the Empire, in addition to full civil and political equality enjoyed by all citizens, the right of cultural self-determination, namely: full freedom of usage of various languages and dialects in public, the freedom to found and maintain educational institutions and meetings of all sorts having as their aim the preservation and development of language, literature and culture of every nationality.

13. The constitutional system of the Russian state will be determined by the constitution.

14. People's representatives are elected by a general, equal, direct and secret ballot, irrespective of their religion, nationality or sex. The party allows within its midst a difference of opinion on the question of national representation, consisting of one or two chambers in which case the second chamber should consist of representatives of the local organs of self-government, organized on the basis of a general vote and spread throughout all of Russia.

15. National representation participates in the realization of legislative power, in the determination of government revenues and expenditures, and in control of the legality and expedience of actions of higher and lower organs of administration.

16. No decision, decree, *ukaz*, order or a similar act not based on the legislative measure of national representation, regardless of its name or place of origin, can have the force of law.

17. A government inventory, which should include all revenues and expenditures of the state, should be established by law, every year. No taxes, dues, and collections for the state, as well as state loans, can be established other than by legislation.

18. Members of national representative assemblies should have the right of legislative initiative.

19. Ministers are responsible to the representatives of the national assembly, and the latter have the right of questioning and interpellation.

Source 3: Extracts from the programme of the Union of Russian People, 1905.

1. ... The Union of the Russian People sets as its undeviating goal a durable unity of the Russian people of all classes and professions to work for the general good of our fatherland – a Russia united and indivisible.

2. ... The well being of the country should consist of a firm preservation of Russian autocracy, orthodoxy, and nationality, and of the establishment of a State Duma, order, and legality.

3. Russian autocracy was created by national wisdom, sanctified by the Church, and justified by history. Our autocracy consists of unity between the Tsar and the people.

Note: Convinced that national well being consists of the unity between the Russian Tsar and the people, the Union acknowledges that the present ministerial bureaucratic system, which separates the pure soul of the Russian Tsar from the people, and which has appropriated a number of rights that truly belong to the Russian autocratic power, has brought our country to grave troubles and should therefore be changed fundamentally. At the same time the Union firmly believes that a change of the existing order should be accomplished not through the introduction of certain restrictive institutions such as constitutional or constituent assemblies, but rather through convocation of a State Duma as an institution which would represent a direct tie between the autocratic will of the Tsar and the right of the people.

4. The Russian people are Orthodox people and therefore the Orthodox faith remains steadfastly the official religion of the Russian Empire. All subjects of the Empire, however, have the freedom of religious worship.

5. The Russian nation, as the gatherer of Russian lands and the creator of the great might of the state, enjoys a preferential position in national life and in national administration.

Source 4: The programme of the Progressive Bloc (comprising Constitutional Democrats, Octobrists and other moderate groups), 1915.

The undersigned representatives of factions and groups in the State Duma and State Council, believing (1) that only a strong, firm, and active government can lead our country to victory and (2) that such a government must be one which enjoys the confidence of the people and is capable of organizing cooperation between all citizens, have come to the unanimous conclusion that such cooperation can only be achieved, and the government gain sufficient authority if the following [minimum] conditions are observed.

1. The formation of a unified government of individuals who have the confidence of the country and are in agreement with the legislative institutions about the need for the rapid implementation of a definite programme.
2. A radical change in the present methods of administration, which are based on a distrust of initiative by the public, in particular:
   (a) strict observation of the principles of legality in government.
   (b) the removal of the dual authority of the military and the civil powers in questions which have no direct relevance to the execution of military operations.
   (c) the renewal of the system of local administration.
   (d) a rational and consistent policy to preserve internal peace, and the removal of discordances between nationalities and classes.

Questions

1. Using Source 4, and your own knowledge, explain why the Progressive Bloc came into existence. (10)
2. Using the extracts in Sources 1, 2 and 3, identify the main differences between the programmes of the Bolsheviks, Constitutional Democrats and Union of Russian People. (20)
3. Using Sources 1 to 4, and your own knowledge, examine the view that Russia's political parties were the best guarantee for the survival of the Tsarist regime. (30)

Total (60)

2. THE COMMUNIST PARTY OF THE SOVIET UNION UNDER THE LEADERSHIP OF STALIN

Source 5: Extracts from *A Short History of the Communist Party of the Soviet Union* (1970 edition). These extracts cover the main developments during the Stalin era.

The Party continued its policy of siting new industries in the vicinity of raw material sources. . . .

A major achievement by the Party was its solution of the problem of accumulating funds for large-scale capital construction, for the financing of all branches of the economy. . . .

The Party and the government extended the utmost aid to the collective farms. Land was given to them for their use in perpetuity. The number of machine and tractor stations serving the collective farms was steadily increased. . . .

Having put Lenin's plan into effect and organised and successfully consummated the building of socialism, the Communist Party thus gave the world a model for the revolutionary remaking of society. ...

The successes of socialism further enhanced the Party's prestige among the people. Its leading position in Soviet society was confirmed by the new [1936] Constitution of the USSR. ...

The Communist Party and the Soviet state, realising that the USSR was threatened with war, took measures to build up the Armed Forces. By the summer of 1941 there were 4,500,000 men serving in the Red Army. ...

The Party worked to increase production of metal, coal and oil. The industrial base in the eastern regions of the country was strengthened. ...

[After the German invasion of 1941] the Communist Party rallied and organised the Soviet people to fight the Patriotic War. It worked out a clear programme for mobilising all the country's resources to defeat the enemy. ...

The Soviet people won their historic victory in the Great Patriotic War because ... the workers and peasants, all the peoples of the Soviet Union, were bound together in real friendship, because the Communist party had fostered and encouraged this friendship.

Source 6: From a speech by Khrushchev to the Twentieth Congress of the Communist Party of the Soviet Union (February 1956).

When we analyse the practice of Stalin in regard to the reaction of the Party and of the country, when we pause to consider everything which Stalin perpetrated, we must be convinced that Lenin's fears were justified. The negative characteristics of Stalin, which, in Lenin's time, were only incipient, transformed themselves during the last years into a grave abuse of power by Stalin, which caused untold harm to our Party. ...

He discarded the Leninist method of convincing and educating; he abandoned the method of ideological struggle for that of administrative violence, mass repressions, and terror. He acted on an increasingly large scale and more stubbornly through unitive organs, at the same time often violating all existing norms of morality and of Soviet laws. ... Collegiality of leadership flows from the very nature of our Party, a Party built on the principles of democratic centralism. ...

Whereas during the first few years after Lenin's death Party Congresses and Central Committee Plenums took place more or less regularly, later, when Stalin began increasingly to abuse his power, these principles were brutally violated ... Central Committee Plenums were hardly ever called. ... In practice Stalin ignored the norms of Party life and trampled on the Leninist principle of collective Party leadership.

Source 7: Extract from Dmitri Volkogonov, *The Rise and Fall of the Soviet Empire*, first published in 1998.

The system designed by Lenin was built by Stalin and the Party. The dictatorship of the proletariat had, long before the adoption of Stalin's 'most democratic' Constitution, become the dictatorship of a single party, which had in turn become the dictatorship of a single leader. By the end of his life, Stalin personified the regime and symbolized a way of thinking and acting. The Russian people believed everything the Bolshevik authorities told them. They submitted to enormous deprivation, endured unprecedented suffering and accepted monstrous sacrifices in the name of a nebulous future.

Source 8: From Graeme Gill, *Stalinism*, first published in 1990.

His personal dominance was enhanced by the decline of the major institutional structures that had dominated Soviet politics before the Stalinist political system had come into being. As effective operating bodies, the central organs of the party ceased to operate. No party congress was convened during this period, the full CC plenum appears not to have met, and while the Politburo, Orgburo and Secretariat may have met on a more regular basis, they exercised little power. The leading state organ, the Council of People's Commissars, also played little role in government affairs. These major institutions were replaced by the State Defence Committee and by the military Supreme Command, or Stavka. These two bodies, linked by Stalin who headed them both, were the main institutional foci of central political life.

Questions

1. Compare Sources 5 and 6 as commentaries on the role of the Communist Party during the Stalin era. How might the differences be explained? (15)
2. 'The Communist Party was incompatible with dictatorship.' Comment on this view, using Sources 5 to 8 and your own knowledge. (30)

Total (45)

4

REPRESSION AND TERROR

ANALYSIS 1: EXPLAIN THE DEVELOPMENT OF THE SECRET
POLICE IN RUSSIA BETWEEN 1826 AND 1991.

Before 1991 Russia had a long history of swift and non-judicial
treatment of people considered to be a threat to society, especially
for political or ideological reasons.

The Tsarist era to March 1917

The political police had its roots during the reign of Ivan the Terrible
(1547–84), who set up a temporary organisation known as the
Oprichniki, or 'Men Apart'. This committed great acts of violence,
including the massacre of most of the population of Novgorod in
1570. A more permanent institution was formed by Peter the Great
(1682–1725): the *Preobrazhensky Prikaz* was more surreptitious in
its methods, concentrating on interrogation in torture chambers rather
than on open attacks on the Tsar's subjects. It survived until the early
nineteenth century when, under Nicholas I (1825–55), it was replaced
by a more administrative structure – the Third Section of the Imperial
Chancellery – with a brief to remove ideological opponents to Tsarist
autocracy and prevent any recurrence of the Decembrist Uprising. By
1861, some 290,000 people had been sentenced to exile, almost
entirely on political grounds.

Alexander II (1855–81) downgraded the Third Section during the
first half of his reign – the 'era of great reforms'. However, the growth

of Populist violence revived the use of repression and the Third Section was replaced in 1880 by the Department of State Police. Under Alexander III (1881–94) and Nicholas II (1894–1917) this was known as the *Okhrana*. It operated entirely outside the law and was used to impose administrative arrest and trial, followed by imprisonment and exile. It also gathered intelligence from abroad about the activities of Russian exiles and penetrated some of the new revolutionary groups. Under Ministers of the Interior Durnovo and Goremykin, during the 1890s, the *Okhrana* kept a low profile, prosecuting political offenders discreetly and avoiding publicity. After 1900, however, the *Okhrana* became more and more active. This was largely to counter the growing threat posed by the Social Democrats (formed in 1898) and the Socialist Revolutionaries (SRs) (1900). At first it relied on agents placed within the revolutionary organisations; Zubatov, who headed the *Okhrana* until 1903, used these both to gather information and to provoke revolutionaries into taking action that would result in arrests. One of these agents was Father Gapon, who led a procession of workers to the Winter Palace to petition the Tsar in January 1905. Following the 1905 Revolution and the partial capitulation of the Tsar to the demands for a constitution, the *Okhrana* stepped up its activities. While on the surface the regime appeared, through the October Manifesto and the 1906 Fundamental Laws, to become more progressive, the Tsar's power was underpinned by a considerable increase in executive arrests, trials, deportations and executions – all carried out by the *Okhrana*. After being 'processed' detainees were either executed in secret or handed over to the Main Prison Administration (GTU), set up in 1879, or to one of its provincial prison branches (TO). Whether or not this system was successful in stabilising the political situation, it certainly provided a precedent for the organisation and methods of secret policing during the Soviet era.

The interlude of the Provisional Government, March to October 1917

The *Okhrana* was identified by the revolutionaries as one of the main symbols of Tsarist repression and its headquarters were sacked and burned on 27 February. The Provisional Government then disbanded the whole organisation and released most of the political prisoners who had been held by the Tsarist regime. Under the new political system, there was no place for administrative arrest, and it was intended that the shadow of the political police should be permanently lifted from Russia. The only initial concession to security made by the

Provisional Government related to the war effort, with the formation of the Counter-Espionage Bureau of the Petrograd Military District. But, as he experienced more and more difficulties in exercising its authority in the wake of military failure, peasant activism and threatened coups, Kerensky began to use the Bureau against the Bolsheviks. Yet the ease with which the Bolsheviks were able to seize the key installations in Petrograd in October suggests that the Provisional Government had lost control over intelligence gathering, the Bureau's original purpose, without reviving fully the Tsarist methods of taking suspected revolutionaries out of circulation.

The Soviet era, 1918–91

The Bolsheviks turned their back on the multi-party system fostered by the Provisional Government, cancelled the elections held in November for the Constituent Assembly and closed the Assembly itself. An alternative system of soviets was set up, dominated by the Bolshevik Party (later known as the CPSU). The Soviet system also gave rise to the reintroduction of the political police. Trotsky, who had been elected president of the Petrograd Soviet, set up the Revolutionary Military Committee, or Red Guard, which overthrew the Provisional Government on the night of 23/4 October (6/7 November) 1917. During the period of the Civil War (1918–21), the Revolutionary Military Committee was extended in two different – but complementary – ways, both at the instigation of Trotsky. The first was the Red Army, which provided 550,000 troops by 1921. The second was political police – the Extraordinary Commission for the Suppression of Counter-Revolution, Speculation and Sabotage, or *Cheka*. This had a dual function: to ensure the total obedience of the regular troops and their officers during the campaigns of the Civil War. The other was to remove any 'counter-revolutionary' influences, increasingly defined as members of other parties, and to eliminate any opposition to the Bolshevik policy of War Communism. These non-military functions were delegated by Trotsky to Dzerzhinsky. As a former prisoner of the Tsarist regime, Dzerzhinsky applied many of the methods of the former *Okhrana*, which the *Cheka* closely resembled.

By 1921 the Bolsheviks had emerged victorious from the Civil War and had established a monolithic political system, while the NEP reduced popular dissent by relaxing some of the former constraints on private enterprise. During this period of greater Bolshevik control, Lenin felt it appropriate to suspend the emergency activities of the *Cheka*, while regularising the political police as the State Political

Administration (GPU) in 1922. This was seen as a more permanent way of strengthening the basis of 'revolutionary legality' while, at the same time, downgrading the emphasis on 'revolutionary terror'. Following the establishment of the Soviet Union by the 1924 Constitution (see Chapter 2), the GPU was expanded into the Unified State Political Administration (OGPU) to reflect the association of other republics alongside the RSFSR. The overall organisation, however, remained firmly in the hands of the Russian component of the CPSU. At this stage there were no plans to re-establish the 'terror' or introduce a permanent successor to the *Okhrana* and *Cheka*.

The rise of Stalin as Lenin's permanent successor made a fundamental difference. Stalin's rule established a command economy (see Chapter 7), a campaign to weaken the nationalities and ethnic groups (Chapter 5), and a personalised dictatorship based on a revised ideology (Chapter 1). In combination, these were sufficient to arouse widespread opposition, which, in turn, could be expected to provoke repressive counter-measures. To this, however, should be added Stalin's extreme antipathy to any alternative strategies and his utter ruthlessness. The result was not so much the revival of the *Cheka* as the establishment of the most extensive political police of the entire century. During the 1930s Stalin's policies demanded victims – whether prominent 'traitors' identified in show trials, or anonymous millions who simply disappeared. The People's Commissariat for Internal Affairs (NKVD) was equally adept at dealing with both. Established in 1934, this ended the previous distinction between the secret police as a regular administration and an emergency form of terror, instead simply combining the two as a permanent system. If Trotsky introduced the paradoxical notion of 'Permanent Revolution', Stalin went a step further by establishing the practice of 'permanent terror'. The NKVD administered the labour camps of the *Gulag*, which 'processed' up to 40 million people, as well as trumping up evidence against Stalin's original Bolshevik rivals – Bukharin, Kamenev, Zinoviev and Rykov – or tracking down and assassinating the arch-enemy Trotsky in 1940. But, just as suspicion generated terror, so also terror produced more suspicion. Under Stalin, this turned inwards. By 1943, the NKVD was considered to be deeply flawed. It therefore gave way to the NKGB (People's Commissariat for State Security), with the special function of purging the ethnic separatism that showed itself during the war with Germany (1941–5). Having completed its task by 1946, the NKGB was in turn replaced by the MGB (Ministry for State Security), which redirected the focus of terror on the population at large. This coexisted with the MVD, or Ministry of Internal Affairs.

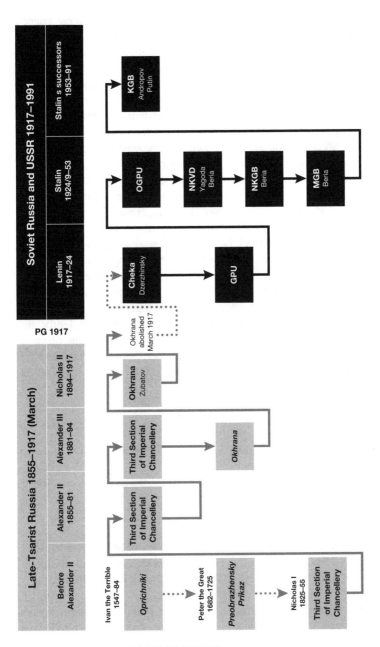

TSARIST AND SOVIET SECRET POLICE

Figure 4.

Stalin's successor, Khrushchev, had the less extreme agenda of maintaining the totalitarian state without the terror. He therefore scrapped the NKGB – but could not do without a lower-key equivalent, the KGB, even if this was now downgraded from a 'Ministry' to a 'Committee' for State Security; in 1954 it was placed under the control of the MVD. Much greater importance was now attached to the KGB's intelligence and espionage functions than to internal security, which could, to a greater extent than before, be entrusted to the MVD and regular police forces. The number of arrests greatly decreased, torture was officially abolished and the *Gulag* system, which had reached gigantic proportions under Stalin, was virtually closed down. By 1956, terror was denounced as a Stalinist practice with no ideological credentials. Yet the Soviet regime remained repressive for the rest of Khrushchev's rule and that of Brezhnev (1964–82), Andropov (1982–4) and Chernenko (1984–5); indeed, Andropov had himself been head of the KGB. Any form of opposition remained illegal, while 'dissidents' such as Sakharov were imprisoned or placed under house arrest. It was not until Gorbachev (1985–91) introduced his policy of *glasnost* that the repression began to fade, along with the remaining totalitarian controls. In 1989 Gorbachev increased the accountability of the KGB to the Supreme Soviet of the USSR. After the collapse of the Soviet Union the Russian KGB eventually became the Ministry of Security. Other states made similar adaptations.

Questions

1. In what ways was there continuity in the use of terror between the Tsarist and Soviet regimes?
2. What were the 'high' and 'low' points in the use of terror in Russia and the Soviet Union?

ANALYSIS 2: 'RUTHLESS BUT EFFECTIVE'. ASSESS THIS VIEW OF THE SECRET POLICE *EITHER* IN TSARIST RUSSIA UNDER NICHOLAS II *OR* IN THE SOVIET UNION UNDER STALIN.

Interpretations of the secret police in the Tsarist and Soviet periods have seen some interesting variations. For example, the NKVD have sometimes been seen as the epitome of ruthless efficiency that underlay Stalin's totalitarian dictatorship; the *Okhrana* similarly represented all that was bad about the rule of Nicholas II – while failing to underpin it effectively. Other views have modified this approach. The Soviet secret police has retained its reputation for ruthlessness but lost the automatic connection between ruthlessness and efficiency. For its part, the *Okhrana* has been credited with at least some more moderate influences, along with a greater degree of success.

Nicholas II (1894–1917)

The 'ruthlessness' and 'efficiency' of the secret police between 1894 and 1917 can be considered under four criteria: as an integral part of the autocratic system, as an instrument of repression and terror, as an obstacle to revolutionary action, and as an influence on official attitudes to reform.

It is clear that the system of secret police was an integral and essential part of the maintenance of Tsarist autocracy. As such, it upheld repressive policies as a norm and used the tactics of terror when necessary. The *Okhrana*, which had replaced the Third Section in 1880, was used by both Alexander III and Nicholas II to prevent constitutional and revolutionary challenges to the status quo based on Tsarist decree. Alone among the major powers of Europe, it had no legal constraints. Its ruthlessness was therefore implicit and its effectiveness lasted until it collapsed with the regime itself. Even then, its influence outlived the regime; according to Andrew: 'Tsarism bequeathed to Bolshevism both a political culture and a legal system in which only the state had rights.'[1]

There has been some debate as to the extent to which the *Okhrana* contributed to the regime's repression and terror. Figes, for example, maintains that there was a direct connection with Lenin's *Cheka*, the latter being influenced by some of the more sadistic measures of the *Okhrana*, especially Orel prison, where Felix Dzerzhinsky had been imprisoned for many years. Even as late as the 1980s the KGB trained its recruits with manuals originally produced by the *Okhrana*.[2] Political executions were also carried out at Kronstadt in secrecy and, according to Hingley, 'in the early twentieth century, the Imperial authorities came nearer to operating a political reign of terror than on any previous occasion'.[3] On the other hand, according to Rogger: 'Unpopular as gendarmes and secret policemen were, they were not so ruthless or efficient as to paralyse the radicals or to silence malcontents.' The regime 'showed a curious inconsistency' in harassing and imprisoning its opponents while, at the same time, permitting 'a surprising degree of personal freedom and public activity'. In 1901 there were about 3,900 internal exiles, who were allowed 'to study or work'.[4] Thus, although the *Okhrana*, at its worst, provided certain precedents for the *Cheka*, there was nothing like the same scale of imprisonment or summary executions.

As an obstacle to revolutionary action, the *Okhrana* experienced varying success. During the reign of Alexander III (1881–94) it had focused largely on tracking down known radicals, especially those involved in assassination attempts. The rise of mass revolutionary parties such as the Social Democrats, formed in 1898, and the SRs (1900) brought about a change of strategy as the *Okhrana* aimed to penetrate such organisations with its own agents. Zubatov, the *Okhrana* leader at the turn of the century, warned that 'we shall provoke you to acts of terror and then crush you'.[5] Although Zubatov was dismissed in 1903, the *Okhrana* maintained an increasingly effective internal surveillance of the activity of the revolutionary parties. The SRs, for example, discovered in 1908 that one of its leaders, Azef, was a double agent. The Bolshevik branch of the Social Democrats was similarly affected, some of Lenin's associates having been uncovered as *Okhrana* agents by 1910. Indeed, Lenin's privately expressed view was that revolution would triumph if 'a few professionals, as highly trained and experienced as the imperial security police, were allowed to organize it'.[6] In fact, the *Okhrana* feared the Bolsheviks less than the other revolutionary activists and sometimes stimulated and encouraged their activities. They were probably more concerned about the Mensheviks, who carried out about 90 per cent of the Social Democrat agitation. Neither group, however, provided any serious threat to the Tsarist system, an indication of the success of the nefarious approach of the *Okhrana* in dealing with them – at least until 1914. On the other hand, the secret police were less adept at dealing with revolutionary groups that had no affiliation to the main parties, operating instead as local cells. These, not the Bolsheviks, Mensheviks or SRs, were responsible for the events of February and March 1917, which culminated in the abdication of the Tsar and the sacking of the *Okhrana* headquarters.

No one has seriously disputed the influence of the *Okhrana*, or its predecessor (the Third Section) on official attitudes to Russian society. The traditional approach is to include them as one of the pillars of autocracy and official conservatism: in other words as a force for slowing social change. This is certainly true of part of the period, especially under Alexander III and in the early years of Nicholas II's reign. There were, however, more positive periods when the secret police were actually a progressive force – although for reasons of security. The *Okhrana* was always mindful of the warning given by the Third Section to Nicholas I that the continuation of serfdom threatened major problems in the future that might actually bring down the Empire. Partly as a result of this advice, Alexander II had declared his intention to emancipate the serfs shortly after his accession in 1855. Now, in the reign of Nicholas II, a parallel situation had arisen. Witte's campaign for rapid industrialisation was creating a large urban-based proletariat that experienced deteriorating working and living conditions. Zubatov (himself a former revolutionary turned police informer) believed that the government should see the wisdom of measured reform. In part, this was to pre-empt the appeal of the revolutionaries to the majority of exploited workers, and in part to broaden the base of the Tsar's appeal by strengthening the benevolent nature of autocracy. For this reason, he set up several trade unions, laying himself open to the allegation that he was fostering 'police socialism'. At the same time, he was careful to keep them under close surveillance. According to Acton, the *Okhrana* therefore developed 'relatively sophisticated techniques of social control'.[7]

Hence 'ruthlessness' was for a time tempered by moderation and far-sightedness. In one sense, however, this was a failure. Zubatov's removal in 1903 and the upheaval of the 1905 Revolution saw a gradual reversion to uncompromising repression. This saw the *Okhrana* marginalised to the role of monitoring revolutionary movements, while mainstream security became the job of military courts of the type that had existed under Alexander II and Alexander III. These accounted for some 14,000 deaths between 1905 and 1906, although it has to be said that 1,126 government officials were also killed and 1,506 wounded – by revolutionaries. There is, however, a more positive side. Tsarist reforms, such as the 1906 Law on Associations, were more or less in line with what Zubatov had proposed, suggesting that the *Okhrana*'s approach before 1903 might well have offered a viable alternative to Nicholas II's obdurate resistance to any sort of social reform.

Any overall assessment of the *Okhrana* must take account of its changing shape and objectives. Sometimes it fitted into the pessimistic conservatism to which Alexander III and Nicholas II inclined – under the ideological influence of Pobedonostsev. Until the late 1890s and after 1905 it can be considered to have been ruthless, but effectiveness became increasingly limited: after 1905 monitoring and surveillance became a fine art but control of law, order and security were handed back to the military. Between 1898 and 1903 there was a brief period of moderation within the *Okhrana* and an attempt to introduce a programme based on limited social reform.

Although this was unsuccessful, it did have two side effects. One was to provide a pattern for social legislation reluctantly conceded by the Tsar after the upheaval of 1905. The other was to blur the boundaries between policemen and revolutionaries long enough for the *Okhrana* to penetrate all organised revolutionary parties, especially the Bolsheviks. This could well explain why the regime was overthrown spontaneously by the masses rather than by Social Democrats or SRs.

Stalin (1929–53)

Stalin's secret police consisted of the United State Political Administration (OGPU) between 1923 and 1934, the People's Commissariat for Internal Affairs (NKVD) from 1934 to 1943, and the People's Commissariat for State Security (NKGB) from 1943 to 1946. Between 1946 and 1953 the functions of the secret police were divided between the Ministry of Internal Affairs (MVD) and the Ministry for State Security (MGB); the latter was recast as the KGB after Stalin's death in 1953. This catalogue of changes suggests one of two things. Either it shows a continuous refinement of an increasingly efficient and ruthless structure, or it indicates that, however ruthless the system, its relative inefficiency led to frequent attempts at reorganisation. Both views have been strongly represented.

One thing has remained unchallenged. Stalin's secret police, in any of its manifestations, was thoroughly ruthless – in terms of its intentions, its methods and the number of its victims. As with the SS and Gestapo it would be pointless to argue otherwise, given the weight of evidence coming out of the Soviet Union after Khrushchev's destalinisation campaign from 1956. The total number of deaths is difficult to calculate but has been put at up to 11 million by Nove and as high as 20 million by Conquest. The secret police were implicated in the majority of these. The OGPU dealt with 'social aliens' during the early 1930s, including intelligentsia and *kulaks*; the NKVD directed the terror and the purges between 1934 and 1941; and the NKGB and MGB deported the nationalities accused of conspiring with the Germans and were also responsible for the revival of the terror in 1949. Between them, the secret police enforced the policy of collectivisation, serviced the show trials, promoted mass terror and spread the culture of informing, and relocated substantial parts of the population. They also ran the *Gulag* system of labour camps. These had a total population of 8 million in 1938, rising to 12 million in 1952. Conditions were appalling and it is believed that at least

25 per cent of *Gulag* inmates died every year. The entire secret police system regarded the use of torture as routine, conducted summary executions on a massive scale – and provided opportunities for extreme forms of sadism. The only measure they did not take was mass industrialised extermination through gas chambers.

Whether there is a direct correlation between ruthless policing and political efficiency is another matter. The argument traditionally pursued in the West is that there was – that the secret police were an integral component of an efficient totalitarian regime under an increasingly personalised dictatorship. Its power derived from a semi-independent status that removed it from normal government constraints and made it responsible to the top CPSU organs and, ultimately, to Stalin himself. Conquest, for example, maintained that Stalin 'had developed direct control of the Secret Police and had set up other mechanisms of power responsible to himself alone and capable, given careful tactics, of overcoming the official hierarchy of Party and State'.[8] It has also been argued that, in standing apart from the normal administrative constraints, Stalin was able to convert a party-based regime into a personal dictatorship and to control each of the political levels involved. In all cases the incentive for action by subordinates was the threat of terror exercised by the secret police and the shadow of summary execution or imprisonment in the *Gulag* camps. The NKVD and NKGB also helped counter the centrifugal forces of nationalism and national self-determination within the Soviet Union through systematic deportations before, during and, especially, after the Second World War.

A re-examination of the whole basis of Stalin's regime suggests a very different view of the effectiveness of the secret police system. Far from ensuring an efficient totalitarian system presided over by personalised dictatorship, the terror and secret police created the most appalling political chaos. J. Arch Getty, for example, maintained that 'Stalin had initiated a movement with vague instructions and ambiguous targets. As the process unfolded on the ground, though, it degenerated rapidly into chaotic and violent struggles based on local conditions.'[9] The problem was that the various levels of the NKVD aimed not just to meet, but to exceed, the quotas of victims set by Stalin. The result was that the initiative and drive from below frequently escaped control from above. In the words of R. G. Suny: 'The requirement to find enemies, to blame and punish, worked together with self-protection and self-promotion ... to expand the purges into a political holocaust.'[10]

There is much to be said for the 'chaos' theory. Its equivalent had, after all, become widely accepted in connection with administration and terror in Nazi Germany: it was therefore logical that eventually it should also find its way into analyses of Soviet Russia. Coercion and terror may have created the semblance of order but fear is rarely a lasting force for stability. In addition to Stalin's paranoia at the centre, which led to frequent changes of instruction to his subordinates, there was also permanent tension between the NKVD and the administration, the army and the local branches of the Party. Because the NKVD tried to use and exploit local prejudices and rivalries, it was often dragged into local politics, which in turn created centrifugal forces within the NKVD itself. Terror therefore became endemic – hardly the pattern of orderly control.

There is a similar contrast in the analysis of the economic impact of the terror and the involvement of the secret police. Traditionally, the NKVD was seen as serving two important economic functions. First, it ensured that policies drawn up by Gosplan were actually carried through: hence, the dekulakisation squads of the NKVD overcame the widespread resistance of the peasantry to the imposition of collective farming between 1929 and 1932, while other units implemented Stalin's orders to purge the senior management level in industry. Second, the NKVD provided a constant reservoir of slave labour to ensure the ambitious targets of the Five-Year Plans could actually be met. The purpose of the *Gulag* was therefore as much economic as it was political – and convict labour was largely responsible for major constructions, such as the Belamor Canal linking the Baltic with the White Sea, or for mining in hostile environments such as Kolyma. It could even be argued that terror provided the means of discouraging the type of consumer aspirations that normally accompanies rapid industrialisation. All this, however, assumes that terror had a *controlled* impact. As we have seen, endemic terror is a force for chaos. In industry, fear of the NKVD created violent swings between initiative and inertia, depending on what seemed the safer course at the time. As a result, production was uneven, resources were inefficiently used, and competition often negative. As far as agriculture was concerned, the brutality of the dekulakisation squads alienated huge numbers of peasants. Many retaliated with unprecedented slaughter of their livestock, while others fled to the towns, creating rural depression and exacerbating urban squalor. The Soviet economy developed a permanent imbalance: agriculture remained crippled in the supposed interest of industry, while the latter, in turn, was never able to foster a balance between heavy and consumer industries. Terror accelerated – but it also distorted and stunted.

An overall perspective emerges that contrasts with the top-down approach of Stalin driving and controlling terror through the agency of his chosen secret police force. Instead, a bottom-up (and largely revisionist) approach is that attempts to exert centralised control were frustrated by local complications that created endemic problems both for the NKVD and for Stalin himself. No one doubts the ruthlessness of the system – but ruthlessness is as likely to undermine efficiency as to enhance it.

Questions

1. 'The activities of the *Okhrana* were destructive to the real interests of the late-Tsarist regime.' Do you agree?
2. How well was Stalin served by his secret police?

ANALYSIS 3: COMPARE THE USE OF REPRESSION AND TERROR BY THE TSARIST AND SOVIET REGIMES BETWEEN 1855 AND 1991.

In the context of Russia, 'repression' amounted to long-term measures to control the population and prevent them from exercising their own initiative. This normally came down to the removal of choice and the promotion of measures in the interests of the regime, whether auto- cratic, as in the case of Tsarist Russia, or totalitarian, as with the Soviet Union. 'Terror' applied to a shorter phase, within the broader context of repression, when more extreme measures were applied to remove opposition and to enforce conformity.

Long-term stability depended on limitations imposed by the state on the freedom and initiative of the Russian people. The degree of repression in this sense depends on whether these limitations out- weighed the more progressive policies designed to emancipate or enable. At first sight, it seems that the balance was more negative in the Tsarist system than in the Soviet Union. Autocracy, for example, was based on an essentially negative view of human nature, as propounded by Pobedonostsev (see Chapter 1): the primary purpose of power was to restrain. Communism, by contrast, aimed to liberate: the constraints of the 'dictatorship of the proletariat' were necessary only as an intermediate stage in the long-term achievement of the 'classless society', in which all forms of coercion would wither away. There also seems to be a contrast between the two systems in terms of whom they enfranchised and what rights they conferred. The Tsarist government allowed only limited representation in local government and tightened up on the electorate for the Duma in 1907; the Soviet Union, on the other hand, adopted an equal franchise in 1936. Similarly, the Russian Empire never allowed autonomy to the nationalities, actually withdrawing from Poland and Finland liberties that had been established earlier in the nineteenth century. The Soviet Union, by contrast, was based on the very principle of federalism, with self-determination built into all the constitutions of the USSR.

In theory, therefore, the Soviet system acted more positively – and with less emphasis on constraint. The practice, however, suggests that the reverse was the case. The repression imposed by the Tsars was considerable – but openly instated through *ukaze* or decree. That of the Soviet regime tended to be more subtle, amounting to measures that cancelled out or limited the more progressive changes: this applied especially to controls exerted by the Communist Party on the influence of the soviets (see Chapter 2) as well as in preventing the nationalities from achieving autonomy in any real sense (Chapter 5). The Tsarist regime was based on absolutism, which allowed for repression as a series of corrective and regulatory measures – as a necessary evil to prevent a greater evil. The Soviet Union came at the problem of control from the opposite direction, claiming to liberate by promoting an absolute good. Its measures were therefore intended to enable rather than disable and to educate rather than repress. An example of this contrast concerned the use of censorship. The controls issued in 1882 by Alexander III were preventive, designed to reduce criticism of the regime by the press and publications. Similarly, higher education was more carefully monitored for 'sedition' under the University Statute of 1887. Under Stalin the approach was formative, the purpose of 'Socialist Realism' being to create new cultural affiliation as well as to destroy the remnants of any 'petty-bourgeois' tendencies in art, music or literature. Repression therefore involved the removal of obstacles to change rather than the prevention of change itself.

Within each regime, there was a variety of intensity in the way in which repression operated. The most consistently repressive leaders within their own systems were Alexander III and Stalin. Repression for them was the minimalist approach, amounting to institutionalised normality operated through their personal decision. In a similar category, although less ruthless in their application, were Nicholas I and

Brezhnev. Others alternated according to circumstances. Alexander II and Khrushchev both relaxed controls during periods of reform (such as Alexander II's emancipation of the serfs in 1861 and Khrushchev's agricultural reforms after 1955), only to reimpose them to deal with what they perceived as the backlash. Nicholas II and Lenin both had salutary reminders about the vulnerability of both regimes to sudden challenges – Tsarism to the 1905 Revolution and Communism to the 1921 Kronstadt Revolt – which forced them to make concessions to at least part of the population. Nevertheless, both subsequently withdrew as much as possible, as quickly as possible. Only one stands out on his own as being hostile altogether to the use of repression in any form. Indeed, Gorbachev's *glasnost* was intended to open up debate as a means of strengthening the regime, the exact opposite of earlier priorities. But, in the process of trying to launch such a challenge, Gorbachev fatally weakened a regime that had always depended on preventing it.

A word about the contexts of the two regimes. Repression is generally seen as more effective in the Soviet Union than in Tsarist Russia because of the nature of modern technology, organisational structures and communications. This means that there is a fundamental difference between the two – absolutism representing the older and more traditional approach, totalitarianism the more modern equivalent. The latter had the advantage of mass-produced propaganda posters distributed by rail during the Russian Civil War, followed by cinematic historical reconstructions created by Eisenstein to reinforce the cults of Lenin and Stalin. Both identified and targeted stereotypical enemies of the regime, apparently making it easier for the Soviet regime to justify harsh measures against them. Indeed, some authorities (such as Tormey)[11] have recently emphasised that the most successful totalitarian regimes have been those able to rely on propaganda and indoctrination – rather than on force – as methods of repression. If this is the case, the Soviet Union, especially under Stalin, can be seen as a weak totalitarianism since it depended on extreme measures, which failed the save the regime in the longer term.

If repression ran through the arteries of Russia, terror acted more in the nature of a pulse beating periodically through Russian history. There were occasions when it reached a climax, just as there were times when repression managed to operate without it. The driving force of this terror is debatable. It is usually seen as coming from a conscious decision made by the leadership of the regime itself. But there is an alternative – that it sprang from that authority's losing the initiative in dealing with the problem of opposition in a more controlled and restrained way.

To an extent terror can be seen as endemic to the Russian political and social condition, implicit in the tradition of reaction and revolution alike. It appeared in the reigns of Ivan the Terrible and Peter the Great, and reappeared in the pogroms of Alexander III and Nicholas II, the Red Terror of Lenin and the purges of Stalin. There is also a continuity between the late-Tsarist and Soviet secret police – the progression from the Third Section to the *Okhrana* and then, via the *Cheka* and OGPU, to the NKVD and the KGB. Sometimes the connection between Tsarist and Soviet periods was direct – the victims of the *Okhrana* became the operators of the *Cheka*. There is even a strong historic and cultural connection, with Stalin's rehabilitation of Ivan the Terrible and the deliberate parallels between the *Oprichniki* and the NKVD. Yet, despite the continuity, the Soviet period does seem to have practised terror on a much larger scale than Tsarist Russia. Within the period covered by this book, the most intense periods of Tsarist terror seem to have occurred in the last two decades of the nineteenth century – under Alexander III and Nicholas II. Yet these paled into insignificance beside the terror of the Lenin and Stalin periods. Under Lenin, terror became a 'cleansing' process, supported by Trotsky as a means of accelerating the dictatorship of the proletariat. 'We shall not', said Trotsky, 'enter the kingdom of socialism in white gloves on a polished floor.' By contrast, Tsarist terror operated to remove perceived threats to the existing system, not as part of the baptism of fire for a new one. The Leninist terror was reactivated by Stalin and given a new twist to ensure personal dictatorship. Under Stalin, therefore, terror entered a phase of reaction while retaining a revolutionary impetus. His purges added a Tsarist capriciousness to ideological bloodletting – and unleashed massive destruction and misery. For this reason Stalin has aptly been called a 'Red Tsar'.

The pulse of terror was a feature of both Tsarist and Soviet Russia. Nicholas I used it selectively, and Alexander II dispensed with it in the 1860s but allowed its use by his officials in the late 1860s and early 1870s – only to have removed it again by 1881. Alexander III sanctioned it in the 1880s, as did Nicholas II between 1894 and 1905; both, however, found it more difficult to justify thereafter. The Soviet regime used to terror on a larger scale during the Civil War (1918–21) but ended the *Cheka* in 1921. Stalin reactivated and massively increased the terror in two waves: 1931–9 and 1946–53. Unlike anyone else in Russian history he made it the norm rather than the exception. This helps explain the revulsion against Stalin from his successor, Khrushchev, and the abandonment of terror as an integral part of the methods of repression by future Soviet leaders like Brezhnev and Andropov, even though the latter had previously been head of the KGB.

We have already seen that repression can be interpreted as the hallmark of either a strong or a weak regime. The same duality can be attached to terror. Normally the strongest exponents of terror are seen as those maintaining their power most effectively – especially Alexander III in the tradition of Nicholas I and Stalin, a combination of Lenin and a latter-day Ivan the Terrible. Yet, it has been argued, this presupposes that the initiative for terror always came from the top and affected those below. An alternative is to see terror as an endemic condition within Russia, fed by social as much as political influences. Although sometimes started by political initiatives, the actual process was determined from below. The worst of the terror in the later Tsarist period manifested itself in the pogroms against the Jews during the 1880s and 1890s: these were not directly instigated by the authorities, although the latter were implicated by their apparent indifference to the plight of those who were being perse-cuted. Revisionist historians have also called into question the extent of Stalin's control over the purges of the 1930s, arguing instead that much of the momentum came from an excess of local zeal (see Analysis 2). Terror, in other words, spiralled out of control.

Repression and terror sometimes, but not always, act in conjunc-tion with each other. But it generally takes a repressive system to produce pulses of terror. Tsarist Russia was a system that sought to preserve itself through institutionalised repression with intermittent but often uncoordinated moments of terror. The Soviet Union aimed in theory to liberate, although in practice the institutions for liberation were subject to repressive constraints: there was therefore more of a contradiction here than in the case of Tsarist Russia. But the revo-lutionary origin and ideological nature of the Soviet regime made it susceptible to more radical manifestations of terror. These reached their extreme form when associated with Tsarist notions of power. In other words, Tsarist repression had a natural affinity to Soviet terror, whereas Soviet repression and Tsarist terror came from different stables.

Questions

1. Who was the most 'repressive' of Russia's leaders between 1855 and 1991?

2. 'The impetus for repression came from above, while that for terror came from below.' Consider this view in the light of Russian history between 1855 and 1991.

SOURCES

1. TERROR, MODERATION AND THE SECRET POLICE UNDER NICHOLAS II

Source 1: Stolypin's views as governor of the province of Grodno, 1902.

One should not be afraid of education or of enlightenment. ... The spread of agricultural knowledge, which no country can afford to deny, depends on general education; the country which is lacking in it will go to ruin. Spread education and you will consolidate the agricultural class which is the most conservative of all classes in the entire world.

Source 2: An order from Tsar Nicholas II to Stolypin (then president of the Council of Ministers), 27 August 1906.

I command the council of ministers to inform me without delay what measures it considers most adequate to undertake in order to carry out my immovable will to uproot rebellion and to re-establish order. ... It seems that only an extraordinary law, promulgated as a temporary measure until peace and quiet are re-established, could give assurance that the government had undertaken decisive measures and would thus quiet everyone.

Source 3: From O. Figes, *A People's Tragedy. The Russian Revolution 1891–1924*, published in 1996.

Zubatov acknowledged that the workers had real and legitimate grievances, and that these could make them into a revolutionary threat. If they were left to the mercy of their factory employers, the workers were almost bound to come under the influence of the socialists. But if, as he advocated, the government set up its own workers' organizations, the initiative would lie with the Tsar's loyal servants. Zubatov's unions aimed to satisfy the workers' demands for education, mutual aid and organization, whilst serving as a channel for monarchist propaganda. To his masters at court, they offered the prospect of a popular autocracy, where the Tsar could appear as the workers' paternal guardian, protecting them from the greed of their bosses and the 'alien contamination of the revolutionaries'. It was the old imperial strategy of divide and rule: the workers would be used to weaken the main threats to the autocracy – the industrial bourgeoisie and the socialist intelligentsia.

Source 4: From S. Phillips, *Lenin and the Russian Revolution*, published in 2000.

Given the subsequent events of the Bolshevik takeover historians have focused a lot of attention on the role of revolutionary groups in the opposition to Tsarism but in the unrest of 1905, sparked off by the hardships of the war against Japan, the revolutionary groups were largely unorganised, small in number and divided amongst themselves. The period after 1905 saw a decline in both organised and spontaneous unrest as economic recovery took place. The Okhrana used ruthless tactics to deal with the revolutionaries. Stolypin set up field courts martial which resulted in the execution of 1,144 people in 1907. The hangman's noose was referred to as 'Stolypin's necktie'.

Questions

1. Study Source 4 and use your own knowledge. Explain briefly the terms '*Okhrana*' and 'field courts martial'. (10)
2. Using Sources 1 and 2, and your own knowledge, compare the attitudes and policies of Zubatov and Stolypin towards popular unrest. (20)
3. Using all of Sources 1 to 4, and your own knowledge, comment on the view that 'Nicholas II and his officials conducted a reign of terror against opponents of the regime'. (30)

Total (60)

2. HISTORIANS AND STALIN'S TERROR

Source 5: From a speech by Khrushchev to the Twentieth Congress of the Communist Party of the Soviet Union (February 1956).

It became apparent that many Party, Soviet and economic activists who were branded in 1937–1938 as 'enemies' were actually never enemies, spies, wreckers, etc., but were always honest Communists. ...

Stalin was a very distrustful man, sickly suspicious; we know this from our work with him. He could look at a man and say: 'Why are your eyes so shifty today?' or 'Why are you turning so much today and avoiding to look me directly in the eyes?' The sickly suspicion created in him a general distrust even toward eminent Party workers whom he had known for years. Everywhere and in everything he saw 'enemies', 'two-facers' and 'spies'.

Possessing unlimited power, he indulged in great wilfulness and choked a person morally and physically. A situation was created where one could not express one's own will.

Source 6: Extract from R. C. Tucker, *The Soviet Political Mind: Studies in Stalinism and Post-Stalin Change*, originally published in 1957.

In the second major phase of Stalinization, which took place in the mid-1930's, Stalin created an absolute autocracy through the suppression of the Bolshevik Party. This meant, in effect, the liquidation of the Soviet ruling class. Here we must refer to Ivan the Terrible in order to elucidate the subjective rationale of Stalin's actions, the method in what might seem to be merely madness. In directing the orgy of treason trials and executions of party cadres, Stalin imagined himself to be acting as Ivan had acted in asserting his absolutism against the ancient landed aristocracy, the Boyars, who were bloodily suppressed on charges of treason and sedition. He even used the pseudonym 'Ivan Vasilyevich'. . . .

One further important point requires mention here. Ivan created an institution known as the *oprichnina*, which was an instrument for the liquidation of the Bovars and a mainstay in his administration of the state. The pre-revolutionary Russian historian Kliuchevsky describes the *oprichnina* as an all-powerful security police. It was organized as a kind of state within the state. The *oprichniki* wore black and rode black horses: their special insignia consisted of a dog's head and a broom attached to the saddle. In the folk memory of the Russian people, the *oprichnina* lingers as a symbol of black crimes and terror, as does its chief, Ivan the Terrible. Stalin unquestionably modelled his NKVD quite consciously upon it. The Soviet security police, originally the terrorist weapon of the Bolshevik Party's dictatorship, became the weapon with which Stalin broke the back of the ruling party. Its functions expanded as its importance rose during the 1930's, until finally, under Stalin's direct guidance, it became a kind of state within the state, an *oprichnina* of Stalinist Russia, inspiring terror, practising torture, watching over everything and everybody, carrying on the kidnapping of Soviet citizens as a matter of settled official policy. In the later Stalin years, the idealizing of Ivan the Terrible was extended to include the idealization of the *oprichnina*. . . .

If Stalin destroyed the Bolshevik Party as a political organism and ruling class, how, we may ask, did he take its place all by himself? What was the Stalin autocracy, considered as an institution? The basic political system has been described here as a complex, three-way, state-party-soviet structure of command and control of society. The autocracy, as Stalin reconstituted it, was a superstructure of command and control, superimposed upon this basic structure, making the Soviet system one single organization in the most literal sense of the word. Concerning the title and detailed operation of the actual organ of the autocracy, there is still some uncertainty. Some sources speak of a personal Stalin 'secretariat.' But according to a refugee account which seems authentic, the organ was something meshed in more closely with the actual machinery of rule. It was the so-called 'special sector' of the Central Committee apparatus, operated by and for Stalin along the lines of a personal secretariat. Through its own special representatives stationed at control positions, this organ operated the police system in accordance with Stalin's bidding. All his directives for trials and purges were funnelled through it. All information was channelled into it.... In short, the superstructure controlled and commanded the control and command apparatus at all key points. It was, as it were, a little gear box through which the entire massive machinery of Soviet rule over nearly 900,000,000 human beings on about one-third of the earth's surface was operated. By manipulating the levers in the control panel, Stalin could cause all kinds of things to happen.

Source 7: An explanation (in 1993) by J. Arch Getty and Roberta Manning as to where the traditional western view of Stalin's terror originated.

Serious academic study of the Stalin period began in the 1950s. Carried out mostly by political scientists and supported by the 'know your enemy' mandate of the Cold War, research on the USSR quickly led to a 'shared paradigm' of Soviet history. That view, which was loosely labelled totalitarian, reflected scholarly consensus in a scientific manner and seemed to explain Soviet reality in a scientific way ...

In a nutshell ... the totalitarian paradigm went as follows. The Soviet system under Stalin consisted of a nonpluralist, hierarchical dictatorship in which the command authority existed only at the top of the pyramid of political power. Ideology and violence were monopolies of the ruling elite, which passed its orders down a pseudo-military chain of command whose discipline was the products of Leninist prescriptions on party organization and Stalinist enforcement of all these norms. At the top of the ruling elite stood an autocratic Stalin whose personal control was virtually unlimited in all areas ... Major policy articulation and implementation involved the actualization of Stalin's ideas, whims and plans, which in turn flowed from his psychological condition.

Source 8: From a revisionist view by R. W. Thurston, *Life and Terror in Stalin's Russia*, published in 1996.

This book argues that Stalin was not guilty of mass first-degree murder from 1934 to 1941 and did not plan or carry out a systematic campaign to crush the nation. This view is not one of absolution, however: his policies did help to engender real plots, lies, and threats to his position. Then this fear-ridden man reacted, and over-reacted, to events. All the while, he could not control the flow of people within the country, job turnover, or illegal acts by managers and many others. He was sitting at the peak of a pyramid of lies and incomplete information, and he must have known it. His power was constrained in fundamental ways, which contributed to his anxiety and tendency to govern by hit-and-run methods. His attitudes and deeds must be situated in the context of vast, popular suspicion generated in part by World War I and the Russian Civil War. Several conclusions follow: Stalin becomes more human than others have portrayed him. And his regime becomes less malevolent but possessed of greater public support than is usually argued.

Questions

1. Compare Sources 5, 6 and 8 as explanations for Stalin's great terror. (20)
2. Using all of Sources 5 to 8, and your own knowledge, examine the view that Stalin 'controlled the terror and the institutions which carried it out'. (40)

Total (60)

5

THE NATIONALITIES

ANALYSIS 1: EXAMINE THE DEVELOPMENT OF
NATIONALITIES WITHIN RUSSIA AND THE SOVIET
UNION BETWEEN 1800 AND 1991.

Russia and the Soviet Union were home to more ethnic groups than
any other country in the world, the result of centuries of expansion
and conquest. The regimes between 1855 and 1991 adopted a
variety of approaches to integrating them into an overall national entity,
sometimes through concessions, sometimes through coercion, but
most frequently through a combination of the two. The main contrast,
however, was between the unitary system of the Tsars and the
federalism adopted as the official policy of the Communist regime.

The Tsars attempted to incorporate most of the peoples they
had conquered directly into Russia. This applied to fellow Slavs such
as Ukrainians and Belorussians, to the Baltic peoples (Estonians,
Latvians and Lithuanians), to the inhabitants of the Caucasus (Armenians, Georgians, Azerbaijanis and Chechens), and Turkic or Asian
groups such as Tajiks, Uzbeks, Tartars, Kazakhs, Azeris, Turkmens,
Kirghiz, Karakalpaks, Uygurs, Bashkirs, Gagauz, Chuvash, Tuvinians,
Buryats, Kalmyks, and 'peoples of the North' such as the Komi,
Yakuts, Mordva, Udmurt and Mari. Successive Tsars had sought to
bring these under Russian administration, although the subjection was
more direct in the case of the European areas than with the central
Asian regions, which were left with a fair degree of social and religious freedom, although this was not accompanied by any formal

political autonomy. By contrast, Alexander III and Nicholas II sought to undermine any separate identity for the Ukraine and Belarus, even to the extent of trying to undermine Ukrainian as a separate language. The administration was controlled from St Petersburg and by local officials who were usually of Russian origin. The large Jewish population was a different case again. Living mostly within the 'pale' of Lithuania, Poland and Ukraine, they had no political influence and experienced such social and religious rights as were afforded them by individual Tsars. Under Alexander II, for example, they were largely ignored by official edicts, but during the reigns of Alexander III and Nicholas II they experienced an increase in persecution and in anti-Semitic pogroms – probably the worst in Europe before the Nazi era.

Two nationalities need particular explanation. Both the Poles and the Finns had a degree of political autonomy in the first half of the nineteenth century, although both were eventually subjected to centralisation and Russification. Poland was deprived of its autonomy, originally granted in 1815, as a direct result of the Polish Revolt of 1863–4, which Alexander II interpreted as a direct attack on the fabric of the Russian Empire. Finland's subjugation came later. Under Alexander II and Alexander III it was permitted to legislate under the 1809 Constitution. Nicholas II, however, saw Finland as a separatist threat, and tried to bring it into line with the rest of the Empire by a series of measures from 1899 onwards. Movements developed in both Poland and Finland for full-scale independence, some even hoping for the collapse of the imperial regime.

This happened in March 1917, as a direct result of military defeat in the First World War. The Provisional Government, which followed the abdication of the Tsar, guaranteed to restore the traditional constitutional rights of the Poles and Finns and to liberalise local government elsewhere. Their commitment to pursuing the war above all else, however, doomed their own power base. The Bolsheviks, who succeeded them in October, had a different policy. Under the Treaty of Brest-Litovsk with the Germans (March 1917), they conceded full independence to Finland, Poland, the Baltic states, Ukraine and Belorussia – a sacrifice which enabled them to win the Civil War and impose their rule on the rest of Russia. A few other areas – Georgia, Armenia and Azerbaijan – declared themselves independent but had been reconquered by the Red Army, along with Ukraine and Belorussia, by 1920.

The Bolsheviks had a difficult choice to make in applying a permanent policy on the nationalities. On the one hand, they had initially sympathised with the principle of national self-determination while, on the other, they favoured democratic centralism as the most feasible approach to implementing Communism. The pragmatic solution was a federal system that guaranteed certain rights for the constituent nationalities. This set the pattern for the whole Soviet state – in the form of the constitutions of 1918, 1924, 1936, 1977 and 1988. These provided more explicit regional liberties than had existed under the Tsarist regime, although whether such liberties were carried out in practice was another matter.

The 1918 Constitution established the RSFSR, which comprised the areas under Bolshevik control. These included Russia and central Asian areas such as Kazakhstan, Uzbekistan and Turkmenia. The Federation was extended in 1922 when the RSFSR signed a treaty with Ukraine, Belorussia, Georgia, Azerbaijan and Armenia. A new constitution formalised the establishment of the USSR in 1924. The rest of the 1920s were probably the heyday of the federal system. Languages in addition to Russian were tolerated and encouraged in the administration and in schools and there seemed to be a more genuine political base to national self-determination than had ever existed before.

Under Stalin (1929–53) the situation became more paradoxical. On the one hand, the 1936 Constitution extended the range of the Federation by a clearer demarcation of constituent members of the Soviet Union. Full republic status was given to the RSFSR, Belorussia, Ukraine, Azerbaijan, Georgia, Armenia, Kazakhstan, Uzbekistan, Turkmenia, Kirghizia and Tajikistan. To these were added Estonia, Latvia, Lithuania and Moldova, when these were annexed between 1939 and 1940. In theory these all had the right to secede from the Union, although in practice this was prevented by the tight control of the CPSU, which was firmly centred on Moscow. On the other hand, Stalin applied measures against individual nationalities, which were unprecedented in their ruthlessness. His punishment for their collaboration with the German invasion of 1941 was mass deportations to remote areas in central Asia, a fate that affected Crimean Tartars, Volga Germans and five groups from the Caucasus, including the Chechens.

Stalin's successors partially reverted to the policies of the 1920s but the Russian and centralising influences continued to be strongly applied by Khrushchev, Brezhnev, Andropov and Chernenko. As part of his policy of *glasnost*, however, Gorbachev (1985–91) allowed a more generous interpretation of 'Republic' status as part of a more progressive series of constitutional reforms from 1988 onwards.

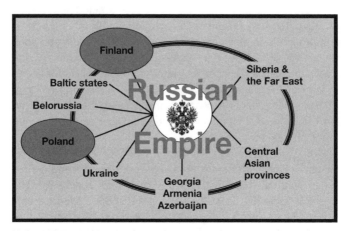

(a) *Imperial Russia*. Direct Tsarist control existed in theory over all areas. Poland and Finland were autonomous at various stages, although this status could be revoked by Imperial edict.

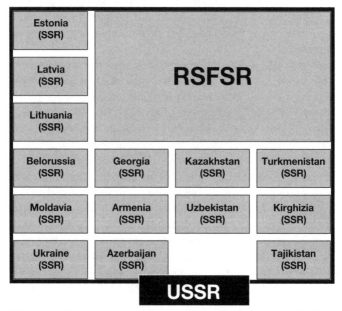

(b) *The Soviet Union – in theory*. This comprised two federations – the RSFSR and the USSR. The latter comprised a voluntary association of 15 autonomous Soviet Socialist Republics (SSRs), each with the right of secession.

IMPERIAL RUSSIA, THE SOVIET UNION AND THE SUCCESSOR STATES

Figure 5.

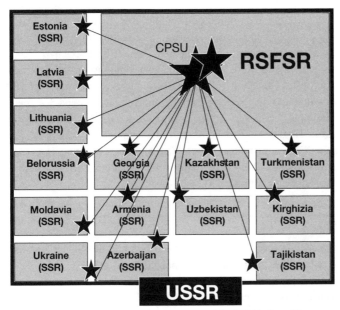

(c) *The Soviet Union – in practice*. The autonomy of the individual republics was nullified in practice by the Communist Party. The central section of the CPSU, based in Moscow, controlled all the republic sections and kept the USSR intact.

(d) *After the Soviet Union*. When centralised control of the CPSU was broken in 1991, the individual SSRs exercised their right to secede from the USSR and became independent sovereign states. The RSFSR became the Russian federation.

Individual republics like Latvia went further in acknowledging the supremacy of their own state legislation over that of the USSR. Following a neo-Stalinist coup against Gorbachev in 1991, many republics asserted their rights under the 1924, 1936 and 1977 Constitutions to secede from the Union; this resulted in the formal dissolution of the USSR on 1 January 1992 and the emergence of 15 independent states: the Russian Federation, Belarus, Ukraine, Estonia, Latvia, Lithuania, Moldova, Georgia, Armenia, Azerbaijan, Kazakhstan, Uzbekistan, Kirgistan, Tajikistan and Turkmenistan. Attempts by the Russian President Yeltsin to establish an alternative system of the Commonwealth of Independent States (CIS) failed to disguise the largest political disintegration in history.

Questions

1. Compare the problems faced by the Tsars and the Soviet leaders in dealing with the minority nationalities in Russia.
2. Compare the policies adopted by the last three Tsars and the Soviet leaders in dealing with the minority nationalities.

ANALYSIS 2: 'THE MOST REPRESSIVE OF THEIR POLICIES, IN RESPONSE TO THE GREATEST OF THEIR THREATS'. TO WHAT EXTENT DO YOU AGREE WITH THIS ASSESSMENT OF THE TREATMENT OF THE NATIONALITIES *EITHER* BY ALEXANDER II, ALEXANDER III AND NICHOLAS II *OR* BY LENIN AND STALIN?

The greatest threats perceived in both cases by the Tsarist and Soviet regimes would have been those most likely to overthrow them. In each case the nationalities featured, but in different ways. They therefore incurred different responses.

The Tsarist system saw ethnic diversity as a fact of life that would have to be contained by a deliberate policy of Russification. This worked as long as ethnic issues did not destabilise the overall political and social structure. When it did, however, it was liable to be seen as a catalyst for chaos and to be treated as such by the harshest measures. This attitude was probably based on the way in which the Russian Empire had evolved – through a collection of conquests and absorptions, any one of which had the potential to destabilise the whole structure at some stage in the future.

The Soviet regime was built on a political revolution that was almost destroyed by the threat of national separatism during the chaos of the last stages of the First World War and the Civil War. Here too there was an overlap between perceived threats of counter-revolution and national self-determination. The initial solution was to concede a measure of national self-determination in order to protect the political system, which meant that the political repression was the more severe. This was, however, neutralised by the parallel imposition of a single-party state, which deprived national self-determination of any practical meaning.

Late-Tsarist Russia

Ethnicity and nationality exercised a key influence on the most repressive policies of the late-Tsarist period. At the same time, these policies could well be based on other fears. A key factor was always likely to be regional opposition to the Russian core of Tsarist autocracy. This, however, existed alongside other pressures based on class; examples were populism (supported by the peasantry), Marxism (based on the urban proletariat), and constitutionalism (supported largely by the middle classes). At times national and sectoral issues merged, as with Poland, the Baltic states, Finland, Ukraine and the Jews. Here nationality acted as a powerful catalyst, incurring a particularly repressive response for the authorities.

One of the main issues concerning the reign of Alexander II (1855–81) was the slowing pace of his reforms after 1865 and the countervailing increase in repression. He was, it could be argued, deflected from initial reforms for two reasons: fear of separatism and fear of radicalism. Two key events were responsible for this change: the Polish Revolt in 1863 and the attempt on his life in 1865 by the student revolutionary, Karakozov. It is debatable as to which of these exerted the greater influence or provoked the more repressive response.

On the one hand, the Polish Revolt must have seemed the more substantial threat, since it involved a precedent for the secession of the subject provinces along the western borders of the Russian Empire. By contrast, revolutionary activity was still in its early Populist phase. Alexander II's Polish policy was harsh and calculated, ending cooperation with local elites, exiling large numbers of nobles, cutting the communication between the Catholic Church and Rome and enforcing, where possible, conversions to Russian Orthodoxy. Attempts were made to eradicate Poland's separate identity through its administrative replacement by a 'Vistula Region', Polish officials were replaced by Russians and Russian became the official medium for education. The harshness extended beyond Poland into areas that had not actually revolted. The Ukraine, although less nationalist than Poland, nevertheless had a growing cultural identity. This was severely damaged by the Decrees of 1863 and 1876 that prevented the publication or import of books in Ukrainian. Severe damage was inflicted on the Ukrainian language and the relative weakness of the Ukraine political movement showed that Alexander's actions were more widespread than counter-measures against rebellion. They were, indeed, part of a broader process of enforced Russification.

On the other hand, Tsarist autocracy was Russian-based and, as such, did not always distinguish between subversion based on nationalism and that due to other motives. Populist groups, such as Land and Liberty or People's Will, were as much a threat to autocracy and centralism since they expressed themselves through local appeals to the peasantry. These could be seen as more dangerous in that they were widespread rather than concentrated in specific areas. As such they required more extensive manifestations of repression, Alexander II conferring special powers on 'regional military dictators' in 1879. These undid many of the powers previously granted to the provincial *zemstva* and established martial law as an official norm in most parts of European Russia. In these circumstances the plight of Poland and the Ukraine was not quite so unique.

Yet the reign of Alexander II remains something of a paradox and it is still difficult to give a clear answer on what were his greatest concerns. The so-called 'Tsar liberator' was also the hammer of the Poles, the leveller of the Ukrainians and the instigator of general martial law. Yet he favoured the Finns (in some ways the most separatist of all the Russian provinces), allowing the Finnish Diet to be called in 1863 and granting what almost amounted to a constitution in 1867. This might appear to swing the weight of repression back to the non-border provinces. But here, again, there were changes, as elements of repression were reversed with the ending of martial law in 1880 and the approval of the plans of Loris Melikov for a general Consultative Assembly. A major reason for the question mark overhanging the reign is Alexander's assassination by People's Will at the very time that the whole nature of future policy was in the balance.

Alexander III made far fewer concessions to progress, establishing a more uniform system of repression that covered political and social issues – as well as the nationalities. The key measures were the

Statute of State Security (1881), which brought the judicial process under administrative control, withdrew the freedom of universities and tightened censorship; all were condoned by Pobedonostsev, Procurator General of the Holy Synod. The whole process was wider and more permanent than the emergency decrees of Alexander II. This applied even more to the treatment of the nationalities. Here two trends became more deliberate: Russification and anti-Semitism. Katkov, Minister of the Interior, increased the pressure on Poland by arguing that 'Poland as a political term is Russia's natural and irreconcilable enemy'.[1] The same principle was applied to any other area that possessed any form of separatist ambition. Alexander III pursued administrative integration and imposed the Russian language, culture and religion in dominance over the indigenous forms; the economic equivalent was integration through heavy industry and communications.

The form of repression that transcended all others was, however, the persecution of the Jews. Anti-Semitism reached a new intensity under Alexander III and Nicholas II, partly under the influence of Ignatiev's memorandum linking Jews with all the negative and insidious influences coming into Russia from the West. Jews were therefore seen as the core of an international conspiracy against Russian traditions as well as the structure of autocracy itself. Measures after Alexander II's assassination therefore included a ban on Jewish resettlement and on the acquisition of property in rural areas. Subsequent regulations prevented Jews from entering the military or medicine and removed them from the electoral roll for the *zemstva*. The worst examples of anti-Semitism were, however, the pogroms that were tacitly tolerated or, on occasion, actively encouraged by the police forces. Indeed, late-Tsarist Russia was probably the most anti-Semitic state in Europe until the Third Reich.

If the reign of Alexander III was one of unrelieved reaction with particular emphasis on national and ethnic minorities, that of his successor was more mixed, even episodic. Until 1905 the security decrees issued by Alexander III were retained and harshly enforced, resulting, for example, in the death of over 1,000 demonstrators on Bloody Sunday in January 1905. The pogroms against the Jews between 1905 and 1906 were even more savage. The authorities were compromised by their inaction, while the Tsar himself blamed the Jews as instigators of all other threats to the regime. He wrote in his diary at the end of 1905 that 'the *narod* became enraged by the insolence and audacity of the revolutionaries and socialists; and because nine-tenths of them are Yids, the people's whole wrath has turned against them'.[2] The fact that some Jews in Poland and the Baltic states did join revolutionary movements – especially the Social Democrats – was probably as much an effect as a cause of this attitude.

After the 1905 Revolution Nicholas II was obliged to introduce more progressive policies. Socially this involved the legalisation of trade unions and a series of agricultural reforms, while politically the State Duma was the first elected assembly in Russian history. Ethnic groups also benefited as Muslims, Poles, Armenians, Jews, Georgians and others were elected to the Duma. Newspapers were more widely published from 1905 in other languages, including Ukrainian and Lithuanian – previously banned or tightly controlled. Yet the concessions were insufficient to win over any of the social or ethnic groups to the regime and there were instances of continued brutality – the Lena goldfields massacre of 1913 and continuing anti-Jewish pogroms being two examples. The regime also lost the opportunity to try to win over the different groups: the Electoral Law of 1907 revised the franchise to exclude a large proportion of the urban working class and peasantry, while nothing was done to adapt the 1906 Constitution to any form of federalism and thereby recognise the role of the different nationalities. The result was that both social and national groups contributed to the disintegration of Tsarist Russia in February 1917.

The last three Tsars were conscious of a variety of threats with which they tried to deal. These were political, social and ethnic. The priorities might differ at any one time but the three were actually interconnected. In the case of Alexander II, the Polish Revolt was probably the key factor in undermining the reform programme, while Alexander III justified his tightening of autocracy by a programme of Russification. Under Nicholas II the whole issue became far more complex, but there is evidence that concessions granted in 1906 were taken back both for political and ethnic reasons – that the two had become merged in the Tsarist concept of the Russian Empire. The problem is that they had also come to influence opposition concepts of the future of the Russian Empire and political solutions now began to clash with ethnic ones.

Lenin and Stalin

Under Lenin (1917–24) the nationalities were seen as one of several key issues concerning the survival of the Bolshevik regime. In some ways they were targeted as the main problem and treated accordingly.

In other ways, however, they received concessions that acknowledged at least a basic right to self-determination.

The Bolsheviks came to power in a country facing military defeat, civil war and disintegration. The first was the most pressing and had to be allayed by the Treaty of Brest-Litovsk in March 1918. This acknowledged the independence of Russia's European borderlands – Finland, the Baltic states, Poland, Belorussia and Ukraine. Lenin and Trotsky considered this necessary to concentrate on the regime's survival against the threats of counter-revolution from the Whites and of alternative forms of democracy from the SRs and the Mensheviks. Yet, in process, the threat of nationalism and national self-determination became increasingly important, as other areas such as Georgia and Armenia also sought their independence from Russia. Eventually the Red Army, reconstituted by Trotsky, included the reconquest of as many nationalities as possible as a part of their victorious campaigns against the Whites under Yudenitch, Wrangel, Deniken and Kornilov. They also extended their counter-attacks on the Green peasant armies in 1921 to mopping-up operations against Ukrainians, Belorussians and Caucasian peoples. In the process the nationalities were dealt with as harshly as were any of the social groups because, militarily, they were seen as part of the same problem. Similarly, the rigours of War Communism (1918–21) affected peasants who may also have been Kazaks, Uzbeks or Russians.

It was, however, characteristic of Lenin's regime to grant concessions – albeit from a position of political strength – to those sections of the population identified as a potential obstacle to future cohesion. An example was the NEP, launched in 1921 to pacify the peasantry. Into this pattern fell the nationalities also. The 1918 RSFSR acknowledged a degree of local self-determination to those ethnic regions left to Russia after Brest-Litovsk, while the USSR (established between 1922 and 1924) recognised the autonomy of areas, such as Ukraine, Georgia and Armenia, which were reconquered during the Civil War. To all such measures there was, however, a limit. The Bolshevik regime controlled the economic concessions to the peasantry by reducing their political influence through weighted votes. Similarly, the principle of autonomy for the nationalities was cancelled out in practice by the centralising influence of the all-powerful CPSU.

During the Stalinist era (1929–1953) the nationalities seemed to experience more obvious extremes of benefit and suffering – again depending on their perceived threat to the regime. On the one hand, the concept of federalism was considerably widened by the 1936 Constitution. The 11 republics, reconstituted from the four of 1924, were the RSFSR, Ukraine, Belorussia, Azerbaijan, Georgia, Uzbekistan, Tajikistan, Kazakhstan, Armenia, Turkmenia and Kirghizia. This seemed broadly in line with the extension of political rights to all sectors of the population through a new and equal suffrage from the age of 20. There was also an apparent attempt to balance social and ethnic representation in the form of a bicameral Supreme Soviet, the Soviet of the Union being elected through equal constituencies, the Soviet of the Nationalities representing the nationally based republics. Could it be that the Stalinist regime had provided a new and more equitable balance between the demands and needs of the social and ethnic sectors of the Soviet Union?

In theory, perhaps. Again, however, both social and ethnic groups experienced counter-measures; under Stalin these were more savage than at any time in the past and conducted through deliberate purges. These were applied to all sectors – including the *kulaks* among the peasantry, the industrial managers and workforce, the membership of the CPSU, and the armed forces. Peasants in the Ukraine were perceived as a threat partly for their resistance to collectivisation after 1929 and partly for their potential separatism. They were therefore purged by the NKVD as Ukrainian *kulaks*. A second round of rural purges in the late 1930s affected the Kazakhs in the same way. The 'old Bolsheviks', seen by Stalin as a particular threat to his personal power within the CPSU, were initially destabilised in their republic status: newer party apparatchiks such as Khrushchev rose rapidly through the ranks of the Ukrainian section of the CPSU under Stalin's sponsorship.

So far it appears that social groups and nationalities under Stalin benefited and suffered more or less evenly in both roles. But this does not go far enough. Under Stalin, mass repression was often con-ducted *primarily* through ethnic channels. This applied particularly to the quotas of victims for each republic and each area. The appropriate branches of the NKVD (and later the NKGB) intensified the pressure on the unfortunate inhabitants in an attempt to exceed the quota. In this way the channels frequently flooded and systematic targeting turned into mass slaughter. In other cases, economic and social policies became doubly repressive in certain areas. The Ukraine, for example, was targeted for the most intensive action against *kulaks* and other 'saboteurs' during the collectivisation campaign between 1929 and 1931, with the mass requisitioning of grain resulting in famine and the death of at least 10 million peasants through starvation. During the col-lectivisation campaign peasants suffered as peasants – but Ukrainian peasants suffered even more than Russian peasants.

The most extreme example of Stalin's persecution of the national-ities occurred in wartime. For most Russians the tight constraints of the 1930s were relaxed between 1941 and 1945 in a desperate effort to focus on winning the war. For the nationalities, however, the repression became increasingly severe. In addition to Germans and Koreans (both considered co-nationals of enemy states, large-scale deportations during the war affected Kalmyks, Balkars, Ingush, Karachaians, Chechens, Crimean Tartars and Meshketians. Millions of these were sent to central Asia; their autonomous republics and districts within the RSFSR were dissolved and were removed from all records. Stalin was therefore reverting to a policy of Russification – but in a much more extreme form than it had ever been applied before. Even more sweeping was the treatment of Ukrainians, Estonians, Latvians and Lithuanians, all of whom were accused of collaborating with the German invaders. It is true that there were *Wehrmacht* and SS units formed from among these nationalities, although subsequent measures were applied with little attempt to target those actually involved. As for the Jewish minorities, those who escaped the *Einsatzgruppen* of the SS or deportation to the Nazi death camps, faced a ban on the practice of their religion, the closure of their institutions, and a prohibition on their publications. During the so-called Doctor's Plot, 15 Jewish leaders were tried and executed in August, 1952, a virtual re-enactment of the show trials of the late 1930s.

The extent to which Stalin saw a threat in the nationalities can be seen in the way in which he treated eastern Europe after 1945. Countries like Poland and Czechoslovakia were dominated by the Soviet Union to prevent the unleashing of separatism *within* the Soviet Union. This, in turn, guaranteed the centralisation of the regime and the continuing operation of the Soviet state in other areas. It also reversed the situation that Lenin had inherited, where the First World War had threatened internal collapse: the Second tamed the national-ities within by subjugating those without. The irony, however, was that, in the longer term, the collapse of Soviet control in eastern Europe led directly to the collapse of the Soviet state itself.

Questions

1. Were the last three Tsars provoked by the minority nationalities into pursuing a policy of Russification?
2. 'Stalin fostered national self-determination within the Soviet Union but persecuted the nationalities.' Do you agree?

ANALYSIS 3: COMPARE THE TREATMENT OF THE NATIONALITIES BY THE TSARIST AND SOVIET REGIMES BETWEEN 1855 AND 1991. HOW EFFECTIVE WERE THEIR POLICIES?

In theory, the change of regime saw a direct transition from rights blurred or removed to rights clarified and conferred. There was, for example, a fundamental difference in the stated attitudes of the two regimes to the non-Russian nationalities. Under the Tsars, minorities of any kind constituted a potential threat to royal absolutism. National minorities were potentially dangerous: most had been brought into the Empire as a result of conquest during the seventeenth, eighteenth and nineteenth centuries and resented attempts to reduce the status of the language and culture. Ignatiev, the Minister of the Interior, con- sidered Polish and Jewish influences particularly insidious – largely because they were concentrated in Russia's western provinces extending from the Baltic states to the Ukraine and Black Sea. In his 1881 Memorandum he warned Alexander II that they were a channel for the penetration of subversive Western influences into Russia. Ethnicity and minority nationalism were therefore seen as agents that could destroy the Russian Empire, especially when allied to revo- lutionary conspiracy or demands for constitutional change. The only real counter to this was absolutism and centralisation – both in a Russian form. The Romanovs emphasised their Russian heritage and, as far as possible, installed Russian officials in key provincial posi- tions. In his early years of revolutionary activity, Lenin had extensive contact with nationalist dissidents and saw their usefulness in under- mining the Empire. After overthrowing the Provisional Government in October 1917, he adopted a new approach to the nationalities issue. The contrast with Tsarist policy is unequivocally stated in the 1971 official Soviet view: 'Millions of people once forgotten and deprived of their rights had now achieved their national statehood.' At the same time this was in a form that guaranteed 'lasting unity'. In the past, 'unity' had 'been based on stifling oppression'. The 'new kind of unity' had, however, come into being voluntarily, as 'an expression of the people's free choice'.[3]

These differences were reflected in the constitutional bases of the two regimes. The main contrast was between a unitary autocracy, based on Russian control, and the federalism of the Soviet Union. The introduction of a new Tsarist constitution in 1906 made very little difference to historic precedent and practice. The Fundamental Laws referred throughout to the 'Russian state', the 'All-Russian Emperor' and 'Russian subjects'. It contained no reference to the non-Russian nationalities, apart from a cursory mention of the 'Grand Duchy of Finland', which was nevertheless 'an inseparable part of the Russian state'.[4] Poland had almost certainly been better off under its 1815 Constitution, which had been abrogated by Alexander II after the 1863 Polish Revolt – and never reinstated. The Soviet constitutions, by contrast, made a point of emphasising the rights of the nationalities. Article 2 of the 1918 Constitution of the RSFSR referred to 'the free union of free nations'.[5] Article 13 of the 1936 Constitution affirmed that 'the Union of Soviet Socialist Republics is a federal state, formed on the basis of the voluntary union' of 'Soviet Socialist Republics', which were 'equal in rights'. There was even a statutory provision for ending this union; by Article 17, 'the right freely to secede from the USSR is reserved to each constituent republic'.[6] This was a contrast to the opening words of the 1906 Fundamental Laws that 'the Russian state is ... indivisible'.[7] The guarantees of rights to self-determination and voluntary secession were reiterated in the 1977 Constitution and were unaffected by Gorbachev's constitutional amendments in 1988. This meant that the Soviet regime opened wide the door of what Lenin had called the 'prison-house of the nationalities'.

Or did it? It is possible to exaggerate the extent of the difference between the two regimes as, indeed, the official Soviet view does. The actual position is rather more complex and somewhat reduces the gap between two apparent extremes.

The Russian Empire actually allowed a surprising degree of autonomy to the nationalities, while the Soviet authorities took particular care to control them. These were often unstated – and certainly unsung – policies, used to provide safeguards against any backlash against the official line. Although it gradually reduced the political autonomy of Poland and launched a cultural offensive in the Ukraine, the Tsarist regime generally allowed economic laissez-faire in its European provinces and religious toleration in central Asia. The result was that the non-Russian European provinces, especially the Baltic states, Poland and Ukraine, were more prosperous than Russia itself; it has been suggested that Russification was, in part at least, a defensive strategy against the conversion of economic power into a political challenge on the traditional regime.[8] The predominantly Muslim areas of Kazakhstan, Uzbekistan, Kirgistan, Turkmenistan and Tajikistan experienced the reverse; their very economic backwardness acted as a magnet for Russian economic interest. Nevertheless, Russification here was limited to economic infrastructural change.

The peoples of an area the size of central and western Europe were otherwise left with minimal interference in their religion, administration, education, social policies and law. This was because the regime preferred not to stir ethnic and religious groups who presented no immediate threat. On the other hand, it was quite capable of following a strategy of 'divide and rule', sometimes backing one ethnic group against another to maintain the balance of power within a particular region; this applied, for example, to the Caucasus area, where the regime tried to control Armenian culture, education and religious practice (even though this was Christian) while making concessions to the Muslim province of Azerbaijan. Russification was therefore far from a blanket policy and was often sensitive to local issues.

The counterpart to a Tsarist regime that did not always seek to dominate its ethnic minorities is a Soviet regime that did. From the start, Lenin had to try to resolve a fundamental contradiction. On the one hand, Marxism as an ideology sought to transcend nationalism, on Marx's premise that 'the working man has no nation'. On the other hand, concessions to national self-determination were necessary for a successful revolution against the Tsarist regime and for the survival of its successor. Unlike many Social Democrats, Bolsheviks as well as Mensheviks, Lenin did not envisage the break-up of the Russian Empire since this would weaken the main objectives of the Communist revolution – the establishment of the workers' state and the preparation for international revolution. Nationalism could therefore be tolerated as long as it did not claim to be exclusive or seek to be repressive. Instead, it had to fit into a socialist structure and to cut all connections with capitalism or imperialism. Although the 1903 Bolshevik Party programme did in theory acknowledge 'the right of self-determination for all nations comprising the state',[9] the practice of this was hedged with qualifications. It is true that full independence was conceded by the Treaty of Brest-Litovsk (1918) to Finland, the Baltic states, Poland and the Ukraine; but this was only under the threat of military defeat by the German armies. The Bolsheviks reconquered the Ukraine during the Civil War (1918–21), at the same time preventing secession by other areas like Georgia and Armenia, while Stalin made good other territorial losses between 1939 and 1945. The Soviet Union used as much force in holding the Empire together as the Tsarist regime had in assembling it in the first place. As for the constitutional guarantees of autonomy, and rights to secession, these were all neutralised by the domination of the whole federal structure by the CPSU. The CPSU was the dominant centripetal influence that made centrifugalism a practical impossibility. Indeed, the role of the Party was more penetrative than the more diffuse system used by the Tsars. Nor was the Soviet Union ever a partnership of *equal* states. Russians controlled the membership of the CPSU and virtually monopolised the key organs. Prominent individuals of non-Russian origins (such as Stalin from Georgia and Khrushchev from the Ukraine) accepted the logic of the channels of power radiating outwards from Moscow and hastened to Russify themselves as an essential step towards controlling the Party and – through careful appointments – the nationalities.

There was, therefore, some blurring of the *actual* differences between the treatment of the nationalities by the two regimes. There were also differences of emphasis within each. Each had – at least by its own normal practice – a relatively progressive phase. In the Empire this applied to the early years of Alexander II's reign – until 1863 – and to the second half of Nicholas II's. The equivalent during the Soviet period was the 1920s – the final years of Lenin and the interregnum between Lenin and Stalin. This decade saw a relative respect for the minority nationalities, accompanying economic and social relations allowed by the NEP from 1921. The CPSU was prob-ably more genuinely representative of the regions than at any other time before the Gorbachev era and other languages were promoted in the administration and in schools. But there were also dark periods within each regime. Alexander II systematically dismantled Poland's autonomy after the Revolt of 1863, while Alexander III (1881–94) and Nicholas II (until 1905) made a more general connection between Tsarist absolutism and Russification at the expense of other national-ities. This period also saw the worst instances of anti-Semitism in the form of pogroms (see Analysis 2). For his part, Stalin deliberately ended the relaxation of the 1920s. His focus was on recentralisation in order to achieve a command economy and prepare for war with the West. Russian domination was revived and there was extensive discrimination against the minority nationalities, who also suffered dis-proportionately from the purges. Although allowed in theory, cultural diversity was in practice subordinated to creeping Russification through 'Socialist Realism'. Even the historic focus was Russian as Stalin revived the reputations of Alexander Nevsky, Ivan the Terrible and Peter the Great. During the Second World War, close parallels were drawn between the Germans and the French invasion of 1812, both of which were labelled the 'great patriotic war'. The period after 1941 is also notable for the enormity of Stalin's retribution against the minority nationalities accused of disloyalty and treason (see Analysis 2). In their scope and savagery these measures exceeded anything in Russia's history since the time of Genghis Khan.

Despite the measures introduced to keep it intact, 'Greater Russia' – or Russia plus its dependencies – imploded twice. Between 1918 and 1921 it lost the western border regions by the Treaty of Brest-Litovsk with Germany and the Treaty of Riga with Poland. Although a small proportion of the Russian Empire, this nevertheless amounted to an area the size of France, Germany and Spain combined. Some of these losses, mainly the western Ukraine, Estonia, Latvia and Lithuania were reclaimed between 1939 and 1941. The second separation came at the end of 1991, when all of the Soviet Socialist Republics (SSRs) opted for their independence as 15 new sovereign states: the Russian Federation, Estonia, Latvia, Lithuania, Belarus, Ukraine, Moldova, Georgia, Azerbaijan, Armenia, Kazakhstan, Turk-menistan, Kirgistan, Tajikistan and Uzbekistan. The two processes of disintegration were marked by mutual similarities and differences.

The main similarities are evident in the influence of ideological and economic factors. Both regimes tried to downplay the importance of nationalism as an ideology but, in the process, succeeded only in strengthening it. Both offered ideological alternatives as a focus for common loyalty, whether in the form of a divinely ordained personal absolutism or of a revolutionary workers' state. Both used Russia's dominant position, within the unitary empire or the Soviet federation, to hold the different nationalities together. Both, however, failed at the end to check the centrifugal force exerted by the minorities. The Soviet approach was particularly flawed. Its assumption was that the ethnic groups in Tsarist Russia were in a 'pre-nationalist' state and could be held securely within a 'post-nationalist' system that acknow-ledged but controlled their 'national identity'. But, like the Tsars before them, the Soviet leadership succeeded only in provoking nationalism by imposing Russian-based controls. Although these were normally presented as 'non-nationalist' measures, the minorities were not convinced; they had to acquiesce – but they remained provoked. There was a similar problem with changing material conditions within the two systems. In both Tsarist Russia and the Soviet Union, the regime tried to set the pace for economic development, whether through Witte's industrialisation in the 1890s or through Stalin's Five-Year Plans. Both, however, largely ignored consumer needs in their emphasis on heavy industry. This was an additional irritant to the provinces (or republics) in the western part of the country, which became increasingly receptive to influences from western and central Europe. It is therefore no coincidence that in the Tsarist period revolutionary movements contained large numbers of non-Russian members or that the first stirrings against the Soviet Union in the late 1980s came from the Baltic states and western Ukraine.

There was, of course, a major contrast between the two situations leading to the collapse of the Russian Empire and the USSR. In 1918 several border provinces became independent states through the agency of two wars (the First World War and the Russo-Polish War). Although the area involved was huge, it did not affect the majority of the nationalities, who were pulled back into line by Lenin in the Civil War and by Stalin between 1939 and 1945. It was a case of a transition from one system to another, with some of the minority groups managing to escape in the process. In 1991 the change was more fundamental. The Soviet Union dissolved peacefully, all of its constituent republics becoming fully independent. Attempts to replace the USSR with a more loosely based CIS met with little long-term success, clearly indicating a preference for unconditional national sovereignty.

The end of the Soviet Union does seem more remarkable than the contraction of the Russian Empire into the USSR, especially since no military catastrophe was involved in 1991. With hindsight, it has become clear that the Soviet Union was a deeply flawed structure, which collapsed under the weight of its own economic problems. Yet this collapse occurred not with untidy chaos at the western periphery, as in 1918, but in an ordered way along all the borders of the individual SSRs. The constitution of 1924 – as updated in 1936 and 1977 – had suddenly gone into reverse. The right to 'voluntary membership' of and 'secession from' the Soviet Union became fault-lines along which Soviet social republics separated from each other and emerged with predetermined frontiers. By contrast, Poland and Finland had, earlier in the century, had to fight for their borders even after their statehood had been acknowledged in 1918. The fault-lines were, of course, unintended; instead, they had been envisaged as the joins within a federal entity, held together by the adhesive influence of the CPSU. Two things occurred to precipitate the change. The first was the growth of dissent within the areas most recently added to the Soviet Union as a result of the Second World War – Estonia, Latvia, Lithuania, the western Ukraine and Moldova. Taking their cue from the 1989 'people's revolutions' against Communist regimes in eastern Europe, they pressed for further concessions within the Soviet Union, exerting a significant influence in other republics as well. The second development was the fortuitous ban placed on the Russian Communist Party following the attempted coup in 1991. This removed the bond between the republics, fully exposing the dividing lines and allowing each republic to exercise to the full its constitutional rights. To rework the original metaphor, Yeltsin produced the key, made but hidden during the Soviet era, to unlock the prison-house erected by the Tsars. The occupants left without ceremony.

Without these constitutional arrangements the violence attending the end of the Soviet Union might have been even more severe than that following the collapse of Tsarist Russia, especially since four of the new states (Russia, Ukraine, Belarus and Kazakhstan) still had nuclear weapons in 1992. The extent of the catastrophe that never happened can be deduced from the actual conflict at the southern edge of Russia itself. The RSFSR had never granted its Autonomous Soviet Socialist Republics (ASSRs) the right to secede and, during the 1990s, the Russian Federation took rigorous measures against Chechnya for attempting to follow the example of neighbouring Georgia, Azerbaijan and Armenia (former SSRs). Serious enough within its own context, the crisis of Chechnya might well have been vastly magnified across the whole region but for those clauses for secession in the constitutions of the USSR. As it is, stability has generally been maintained between (if not always within) the new states. The central Asian republics are among the more moderate Islamic regimes, while, in Europe, the Baltic states have joined the European Union and may well be followed eventually by Ukraine and Moldova. The contrast with the volatility in eastern Europe between 1918 and 1945 could not be greater. On the other hand, allowing a similar concession within the constitution of the RSFSR could have released up to 50 more independent states and Russia itself could well have shrunk to the size of fifteenth-century Muscovy – the core upon which the Russian Empire was built. The Chechen crisis might have been avoided – but the other effects of this development would have been incalculable.

Questions

1. Was the Soviet Union any less a 'prison-house of the nationalities' than Tsarist Russia had been?
2. Was the secessionist clause within the Soviet constitutions of 1924, 1936 and 1977 the 'fatal flaw' within the USSR?

SOURCES

1. THE POLICIES OF ALEXANDER III AND NICHOLAS II TOWARDS THE NATIONALITIES

Source 1: The 15 largest nationalities in the European part of the Russian Empire in 1897 (in millions).

Russians	55.7
Ukrainians	22.4
Poles	7.9
Belorussians	5.9
Jews	5.1
Kirghiz	4.1
Tartars	3.8
Germans	1.8
Lithuanians	1.7
Georgians	1.4
Bashkirs	1.3
Armenians	1.2
Latvians	1.2
Estonians	1.0
Moldavians	1.0

Source 2: From M. Lynch, *Reaction and Revolutions: Russia 1881–1924*, published in 1994.

These restrictive measures were accompanied by a deliberate policy of Russification, which was an attempt by Alexander III's government to restrict the influence of the national minorities within the Russian Empire. Russian was declared to be the official first language, thereby extending the traditional policy of making it the form in which law and government were conducted throughout the Empire. The effect of this was to give officials everywhere a vested interest in maintaining the dominance of Russian values at the expense of the other national cultures. Discrimination against non-Russians, which had previously been a hidden feature of Russian public life, became more open and vindictive in the 1890s. State interference in national forms of administration, education and religion became frequent and systematic. The nationalities that suffered most from the discrimination of these years were the Baltic Germans, the Poles, the Finns, the Armenians and the Ukrainians. With hindsight, the tsarist policy of Russification can be seen as peculiarly ill-judged. At a critical stage in its development, when cohesion and unity were needed as never before, Russia chose to treat half of its population as inferiors or potential enemies.

Source 3: From R. G. Suny's chapter on 'Nationality Policies', a contribution to a larger work on Russia, published in 1997.

The variety of political entities within the Russian empire, from the Grand Duchy of Finland and the Viceroyalty of Caucasia to the khanates of Bukhara and Khiva, were indelible reminders of the stages of expansion that continued until the last days of Romanov rule.

Non-Russian peoples were governed in a contradictory system that involved indirect rule in some places, direct military government through local elites assimilated into the Russian administrative system in others, and various forms of constitutionalism (in the Grand Duchy of Finland and, until 1863, the Kingdom of Poland). Among the effects of tsarism was the imposition of a new state order on societies that had little contact with strong state structures, new regulations and laws, the spread of serfdom to certain regions, such as Georgia, and the enforcement of new taxation. This administrative 'Russification', the extension of bureaucratic absolutism over non-Russian subjects, was accompanied by a spontaneous self-Russification that many non-Russians found advantageous in the first two-thirds of the nineteenth century. But after 1881, when the government adopted more stridently anti-national and anti-semitic policies that threatened a forced cultural homogenization, even ethnicities which had been Russophilic, such as the Armenians, turned hostile to the tsarist regime.

Questions

1. Study Source 1 and use your own knowledge. Comment briefly on the ethnic diversity of the Russian Empire at the end of the nineteenth century. (10)
2. Study Sources 2 and 3. With reference to your own knowledge of Alexander III and Nicholas II, examine the similarities and differences between the explanations given in Sources 2 and 3. (20)
3. Study Sources 1, 2 and 3 and use your own knowledge. 'The source of all their problems.' How far do you agree with this assessment of the policies of Alexander III and Nicholas II to the nationalities? (30)

Total (60)

2. DIFFERENT PERSPECTIVES ON THE NATIONALITIES UNDER THE TSARIST AND SOVIET REGIMES

Source 4: Extracts from (a) *A Short History of the CPSU*, and (b) *A Short History of Soviet Society*. (These were written by a committee of Soviet historians and published in the USSR in 1970 and 1971.)

(a) Tsarist Russia was one of the largest colonial empires. The non-Russian peoples, who comprised more than half the population, were denied all political rights. They were brutally exploited, humiliated and insulted. The tsarist officials wielded arbitrary power. The non-Russian regions in the East were turned into sources of raw materials and doomed to economic backwardness. Some of the non-Russian peoples were driven from their ancestral homes and their land was turned over to Russian landowners and well-to-do peasants. The national culture of the non-Russian peoples was trampled and suppressed. The tsarist government deliberately fomented national strife, setting one nation against another, and provoking Jewish pogroms and massacres between Armenians and Azerbaijanians. In fact, tsarist Russia was nothing less than a prison of nations.

(b) A number of non-Russian republics were set up on the territory of the former Russian Empire after the October Revolution which had burst asunder the chains of national oppression. Millions of people once forgotten and deprived of any rights had now achieved their national statehood and were establishing Soviet power. This did not, however, in any way imply that the state was weakened and dismembered as a result. The self-determination of the peoples of Russia and the simultaneous establishment of Soviet power and national statehood which created conditions favourable to the development and advance of the national minorities provided guarantees of a firm and lasting unity. In the past 'unity' had been based on stifling oppression but the new kind of unity came into being voluntarily; it was the expression of the peoples' free choice, for they realised and appreciated the vital importance of joining forces.

Source 5: An interpretation by Edward Acton, *Russia: The Tsarist and Soviet Legacy*, published in 1995.

(a) [On Tsarist Russia at the turn of the nineteenth century m]ounting social tension was accompanied by the swift development of national consciousness among the Empire's ethnic minorities. ... The last two Tsars pursued a heavy-handed if uneven policy of Russification, motivated sometimes by concern to create a uniform legal order and administrative system, but accompanied by measures promoting Russian culture and Orthodoxy and discriminating against minority languages and religions. This tended to push even relatively mild cultural movements, such as that in the Ukraine, in the direction of political protest. The dynamics of the process varied widely.

(b) [On Soviet Russia in the 1920s t]he Party's political monopoly seemed indispensable in establishing control over areas regained from the Whites, particularly where national separatist feeling was pronounced. One-party rule was the fundamental premise underlying the Constitution of the Soviet Socialist Republics (USSR), ratified in 1924, which created a quasi-federal union between the Republics of the Ukraine, Belorussia, and Transcaucasia, and the giant Russian Socialist Federative Soviet Republic (RSFSR). The Constitution not only recognized separate governments for each Union Republic, each with its own flag and symbols of sovereignty, but boldly proclaimed their right of secession from the Union. Yet this did not reflect the slightest willingness to countenance independent policy-formation by the minority republics, still less any future break-up of the Union. . . . The premise of concessions to the minorities on the constitutional structure and scope of cultural autonomy was the Party's monopolization of political life throughout the USSR.

Source 6: The view of Sheila Fitzpatrick in *Changing Western and Soviet Perspectives* part of a larger work published in 1993. This extract anticipates future histories of the nationalities in Russia.

Perhaps even more importantly, the same is true, only to a greater degree, for all the non-Russian peoples and republics. They will be writing their own nationalist (quasi-separatist) histories, distinct from the Russian-dominated 'official Soviet' version given in the old history books. National heroes and martyrs (many of the latter being victims of Stalin's regime) will appear, along with hitherto unmentionable episodes of inter-ethnic conflict and oppression by Moscow.

This means that, for the first time, real diversity of historical interpretation will arise out of the ethnic diversity of the multi-national and multi-ethnic Soviet state. This point can be appreciated if one considers the recent territorial dispute between the Armenians and Azerbaidzhanians over Nagorno-Karabakh, an issue which was unknown to the outside world before perestroika. There is a legitimate Armenian historical perspective on this issue and an equally legitimate Azerbaidzhanian one. Future historians will no doubt also find a third perspective in the central archives, namely that of Imperial Russian and Soviet administrators trying to cope with the long standing ethnic conflicts of the region.

Questions

1. Examine the similarities and differences between the interpretations in:
   - Sources 1(a) and 2(a) or
   - Sources 1(b) and 2(b). (20)
2. Using all the sources and your own knowledge explain whether you agree with the view that the nationalities were engaged primarily in a struggle against centralising authority in Russia between 1855 and 1991. (40)

Total (60)

6

THE IMPACT OF WAR

ANALYSIS 1: EXPLAIN THE IMPACT OF WAR ON RUSSIA'S INTERNAL DEVELOPMENT BETWEEN 1854 AND 1991.

Von Clausewitz defined war at the beginning of the nineteenth century as 'the continuation of policy by other means'. This put the emphasis on foreign policy and diplomacy and reflected the view of most leaders that they can control the nature of military conflict. There is, however, another side to war – its impact on the internal situation of the country involved. This is much more unpredictable. In most circumstances the experience of war interacts with political and social pressures; war is therefore a catalyst for change. This acts in one of two ways. The catalyst can either initiate change, perhaps against a previous trend. Or it can accelerate the pace of a previous trend to bring about more quickly a change that might have occurred anyway. During the period 1854–1991 Russia was involved in ten major wars, all of which played an important part in its internal development.

War was both a reason for – and an effect of – key adjustments in Tsarist policy on autocracy. The first of these was the decision of Alexander II, immediately after his accession in 1855, to introduce major reforms, even though Nicholas I had generally resisted change. A key factor was Russia's poor performance in the Crimean War (1854–6), a reflection on the recruiting system, the military leadership, the supply chain and the bureaucratic inefficiency. The result was a series of reforms, beginning with the emancipation of the serfs in 1861 and proceeding to the updating of local government (1864 and 1870), changes in military organisation and the recruiting system (1874) and improvements in education (1863–4). Such developments were intended to strengthen, not weaken, the autocratic base; they also increased Alexander II's awareness of Russia's advantages as a modernised power against its traditional rival – the Ottoman Empire. He was therefore prepared to take up arms, on behalf of the Sultan's Christian subjects, in the Russo-Turkish War (1877–8). But, although Russia won the war, it lost the peace that followed, the bilateral Treaty of San Stefano being substantially altered at the international Congress held in Berlin in 1878.

The lesson, that Russia needed a more powerful infrastructure if it was to hope to impose its will, was not lost on Alexander III (1881–94). During the late 1880s he encouraged investment from the Western powers, initially from Germany and then from France. He also set in motion a series of economic reforms that were planned and executed by his Finance Ministers, Vyshnegradskii and Witte. These emphasised heavy industrial development as part of an industrial revolution that would strengthen Russia's military infrastructure and guarantee the future security of Tsarist autocracy. The process was continued, and accelerated, by Nicholas II, who succeeded Alexander III in 1894. The next ten years, however, saw two interconnected trends that threatened the whole base of the regime. On the one hand, the Tsar became increasingly confident in both domestic and foreign policy, the latter leading directly to the Russo-Japanese War (1904–5). On the other, industrialisation resulted in a greatly enlarged urban proletariat, especially in St Petersburg, which played an important role in the 1905 Revolution following Russia's defeat in the Far East. The whole cycle seemed to repeat itself between 1906 and 1914. Defeat in 1905 provided an impetus for further industrialisation and domestic reform, which, in turn, encouraged another period of active foreign policy backed by a programme of rearmament.

The result was Russian involvement in the First World War (1914–18). The importance of this development is considered in the first half of Analysis 2. At first the war united the population against a common enemy. But subsequent military defeat imperilled the regime itself. The deficiencies of autocracy were exposed by the Rasputin escapade, in turn caused by the delegation of authority to Alexandra during the Tsar's absence at the front. Revolutionary groups were able to use the war to promote their own causes, while the serious disruption of communications led to hunger riots and brought the population out in largely spontaneous revolt in March 1917.

The First World War continued to exert a major influence after the abdication of Nicholas II. It prevented the Provisional Government from introducing key constitutional and social reforms, undermined the credibility of the Mensheviks and SRs who had cooperated with Kerensky, and gave the Bolsheviks the only realistic chance of seizing power that they had ever had. After October 1917, the First World War nearly claimed its third victim, but the Bolshevik regime survived through hasty withdrawal in March 1918 by the Treaty of Brest-Litovsk.

Just as the First World War had exerted a powerful force for the collapse of two regimes, the Russian Civil War (1918–21) helped determine the type of system that eventually emerged – and the direction that this was to take in the future. In the process of defeating their opponents (whether alternative revolutionaries or White counter-revolutionaries), the Bolsheviks set up a monolithic regime based on single-party control. The emergency of war also meant the extensive use of coercive institutions such as the *Cheka* (see Chapter 4). Although there were some concessions, for example a federation for the nationalities (see Chapter 5), what was established between 1918 and 1924 remained the basis of the Soviet regime for the next 70 or so years. The most savage civil war in European history also influenced that regime's expectations of what sacrifices the population could be expected to make in the future. There was an added incentive for Stalin to rebuild the industrial infrastructure through a ruthless command economy. The Civil War therefore forged the new regime, which had emerged from the destruction of its predecessors by the First World War.

Two minor wars followed during the next 20 years. These were less total in their impact – but they did play an important part in *adjusting* the course of internal developments. In the Russo-Polish War (1920–1), the Bolsheviks lost a substantial part of the Ukraine as Poland extended its frontier eastward. It heightened the regime's awareness of its vulnerability to the west, and especially to Poland's unquestioned superiority in a traditional cavalry war. This had a dual impact. In the immediate term it influenced Lenin's decision in 1921 to introduce the NEP to minimise the chances of internal revolt in the wake of military defeat. In the longer term, however, it was a key factor in Stalin's decision to accelerate the development of Russia's heavy industry through his Five-Year Plans and, more specifically, to gear industrial development to armaments in the form of aircraft, tanks and heavy vehicles (see Chapter 7). For Stalin, Poland had signalled, in the clearest way, the end of nineteenth-century warfare in twentieth-century Europe. The Russo-Finnish War (1939–40), which emerged from a border dispute in Karelia, also brought a change of direction. Because the performance of the Red Army was less effective than expected, Stalin took the hint that his purges within the armed forces between 1937 and 1939 had been too vigorous. His decision to suspend them and reinstate those officers who had not actually been executed probably saved the Soviet Union from total collapse in the face of Hitler's surprise attack in 1941.

The impact of the Second World War (1941–5) is much more controversial now than it seemed to be before 1991. Then it was generally accepted that, despite the immense destruction to Soviet infrastructure brought by the Nazi invasion, Stalin's Five-Year Plans had enabled the Soviet Union eventually to crush Germany and, after 1945, to become one of the two superpowers, with a greatly expanded role in eastern Europe. With the hindsight of the collapse of the Soviet Union in 1991, it is now argued that Soviet victory was achieved despite, not because of, the planning system and that the impact of the Second World War was ultimately destructive, preventing the Soviet system from modernising to meet the demands not so much of the 1950s and 1960s but of the 1970s and 1980s. These issues are dealt with in greater detail in the second half of Analysis 2.

The Soviet Union after 1945 was considerably affected by the Cold War (1945–89). Although this did not involve actual fighting, a great deal of investment was poured into preparation for war – in the form of permanent standing armies, a greatly enlarged navy (especially after the 1962 Cuban Missile Crisis) and both strategic and tactical nuclear weapons. In addition, the Soviet Union had to maintain its dominance in eastern Europe and its ideological influence in south-east Asia, Africa and Latin America. Such commitments created enormous pressures on the internal structure of the Soviet state. Unlike the United States, the Soviet Union could not finance its Cold War commitments *and* experience a rapid development of consumer industries. Nor could it hope to compete with the West in terms of high technology, a deficiency that became increasingly apparent by the late 1970s and early 1980s (see Chapter 7). Meanwhile, the ideological confrontation with capitalism meant that it was difficult to relax the totalitarian controls over the population, even if the mechanism of terror was suspended after the death of Stalin.

Hence, although the Cold War provided the Soviet Union with a period of political and military power and security, this was largely illusory because it worked against the economic growth that alone could guarantee the permanence of the regime. At first sight it is strange that the same country that had withstood the German onslaught in 1941 – and emerged as a victorious superpower in 1945 – lost a much smaller war in Afghanistan (1979–88) and experienced economic and political crisis as a direct consequence. The Afghanistan experience was the culmination of all the problems that had consumed the Soviet Union during the Cold War. It defeated Gorbachev's attempts to deal with the economic crisis through *perestroika*; it provoked strong internal opposition to a regime that was trying to ease social controls by allowing for more openness or *glasnost*; and military failure provoked a neo-Stalinist coup in 1991 against Gorbachev's policies. It is ironic – but entirely in keeping with the vulnerability of the Soviet system – that the regime could survive major blows but not a slow and steady economic stratification.

Questions

1. Which of Russia's wars in the period 1854–1989 'initiated' internal change and which ones 'accelerated' changes already under way?
2. In terms of its domestic impact, which was the most important of the ten wars fought by Russia between 1854 and 1989?

ANALYSIS 2: 'A TURNING POINT IN THE FORTUNES OF THE RUSSIAN REGIME'. DISCUSS THIS VIEW IN RELATION TO *EITHER* THE FIRST WORLD WAR *OR* THE SECOND WORLD WAR.

'Turning point' denotes a significant change of direction as a result of a particular event or combination of events. The implication is that the trends after the event differ significantly from the trends before it – and that the event itself was responsible for this change. There are two broad perspectives on this.

On the one hand, events can be seen as the determinant of trends. After all, what is a trend but an interpretation of how events relate to each other? Some events are clearly more significant than others and, as such, are likely to alter the direction taken by the trend. The event acts as a hinge, in retrospect appearing to dominate a sequence and thereby bringing about a changed sequence in the future.

On the other hand, 'turning point' can be a simplistic concept that attributes too much influence to one particular event at the expense of other possibilities. Is the particular event seen within too simple a trend, perhaps giving rise to a 'Whig' or 'value-based' view of history? Or is the trend imposed on the event really a formula, in which the event is deduced to be a catalyst for predictable change? This would incline more towards a deterministic or Marxist approach.

The fact is that Tsarist Russia died during the First World War, while the Soviet regime outlived the end of the Second World War by 46 years. The concept of 'turning point' can be applied in very different ways to both of these developments, reflecting different historical perspectives and also an increasingly complex historiography.

The First World War (1914–18): a 'turning point'?

Two main arguments are possible, reflecting the state of Tsarist Russia between 1914 and 1917. These have already been mentioned elsewhere as the 'Optimist' and 'Pessimist' views. The First World War plays a major role in this controversy.

The 'Optimist' view stresses the viability of Tsarist Russia after the turn of the century. The First World War is seen as a turning point, first in that it made a real difference to the political system of Russia and, second, in that without it revolutionary change probably would not have occurred. The basic assumption behind this argument is that the Tsarist regime had, within it, the capacity to survive into the future – and certainly well beyond 1917. It is true that it had serious flaws but these need not necessarily have been fatal. The regime proved surprisingly resilient and it took a number of crises occurring simultaneously to bring it down. The First World War was a 'turning point' in that it made this happen.

The resilience of the Tsarist regime was clearly shown during the first decade of the twentieth century. It had not been overturned by the 1905 Revolution; despite suffering military defeat in the Russo-Japanese War, the army remained intact to see off the urban and rural uprisings. Indeed, the regime seemed to have recovered some of its composure through a cautious policy of damage limitation that allowed for a series of controlled constitutional, economic and social reforms between 1906 and 1913. The First World War destroyed this composure – and any equilibrium that lay behind it. Military defeat by the German armies from 1915 onwards brought two particularly destructive influences. One was political upheaval. When Nicholas II misguidedly took over the high command at the front he left behind a political vacuum in Petrograd that was filled by the arbitrary despotism of Alexandra and Rasputin – which it is safe to say would not have occurred in other circumstances. The resulting incompetence alienated the Duma, the bureaucracy and even the military and naval commanders. The other war-induced catastrophe was food shortages and distribution problems, which combined with a particularly harsh winter at the end of 1916 to inflame popular radicalism.

The two ingredients for revolution were therefore a direct result of impending military defeat. The March Revolution, which brought down the Tsarist system, developed in two stages. The first was the spontaneous uprising in March. Here it has to be asked why this succeeded then, when it had failed before. The essential reason was its size, which was unprecedented because of the suffering brought by the war, and the breakdown of the forces of law and order, which had not happened in 1905. Even more significant was the involvement of constitutionalist and even conservative elements to prevent the descent into chaos. The actions of the Duma to establish the Provisional Committee and force the abdication of the Tsar were again unprecedented and unimaginable outside the context of impending defeat.

The 'Optimist' argument goes further. None of the participants in the March Revolution would have chosen the regime that was to come to power in October 1917. Nor should any natural impetus be deduced moving towards a Bolshevik takeover. The Provisional Government could have succeeded in setting up a permanent successor to the Tsarist system. That it failed to do so was due to the continuing impact of the war. This prevented the Provisional Government from addressing popular demands for land redistribution, industrial reorganisation and constitutional reform. Instead, the real beneficiaries were the Bolsheviks, who were able, in Lenin's words, to 'turn the capitalist war into a civil war'. Historians are now divided as to whether the Bolsheviks launched a minority conspiracy-based coup or whether they led a popular backlash against an unpopular government. But, either way, it was the war that made the crucial difference – in breaking the pattern of traditional loyalties. Without the war the Bolsheviks could not have overthrown the Provisional Government: they had, after all, already shown themselves incapable of threatening its predecessor.

The First World War was therefore a turning point – which actually turned twice. It might have turned a third time but for the armistice at Brest-Litovsk in March 1918. Lenin and Trotsky both recognised the destructive impact of the First World War and sought to be free from it so that they could win the Civil War and guarantee their survival.

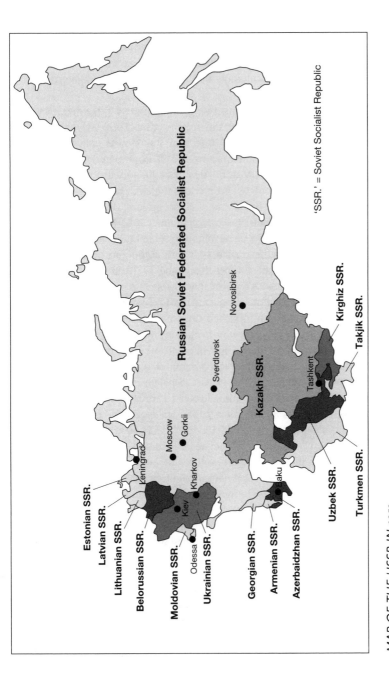

MAP OF THE USSR IN 1953

Figure 6.

'SSR.' = Soviet Socialist Republic

Russian Soviet Federated Socialist Republic

Novosibirsk

Sverdlovsk

Kazakh SSR.

Tashkent

Kirghiz SSR.

Takjik SSR.

Moscow

Gorkii

Leningrad

Kharkov

Turkmen SSR.

Uzbek SSR.

Baku

Kiev

Odessa

Estonian SSR.

Latvian SSR.

Lithuanian SSR.

Belorussian SSR.

Moldovian SSR.

Ukrainian SSR.

Georgian SSR.

Armenian SSR.

Azerbaidzhan SSR.

Against all this is the 'Pessimist' view that the First World War could not have been a turning point because all the reasons for the overthrow of the Tsarist regime were already in place. Survival might have been prolonged – but for how long? What the war actually did was to accelerate a change that could already be anticipated by 1913.

By this analysis, Russia was being inadequately governed. This was due to mistakes made by the regime after 1906, which were compounded by war. It is quite true that the 'power vacuum' and exercise of 'arbitrary despotism' from 1915 contributed directly to the collapse of Tsarism in March 1917. But these were not sudden aberrations brought about by a unique situation. Rather, they were latent tendencies inherent to the Tsarist system; the war merely released them. Ever since its inception in 1906, Nicholas II had systematically attempted to undermine the 'constitutional experiment' by insisting on the clauses protecting the 'autocratic power' in the Fundamental Laws, by dissolving the Duma in 1906 and 1907 for questioning his government's policy, and by issuing an edict to narrow the franchise in 1907. For some time he had been under the influence of Alexandra who, in turn, had become dependent on Rasputin well before 1915. Autocracy was already defying constitutional constraints and actively seeking a transition to arbitrary despotism. The Tsar's decision to take on the high command in 1915 was the occasion for this – but hardly the cause. Similarly the constitutionalist opposition did not suddenly materialise in 1915. The Progressive Bloc developed within the Duma as a broad influence for constitutional control. The situation between 1915 and March 1917 gave it a more specific concern – but did not define its overall purpose. An overall 'Pessimist' slant, therefore, might be that autocracy was failing entirely to come to terms with legitimate constitutionalist demands, thus ensuring its own demise. The war merely accelerated this.

A second 'Pessimist' argument is that Russia had become ungovernable before the outbreak of war. Several schools of historians have emphasised the powerful build-up of popular opposition from the lower levels of society that challenged the whole political structure – whether autocratic or constitutionalist. A Marxist perspective would emphasise the development of the urban proletariat and a 'socialist' rejection of the values implicit in 'feudalism' and 'bourgeois capitalism'. The Soviet variant of this is that Lenin and the Bolshevik party provided the leadership and organisation to enable the proletariat to seize power from a corrupt Provisional Government in October 1917. The war was therefore a catalyst only: it was the means whereby the dialectical process could be accelerated but not the reason for this process in the first place. Recent revisionist historians – both in the West and in post-Soviet Russia – have emphasised the growing power of opposition from the rural peasantry as well as the urban proletariat, along with the capacity of both sectors to establish their own organisational structures independently of any Bolshevik influence. These were already causing the regime serious difficulties before 1914. Rather than military defeat bringing about social alienation, it was the deepening rifts in society that ensured military defeat.

There would appear to be one possible point of contact between two very different views on the impact of the First World War on Russia. Even allowing for the underlying continuity stressed by the 'Pessimists', we can still see a possible application of the idea of 'turning point'. The First World War may not have been a turning point in 'causing' the Russian Revolution. But, it could be argued, it did ensure that the successful *pattern* of Revolution would be eventually be the Bolshevik one. This perspective could be given a liberal or a Marxist slant. Using the former, the March Revolution was what had always been in the pipeline – with or without the war – but the October Revolution was the direct result of the distortion of the March Revolution *by* the war. A Soviet Marxist approach would be that an underlying dialectical process made revolution inevitable since this meant the transfer of power from one class to another. But the war made it possible to speed up the operation of the dialectic to move swiftly from the overthrow of Tsarism to the overthrow of the liberal regime that followed. The emphasis would therefore be on the war leading to *fulfilment* rather than distortion.

The Second World War (1941–5): a 'turning point'?

Again, there are two contrasting approaches in considering the influence of the Second World War, in this case on the development of the Soviet regime. One is that the war acted as a 'turning point' in the sense that it was the key factor behind the major changes that occurred from the 1940s onwards. The other is that internal developments, already set in motion during the 1920s and 1930s, worked their way through the period after 1945 with help from – but not necessarily because of – the experience of war. In each case there is a positive and a negative slant, with the 'turning point' and 'continuity' being seen as either a strengthening or weakening influence on the regime.

The main argument in support of the war as a 'turning point' is that the Soviet Union was transformed into a superpower as a direct result of the experience of war between 1941 and 1945. The eventual defeat of Nazi Germany had involved the occupation by the Red Army of a swathe of eastern Europe by the beginning of 1945. This extended Soviet territory and influence to a degree that would have been quite impossible in peacetime. Estonia, Latvia and Lithuania were reoccupied, along with other areas lost by the Treaties of Brest-Litovsk (1918) and Riga (1921). In addition, Communist regimes were installed in five states that had previously been strongly anti-soviet – Poland, Czechoslovakia, Hungary, Bulgaria and Romania – all of which were brought within the scope of the Soviet-dominated Council for Mutual Economic Assistance (1948) and the Warsaw Pact (1955). At the same time, Germany was divided, the eastern zone becoming in effect a Soviet satellite. The descent of the 'Iron Curtain' was, therefore, a direct result of two processes: the collapse of Nazi Germany and the expansion of Soviet Russia to fill the vacuum this left. It is hard to see how the latter could have occurred without the former. During the early years of the Soviet state, Trotsky had forecast that Communism would spread to other countries through 'Permanent Revolution'. The failure of uprisings in Germany, Hungary and northern Italy had, however, proved this policy to be inappropriate. The real vehicle for Communist change was not revolution but war, which enabled Stalin to succeed where Trotsky had failed.

The war could be seen as a 'turning point' in another – more negative – sense. Although it released the Soviet Union as a new superpower, its impact was such that this power lacked the resources for long-term success. Hence the moment of victory, which defined external expansion into eastern Europe, was also the start of a long period of internal decay that led to the collapse of the Soviet state in 1991. It impoverished the USSR so badly that the effort spent in recovery prevented the sort of growth necessary to keep up with the Western economies. The combination of trying to offset the destruction by using rigid planning was ultimately lethal to proper economic development. Stalin's successors became increasingly aware of the problem. Under Brezhnev (1964–82), for example, the Soviet Union was reduced to importing high technology and grain from the West (see Chapter 7), while Gorbachev (1985–91) attempted to modernise the economic structure through a belated policy of *perestroika*. The situation was exacerbated by another consequence of the Second World War. The Cold War brought a struggle for worldwide supremacy that the Soviet Union lacked the resources to win. The economy was further distorted by massive expenditure on nuclear weapons in a crippling arms race with the United States (which had, of course, emerged from the Second World War as the first nuclear power). Even Soviet control over eastern Europe ceased to provide the security originally envisaged. It eventually became a timebomb as national resistance developed during the 1970s and 1980s in Poland, Hungary, Czechoslovakia, Bulgaria and Romania, culminating in the overthrow of pro-Soviet regimes in 1989. Their success had a knock-on effect within the Soviet Union itself as demands occurred for independence in the Baltic states and Ukraine. The break-up of the Soviet Union in 1991 was, above all, due to the breakdown of the bond between the nationalities. The process was activated by the impact of nationalism in eastern Europe against the territorial and political settlement resulting from the Second World War.

So far we have seen that the war exerted an apparently contradictory influence on the Soviet Union – as a 'turning point' that turned both ways. There is, however, an alternative perspective. This would emphasise an underlying continuity in the development of Soviet history. As in the case of the First World War, the Second World War was an 'accelerator' rather than a 'turning point'. Any problems and contradictions were already implanted in the whole Soviet system. The impetus – both positive and negative – therefore came from *within* the regime rather than through the agency of war. The infrastructure of the Soviet Union was all in place before the outbreak of war in 1941 – and continued after its conclusion in 1945. Stalin had already introduced the command economy, based on the first three Five-Year Plans, and maintained it through his fourth and fifth Plans from 1946. The 1936 Constitution remained intact until the comparatively minor changes made to it by Brezhnev in 1977. The Party structure was largely unchanged, apart from a brief experiment by Khrushchev with a Presidium instead of the Politiburo. Even the regime's priorities were unaffected. The emphasis after 1945 was the development of Soviet industry to underpin the Soviet Union as a nuclear superpower: this could be seen as the logical continuation of Stalin's aim in the 1930s to create a military power capable of holding off any future threat from the West. What the war did was to confirm Stalin's power and, with it, the direction of policies already under way. This was hardly a 'turning point'.

Another alternative is to see the war as a temporary reversal that, however, had no permanent effect – a 'turning point that failed to turn'. The internal developments making the Soviet Union what it was after 1945 had all occurred before 1941. If anything, the war had interrupted an underlying continuity, which was resumed as soon as it was over. This can be supported by examples from the economy, politics and the nationalities. Revisionist historians have shown that the centralised planning system, built up during the 1930s, was relaxed between 1942 and 1945 in favour of more decentralised and local-based structures for decision-making and armaments production. Immediately after the war, however, Stalin resumed his pre-war industrial and agricultural policies in the Fourth and Fifth Five-Year Plans, introduced in 1946 and 1951. Similarly, the use of the Politburo and the party apparatus was almost entirely suspended in wartime, to be replaced by the State Committee for Defence (GOKO); again, this was reversed in 1945. Another trend of the late 1930s reappearing after 1945 was the deliberate use of terror: the period between 1948 and 1951 was almost a duplicate of 1938–40. Strangely, the Second World War seems to have modified the totalitarian nature of the Soviet regime – but only while it was being fought. After 1945 Stalin felt impelled to restore the sort of political control he had exercised during the 1930s and to reduce the influence of the military.

With such a variety of interpretations an overall synthesis is difficult. But there is one possibility. As a result of the collapse of the Soviet Union in 1991 we have become more conscious of the rigidity and inflexibility of the Soviet regime. This points to an underlying continuity – the development by Stalin of a command economy and bureaucratic structure that defined the future of the Soviet state. These were suspended during the Second World War but reinstalled after 1945 – clearly an opportunity missed to make a fresh start. At the same time, victory in the war enlarged the Soviet Union and expanded its influence across eastern Europe in a way that could not have occurred in peacetime, while the collapse of Nazi Germany created a power vacuum that was filled by the Cold War. The Second World War was therefore a turning point in that it created new opportunities and problems. But the regime ultimately failed in its response to these because it was impeded by a rigid structure that the war had *not* changed.

Questions

1. Tsarist Russia collapsed in 1917, the Soviet Union in 1991. Was either failure 'inevitable'?
2. 'In terms of influencing Russia's regimes, the First World War was a turning point, whereas the Second World War was not.' Do you agree?

ANALYSIS 3: COMPARE THE TSARIST AND SOVIET REGIMES AT WAR.

Late-Tsarist Russia was at war for a total of 9 years out of the 62 between 1855 and 1917, the Soviet Union for 17 of its 73-year lifespan. Comparisons can be made between them on the basis of the role of war within each system; the diplomatic prelude to war; the military development and use of Russia's infrastructure; and mobilisation of the population.

In a very real sense Russia itself was the product of war. The Tsarist empire had been built up by a series of conflicts. It had become a great power through involvement in wars against other European states, especially in the eighteenth and early nineteenth centuries. At the same time it had become a multi-ethnic empire with the rapid expansion of its eastern and southern frontiers in Asia. Indeed, it was success in war that confirmed the power and authority of the Tsarist regime. By the end of the nineteenth century, however, the process of expansion had become more difficult, although it was considered no less natural as a function of the regime. The experience of Communism was somewhat different. Its method of progression was normally by revolution – the action of one class against another rather than one ruling class against another. Nevertheless in Russia Communism came to terms with war in three ways. At the outset, Lenin adopted the strategy of turning an imperialist war into a civil war – and using this to generate revolution. Then, once the revolutionary regime had been established, war was used to mobilise the dictatorship of the proletariat. In the longer term, war became the agent through which Communist regimes were imposed elsewhere. In several respects, therefore, the Soviet Union developed a semi-Tsarist momentum for expansion.

The diplomatic background to war also contained similarities and differences between the two regimes. There was, in particular, a surprisingly pragmatic approach to diplomacy – sometimes as a direct response to initiatives from Germany. Alexander II and Alexander III, for example, were drawn into complex negotiations with the European powers as a result of the diplomacy of Bismarck, while Stalin adopted an even more tortuous response to Hitler. In both cases the ultimate objective was Russia's security, although the eventual outcome was the opposite to that originally envisaged. In the case of Alexander II and Alexander III, the preferred option was agreement with Germany, in the form of the Dreikaiserbund of 1872. Under Nicholas II, however, this gave way to an alliance with France in 1894 and accommodation with

Britain in 1907. Stalin made the opposite switch, in response to the initiatives of Hitler. His initial preference for an alliance with Britain and France to contain Germany gave way in 1939 to the Nazi–Soviet Pact. There, however, the similarities ended. The Franco-Russian alliance was the basis for Russian participation in 1914 in the Great War, while the reason for Soviet involvement in the Great Patriotic War was the unexpected invasion launched by Hitler in 1941 in direct contravention of the Nazi–Soviet Pact.

How effectively did the two regimes develop Russia's infrastructure in preparation for war? Both gave priority to the development of heavy industry – with a specific commitment to rearmament. Alexander III and Nicholas II deduced the need for heavy industrial development from the lame ending to the Russo-Turkish War (1877–8) and the growing challenge from Germany and Austria-Hungary in the Balkans. But the achievements of Vyshnegradskii and Witte in the 1890s were misused in the misjudged and unsuccessful war against Japan (1904–5). The most serious development, however, was Russia's premature involvement in the Great War: any prospect for Russian success here needed the completion of a second round of industrialisation, started in 1906, and the completion of Russia's rearmament which was – ironically – scheduled for completion in 1917. To make matters worse, Nicholas II employed disastrous tactics during the war, in mistaken imitation of the 1812 campaign. This unfortunate combination was to cost the Tsar both his regime and his life. The experience of Stalin provides an interesting parallel. The lesson he deduced – this time from the Great War – was that Russia needed to be better prepared through the strengthening of Russia's industrial infrastructure. This is the key factor behind his launching of the Five-Year Plans. 'We are', he said in 1929, 'fifty to a hundred years behind the advanced countries. We must make good this distance in ten years. Either we do it, or they crush us.'[1] Like Nicholas II, however, he seriously misjudged the next step. Convinced that Germany would not strike first, he prepared the Soviet Union for an offensive war, which was entirely negated by Hitler's invasion of 1941. But there was a key difference between Stalin and Nicholas II. The Soviet Union eventually emerged from the Great Patriotic War triumphant and with the residual capacity for reconstruction; the Tsarist regime, on the other hand, had already perished. In one way, the Soviet Union went well beyond Tsarist Russia by establishing itself as a global superpower based upon a universalist ideology. There was no equivalent during the Tsarist period, during which objectives were more limited and finite. Yet the end result was the same. The Tsarist regime collapsed because its industrialisation failed to meet the demand of sustained conflict with Germany. The Soviet Union was worn away by the demands of maintaining stockpiles of nuclear weapons and the world's largest navy and standing army. In both cases the infrastructure for war was both strengthened – and destroyed.

Another basic resource in war was the population itself. How effectively was this mobilised by the two regimes? During the late-Tsarist period the potential for effective control was limited, since wars were likely to destabilise both socially and regionally. The Tsar's armies were a microcosm of society in that the recruits were drawn predominantly from the peasantry and urban proletariat, the officers from the middle classes and nobility; the social groups, in turn, over-lapped a variety of nationalities, including Russians, Poles, Ukrainians, Finns, Tartars and many others. War always carried with it a poten-tial risk. It might – as in 1812 or in 1914 – rally and unite disparate groups against a common enemy. Alternatively, if it went wrong, it could well emphasise their disparity, opening up social discontent to the influence of revolutionaries and tempting national minorities to break away. Although built up by war, imperial Russia was imperilled by its recurrence – a contradiction that eventually resulted in its destruction. War acted in the opposite way in the Soviet system: once the regime had become fully established, war – or the anticipation of war – helped create centripetal forces rather than the centrifugalism of the Tsarist period. Hence the Civil War forged the one-party regime and ended political pluralism, while anticipation of war with the West underlay the development of Stalin's command economy and the imposition of tight controls on the peasantry and proletariat. The nationalities, it is true, attempted to secede in the Great Patriotic War (1941–5) – but were forced back into the federal system of 1924 by ultimate victory over Germany. In contrast to Tsarist Russia, the Soviet Union learned to live with war or the prospect of war.

But perhaps it learned too well. The Cold War confirmed the existence of a regime that was in control of its people – but only if the siege mentality was maintained. This meant that there was no prospect of economic or social change of the type needed to enable the Soviet Union to compete with the West. The gap with the 'advanced countries' therefore opened up again. This time, how-ever, the structure created by Stalin to close it succeeded only in destroying itself. Tsarist Russia, built on war but stabilised by peace, died at war. The Soviet Union, forged in war, died of the problems brought by peace.

Questions

1. Which was better able to adapt itself to war – the Tsarist regime or the USSR?
2. Was either the Tsarist or the Soviet regime 'warlike'?

SOURCES

1. THE IMPACT OF THE FIRST WORLD WAR ON RUSSIA

Source 1: The warning of Minister of the Interior Durnovo in a memorandum to Nicholas II, about the possible effects of war on Russia.

Certainly Russia, where the masses without doubt instinctively profess to socialist principles, represents an especially favourable soil for social tremors. If the war ends in victory, the suppression of the socialist movement will not pose any difficulties. But in the case of defeat, the chance of which in a struggle with such an opponent as Germany it is impossible not to foresee, social revolution will inevitably manifest itself in its most extreme forms and Russia will be plunged into hopeless anarchy, the end of which cannot even be foreseen.

Source 2: The views of Trotsky on the influence of war.

Revolution directs its blows against the established power. War, on the contrary, at first strengthens the state power which, in the chaos engendered by war, appears to be the only firm support – and then undermines it. Hopes of revolutionary movements are utterly groundless at the outset of a war. But this is only a political delay, a sort of political moratorium.

Source 3: Extracts from letters from the Empress Alexandra to Nicholas II in 1915.

Never forget you are and must remain autocratic Emperor – we are not yet ready for a constitutional government. God anointed you at your coronation. He placed you where you stand.

Dearest, I heard that that horrid Rodzianko and others beg the Duma to be at once called together – oh please don't; it's not their business. They want to discuss things not concerning them and bring more discontent. They must be kept away.

No, hearken to our Friend. He has your interest at heart – it is not for nothing God sent him to us – only we must pay attention to what he says.

Source 4: Adapted from Michael Karpovich, *Imperial Russia 1801–1917* (1932).

On the eve of the World War Russia was profoundly different from what she had been in the beginning of the nineteenth century. In spite of the deadweight of the past and the acute contradictions of the present, it was a steadily and rapidly progressing country. In view of this progress it would be hardly correct to assert that the revolution was absolutely inevitable. Russia still had to solve many complicated and difficult problems but the possibility of their peaceful solution was by no means excluded. To this hope of peaceful evolution the war dealt a staggering blow. It caught Russia in the very process of internal reorganisation.

Source 5: Adapted from Edward Acton, *Rethinking the Russian Revolution* (1990).

In the light of recent research the traditional view of the revolution as the fortuitous product of war is unacceptable. Before 1914, neither peasant land-hunger nor working-class militancy were abating. Middle-class pressure for liberal reforms was ineffectual. At the same time the gradual erosion of the regime's social base and its repressive power pointed firmly towards a revolutionary upheaval likely to be fatal to tsarism and liberalism alike.

Questions

1. What does Source 2 reveal about the expectations that Trotsky had in 1914 for opposition to the Tsarist regime? (10)
2. Use your own knowledge to explain the reference in Source 3 to 'our Friend' who has 'your interest at heart'. (10)
3. Compare the arguments in Sources 4 and 5 as to the effect of the First World War on the development of Russia. How would you explain the differences between them? (10)
4. Compare the value of Sources 1 and 2 to the historian studying the anticipated impact of the First World War on Russia. (10)
5. Using any of Sources 1 to 5, and your own knowledge, explain how the First World War undermined the Tsarist regime. (20)

Total (60)

2. THE IMPACT OF THE SECOND WORLD WAR ON THE SOVIET UNION

Source 6: From N. A. Voznesensky, *The Economy of the USSR during World War II*. (This is a book commissioned by Stalin and published in 1948.)

The Soviet people is reconstructing the national economy of the USSR with its heroic efforts, and will surpass the pre-war level of production and overtake economically the main capitalist countries.

Source 7: From Y. Polyakov, ed., *A Short History of Soviet Society*. (This is the 1971 edition of the official Soviet history. It does not mention Stalin at any point.)

The Great Patriotic War waged by the Soviet people against fascism divided the life of the country into two periods as it were. Events were referred to as having happened before or after the war. Although over a quarter of a century has now passed since those memorable years, people are often found referring to the last 26 years as the post-war period. If we look back over the intervening years from the historical angle, in order to analyse the socio-economic and political processes which have characterised life in the USSR since the Great Patriotic War, it is then possible to distinguish two main stages. The first of these covers the period 1946–1958, the time the country required to regain its pre-war economic level and to a large extent exceed it. The formation of the world socialist system and the consolidation of the Soviet Union's economic and defence potential had brought about a change in the international balance of power that was to socialism's advantage, provided a powerful guarantee against the restoration of capitalism and assured the ultimate victory of socialism in the USSR.

By the end of the fifties it was clear that a new stage in the Soviet Union's social development was at hand. In January 1959 the 21st Congress of the CPSU formulated this thesis and included it in its decisions. In the light of this fact we would do as well to take a look at the more important events which took place in that period in the life of the Soviet people and the path traversed by the country in the course of 12 years of peace-time development.

Source 8: From *The Memoirs of the R. Hon. Sir Anthony Eden*, published in 1960. (Eden had been British Prime Minister between 1955 and 1957.)

For a quarter of a century, Stalin ruled a vast empire in the manner of an eastern despot, made more terrible and more effective by a modern technique of persuasion and repression. Ruthlessly, he had driven his country into the front rank of the world's industrial powers. Against all expectation, he had mobilized the heroism of the Russian people, and urged them to the untold sacrifices which made possible the defeat of the German invader. The victory won, he gave no pause. His armies remained to hold in subjection the territories through which they had advanced to the west. He extracted from his exhausted countrymen their last ounce of strength to rebuild their devastated land, and to prepare for the next stage of communism's aggrandisement. However malign its purpose, the scale of Stalin's achievement was stupendous, dwarfed only by its cost in human suffering.

Source 9: From Michael Lynch, *Stalin and Khrushchev: The USSR, 1924–64*, published in 1990.

The appalling sufferings of the Soviet population had not diminished Stalin's grip upon the country. Indeed, the Soviet victory and his part in it had made his position within the USSR unassailable. When Stalin turned to the consideration of Soviet economic reconstruction after the ravages of war, it was with no thought of rewarding the people for their efforts. If anything, he was even more suspicious of the outside world than he had been before 1941. He called upon the nation to redouble its efforts. Defence and the recovery and expansion of heavy industry were again to be the priorities. Little appeared to have changed in his economic thinking since 1928. Adjustments were made in the structure and personnel of the central planning departments but these were of only minor importance; the basic economic strategy remained the same.

Source 10: From Chris Ward, *Stalin's Russia*, published in 1993. (At the time of publication, the author was a Fellow of Robinson College, Cambridge, and a major influence on revisionist ideas about the Soviet Union.)

While the structures and predilections of pre-war Stalinism resurfaced after 1945 – party purges, the command-administrative system, the emphasis on group A industry, the reimposition of collective farming – the attempt to reassert control over an economy and society profoundly transformed by the experience of 1941–5 looks more haphazard and less successful than was once thought. Moreover, it now seems that whilst the Russo-German conflict strengthened the regime and legitimized the Generalissimo as a symbol of the will to victory, Stalin's personal power was threatened: the prestige of the Red Army's commanders stood very high in 1945 and new clusters of client-patron relationships emerged during the war – in Leningrad and behind the Urals, for example – about which he probably had scant knowledge and over which he may have exercised limited control. . . .

... This was no self-confident tyrant in charge of a smoothly functioning totalitarian regime, but a sickly old man; unpredictable, dangerous, lied to by terrified subordinates, presiding over a ramshackle bureaucracy and raging, like Lear, against failure and mortality.

Questions

1. Compare the arguments in Sources 9 and 10 about Stalin's power and intentions for the Soviet Union after 1945. (20)
2. Using all of Sources 6 to 10, and your own knowledge, examine the view that the Second World War had comparatively little positive impact on the Soviet Union. (40)

Total (60)

7

AGRICULTURE AND INDUSTRY

ANALYSIS 1: WHAT WERE THE KEY DEVELOPMENTS IN
RUSSIAN AGRICULTURE AND INDUSTRY AFTER 1855?

Both Tsarist and Soviet Russia faced two key issues in the development of the economy. One was periodic increases in the pace of
industrialisation, the other periodic attempts to promote efficiency in
agriculture. This analysis provides the overall perspectives to these
changes.

Agriculture and industry to 1914

Alexander II, who came to the throne in the middle of the Crimean
War, pursued a policy that was largely a reaction to the threat of
economic collapse. His measures included the establishment of the
state bank and the Ministry of Finances in 1860 and the exploitation
of new forms of revenue, including an excise tax on spirits. Aside from
these institutional and fiscal reforms, his main concern was with agriculture rather than industry. But measures like the emancipation of
the serfs (1861) had mixed effects (see Analysis 2); productivity actually declined, probably held back by the prevalence of subsistence
farming and the complexity of redemption payments and land tenure.
Industry was a lower priority. Although by 1881 the railway network
had increased by 2,000 per cent and the number of factory workers
by 150 per cent, this was from a very low base. As yet there was no
industrial spurt of the type occurring in Britain, Belgium or Prussia.

The reign of Alexander III (1881–94) saw the beginning of a shift in emphasis. He was less concerned with bringing further change to agriculture; indeed, his instinct was to leave things as they were in the rural areas and focus on law and order. Instead, he placed a stronger priority than Alexander II on industry. Behind this decision was a determination to strengthen his political base within Russia and to assume more direct leadership of Slavs elsewhere in Europe. This combination of autocracy and pan-Slavism required a much stronger industrial-military infrastructure to deal with internal threats and external challenges, especially from Austria-Hungary. It was this reign, therefore, that launched the policies of Vyshnegradskii (Finance Minister 1887–92) and his successor, Witte (1892–1903). Their priorities were investment from abroad and state subsidies to heavy industry. The source of loans was Germany until 1890, thereafter France.

The neglect of agriculture contributed to the poor harvest and severe famine of 1991. Yet the first decade of Nicholas II's reign saw a continuation of the one-sided policies of his predecessor. During the 1890s agriculture was largely ignored as the regime refused to take any action on the burdens of redemption payments or scrap the enervating influence of repartitional land tenure. By contrast, industrialisation forged ahead under Witte. Capital was derived from French investments, increased taxation at home and protective tariffs on imports. Priority was given to heavy industry (especially steel, coal and oil) and railways. By 1900 Russia had achieved an annual growth rate of about 10 per cent and the trans-Siberian railway was nearing completion. But the very success of industrialisation brought its own problems. Nicholas II drew the wrong message from the strengthening of the industrial infrastructure, assuming that this would enhance the prospects of success abroad. A period of aggressive and careless diplomacy brought war with Japan in 1904 – and military defeat in 1905. Autocracy, which was supposed to have been strengthened by industrialisation, came the closest it had ever been to overthrow during the revolution of 1905.

The regime was, however, given a second chance. It bought time by introducing a series of reforms, including a new constitution in 1906. It also realised the importance of a more balanced economic policy. Industry experienced a second period of rapid growth down to 1913, but this time attention was also given to agricultural reform. Between 1906 and 1911 Stolypin introduced measures to increase agricultural production through the consolidation of land holdings and more intensive farming measures. He aimed to develop a wealthy layer of peasants (or *kulaks*) who would benefit from the loans provided by the state and underpin Russia's modernisation of agriculture. By 1913 the approach was already beginning to pay off in greatly increased production and exports in grain and other items. It seemed to many observers that, given political stability, a balanced Western-style economy was now in prospect.

Agriculture and industry since 1914

What actually happened was the reverse. A period of conflict and political instability had economic results more devastating than could ever have been foreseen. Eight years of continuous conflict, through the First World War and the Russian Civil War, brought extensive destruction of industrial infrastructure, disruption of communications and neglect of the land. The First World War also prevented two regimes from providing solutions and, but for the Treaty of Brest-Litovsk in March 1918, would have brought down the Bolsheviks as well. But it was the Civil War that inflicted the greatest economic and social damage. Civilian deaths between 1918 and 1922 totalled over eight million and destruction was massive. In some areas, starvation caused the breakdown of normal social structures and even resulted in cannibalism. Agriculture was set back by several decades and the industrial developments of Witte were dislocated. Psychologically the Civil War had a profound impact. It has been seen by recent historians as perhaps the main reason for the emergence of totalitarian dictatorship in Russia and for the accompanying growth of a command economy (see Chapter 6).

The main economic problem confronting the Bolshevik regime was to mobilise and restore the economy in a way that would provide a productive balance between industry and agriculture. This balance proved elusive; what followed was the dominance of one sector and the exploitation of the other. Marxist-Leninist ideology tended to stress industrialisation. Lenin started with this premise and his policy of War Communism (1918–21) requisitioned agricultural produce to feed the towns that were being mobilised for industrial revival. Its failure meant a tactical retreat into the NEP (1921–4). This restored a partial market economy to agriculture, which increased the cost of living in the towns. Just how long this was supposed to last was a matter for debate during the 1920s, with Bukharin favouring an evolutionary progression towards state control (if necessary at 'the pace of the peasants' slowest nag') and Stalin eventually imposing radical changes that favoured industry at the expense of agriculture.

Indeed, the Stalinist era (1929–53) is generally associated with the imposition of a command economy. In theory this was based on a more rational use of the Soviet Union's resources, as determined through quotas to collectivise land and targets set in a series of Five-Year Plans, reinforced by large pools of labour provided by the *Gulag* system. The results have been extensively debated by historians. There is little disagreement that agriculture was adversely affected, especially during the early 1930s. Throughout the entire period, for example, the grain harvest never reached the levels of 1913 and there were catastrophic decreases in the number of livestock: the number of cattle fell from 70 million in 1928 to 34 million in 1932. Stalin's legacy was a permanently crippled agricultural base that posed insoluble problems to future leaders such as Khrushchev, Brezhnev and Gorbachev.

There is greater controversy over industry. One view is that the command economy worked here. The Five-Year Plans between 1928 and 1941 equipped the Soviet Union with the industrial infrastructure and armaments to overwhelm Nazi Germany in the Second World War. Similarly, the Fourth and Fifth Five-Year Plans (1946–55) provided the basis for the emergence of the Soviet Union as a superpower, with a vast standing army and nuclear weapons. On the other hand, the command economy placed undue emphasis on heavy industry, so starving consumer industries that the overall economy was permanently distorted by the absence of a broadly based consumer sector. This was in complete contrast with the West, where economic growth depended primarily on consumerism.

The gap opened up under Khrushchev and, even more, under Brezhnev. This time the lack of a private sector proved to be the most important factor. Agricultural productivity remained low and state-directed initiatives such as Khrushchev's virgin-lands scheme proved a disaster. Brezhnev failed in his attempts to raise productivity and by the mid-1970s the Soviet Union was having to import grain from North America. Industry was badly affected by inadequate funding for research and development, especially in high technology. Here the absence of private enterprise proved a major handicap and, again, computer and drilling technology had to be brought in from the United States. The collapse of detente in 1980 deprived the Soviet Union of these props to its economy and, from 1985, Gorbachev tried through a policy of *perestroika* (restructuring) to introduce a degree of private enterprise. This was, however, unable to prevent the further spiralling of the economy and the collapse of the Soviet system at the end of 1991.

Questions

1. Why was agriculture a problem both for the Tsars and for the Soviet leaders?
2. Why did the last two Tsars and the Soviet leaders give priority to industrial production?

ANALYSIS 2: CAN THE ECONOMIC POLICIES OF *EITHER* WITTE *OR* STALIN BE CONSIDERED A 'TURNING POINT' IN RUSSIAN HISTORY?

Sergei Witte, appointed Finance Minister in 1892, was entrusted by Alexander III and Nicholas II with the task of transforming Russia's industrial infrastructure, including rail transport. By 1903 he had presided over the most rapid economic changes of the nineteenth century. Another period of hectic activity occurred at the instigation of Stalin (1929–53) through a series of Five-Year Plans. Like Witte, Stalin emphasised the priority of heavy industry and claimed a transformation exceeding anything from Russia's past. Both Witte and Stalin have been credited with introducing a 'turning point', the basic definition of which has already been considered. As in the previous chapter, it is possible to argue this both ways.

Witte

The argument in favour of Witte's 'great spurt' of industrialisation being a turning point is well known. After centuries of relative stagnation, Russia's economic infrastructure expanded rapidly and Russia became one of the great powers. This had major implications for foreign policy and international relations. It also meant that future Communist regimes had an important base upon which to build. The scale and rapidity of Witte's industrialisation were unusual. He was therefore crucial for the modernisation of the infrastructure of Russian industry, which showed the largest sustained growth since the reign of Peter the Great. For example, he achieved an industrial growth rate averaging nearly 10 per cent per annum by 1900. He also developed energy resources, coal output increasing from 3.2 million tonnes in 1895 to 35 million tonnes in 1914. This was accompanied by a 350 per cent growth in rail network and the construction of most of the trans-Siberian line. This was all achieved while maintaining a sound balance of payments. The foundations established by Witte also meant that future regimes had something to build on.

Further industrialisation occurred in Soviet Russia, taking forward the achievements of the 1890s. Lenin, for example, focused on the electrification of industry, while Stalin's Five-Year Plans (1928–32, 1933–7, 1938–41, 1951–5) followed the same basic pattern established by Witte, namely heavy industry, with extensive potential for rearmament. In both periods the state provided the specification for expansion, setting the targets and the pace for their achievement.

But does this approach not overemphasise Witte's importance and encourage a view that his role was both progressive and definitive? Instead, within the broad scope of Russian history, it may be that Witte was one of many contributors to Russian industrialisation and, furthermore, that his contributions were not crucial to the future. They have to be seen within the broad scope of Russian industrialisation, in which there were several stages, all of equal importance to Witte's. There is, therefore, a stronger argument for steady evolution. The first major wave of industrialisation had occurred during the reign of Peter the Great (1682–1725). This was the real turning point; Witte was merely reviving Peter's emphasis, perhaps oiling the hinge of the original change rather than initiating a new one. There had also been contributions from other reigns, including Catherine the Great (1762–96) and Alexander I (1801–25). Nor could it be said that Witte developed his policy from scratch. His immediate predecessor as Finance Minister was Vyshnegradskii, who had advised Alexander III in 1892 about the necessity for expanding Russia's industrial base. Witte merely built on Vyshnegradskii's ideas, which can, in any case, be seen as one of the periodic revivals of the original Petrine impetus. Indeed, there was nothing new about the method proposed by either Vyshnegradskii or Witte. Modernisation through a combination of state capitalism and private enterprise had been the broad pattern of all previous industrial changes in Russia.

Another strand in the argument against Witte's achievement being a turning point is that the changes were restricted by the deficiencies upon which they were based. Some of these were serious. State capitalism meant in practice seeking investment from abroad as well as increasing revenues at home. This resulted in excessive dependence on French loans. Interest rates were set artificially high, designed to attract foreign capital and impeding the smaller-scale entrepreneurship that had characterised the earlier phases of the industrial revolutions in Britain, Belgium and Germany. The extent of the state's involvement in Russian industrialisation meant a strong emphasis on heavy industry at the expense of consumer goods. Growth could also be impeded by inertia and even by resistance to change that seemed to carry no material benefit to the workforce. Qualitatively, therefore, changes were limited. Russia was still backward when compared with Germany and the US. To make matters worse, the economy was affected by the recession that hit Russia at the end of the 1890s.

As for the future, the importance of Witte can also be downgraded. Much of the infrastructure he created was destroyed by a combination of the First World War (1914–18) and the Civil War (1918–21). The real impetus for industrialisation had eventually to come from Lenin and, more especially, Stalin. The latter established the infrastructure that made the crucial difference in the conflict with Nazi Germany. A major factor in the difference between defeat in the First World War and victory in the Second World War was that, in the latter, Soviet industries massively out-produced those of Germany in terms of tanks, aircraft and other armaments. The basic reason is that Stalin's Five-Year Plans had been far more extensive than anything envisaged by Witte. Even Witte's method for financing industrial change had little future influence. State capitalism was replaced by Communism and a much more rigorous command economy.

This case for continuity does not, however, prevent the application of 'turning point' in a deeper and more fundamental sense. The industrialisation of the 1890s greatly increased the social and political tensions within Russia, making revolution more likely as an outcome. It also increased the size of the urban proletariat and made it more receptive to political radicalism. Industrialisation affected the key industries that encouraged heavy concentrations of industrial workers, such as engineering, mining, oil, steel and munitions. These concentrations increased rapidly during the 1890s and after 1900, with two main effects. One was a rapid deterioration in working and living conditions. This was precisely the time that Marxism was making headway; the RSDLP was formed in 1898 and further radicalisation occurred with the 1903 Brussels split between Bolsheviks and Mensheviks. Some revisionist historians have gone so far as to argue that factory-floor committees in these industries developed ideas and strategies that influenced Marxist leaders like Lenin and Martov. There was thus a two-way process of change. The expanding proletariat were influenced by Marxist ideas coming in from abroad and being adapted by Russian Marxist leaders. At the same time, they were also influencing the way in which the ideas were being interpreted by the Marxist parties. Compared with the earlier predominance of Populism, based on an appeal to the peasantry, this emergence of urban-based agitation was a major switch of direction.

Its success, of course, depended on a sudden collapse of confidence in the Tsarist regime. Paradoxically, although the reverse occurred with Witte's industrialisation, the effect of this eventually benefited Marxism. The underlying purpose of Witte's policy was not to develop a modern capitalist state, with more liberal political institutions, but to enhance the autocratic power of the Tsar and to increase Russia's military strength in relation to other powers. The dynamic of a revived Tsarist regime would therefore be expansionist, making war more likely and raising the possibility of military defeat and sudden political instability. The real turning point of the Witte period was therefore the new confrontation between a radicalised proletariat and a confident autocracy willing to take liberties with its own safety. More than any other developments to date – more even than the subversive violence of the *narodniks* – this raised the spectre of revolution. The defeat of the Tsar's new war machine in the Russo-Japanese War meant that the urban working proletariat had the opportunity to revolt in 1905; although this was unsuccessful in overthrowing the regime, it did mark the beginning of organised radical resistance and, in this sense, provided a 'dress rehearsal for 1917'.

Stalin

The main argument in favour of the Five-Year Plans being a 'turning point' is that industrialisation was accomplished rapidly and an infrastructure was built up so effectively that it guaranteed the very survival of the Soviet Union in its period of greatest crisis. Here the whole emphasis is on the planned and command economy as a departure from the past. It abandoned all notions of private enterprise and involved the state on a massive scale. The emphasis on 'gigantomania' involved the unprecedented construction of new industrial cities such as Magnitogorsk and the rapid expansion of heavy plant and steel production. The actual production figures illustrate the sheer scale of the change. The First Five-Year Plan (1928–32) raised steel production from 3 to 6 million tons, coal from 35 to 64 million and oil from 12 to 21 million. The Second Five-Year Plan (1933–7) increased the figures to 18 million tons for steel, 128 million for coal and 26 million for oil. The last complete figures for the Third Five-Year Plan before it was interrupted by the 1941 German invasion were 18 million, 150 million and 26 million respectively.

This development has been seen as the key factor in the survival and eventual victory of the Soviet Union during the Second World

War. Hutchings, for example, has argued that: 'One can hardly doubt that if there had been a slower build-up of industry, the attack would have been successful and world history would have evolved quite differently.'[1] Heavy industrialisation had made it possible for the Soviet Union to rearm in a more direct sense. The military infrastructure expanded in an unprecedented way. In 1933, for example, defence comprised 4 per cent of the industrial budget; by 1937 it had risen to 17 per cent and by 1940 to 33 per cent. In this way, heavy industrialisation therefore translated into ultimate survival, with Soviet wartime armaments rapidly out-producing Germany's in terms of tanks, aircraft and heavy artillery. Particularly important was the industrialisation of western Siberia in the 1930s; Siberian factories were well beyond the range of German bombers and fed Soviet forces with a regular supply of munitions.

The industrial changes of the 1930s, reactivated in the Fourth and Fifth Five-Year Plans, also established the infrastructure of a future superpower with a nuclear capability based on the atomic bomb in 1949 and the hydrogen bomb by 1953. Along with the massive conventional military presence in eastern Europe, the development of a worldwide navy, and work on missile technology, this ensured that the Soviet Union was able to move from a state under threat from the West to one which felt able to sustain a cold war with it. The Five-Year Plans were therefore a double turning point, ensuring the Soviet Union's survival and then maturation as a superpower.

But perhaps all this attributes too much to the influence of Stalin. His contributions to heavy industry were by no means unique and were not without precedent. The importance of heavy industry – and of state involvement in its expansion – had already been established by Witte, who had ensured that a considerable amount of infrastructure was already in place before the Soviet era. What Stalin had done was to intensify and extend it rather than to create it from nothing as *A Short History of the CPSU* often claimed. Nor, it has been argued, were the first three Five-Year Plans the main factor in Soviet victory in the Second World War. Recent research has shown that setting targets did not in itself constitute effective planning – let alone delivery of results. It was one thing for the central administration, including Gosplan, to draw up target figures for the different components of industry, but quite another to develop the mechanism whereby these might be achieved systematically. There was, for example, little overall consistency in the pace of the Five-Year Plans. This was due largely to the disruption caused by local influences. Although complexity seemed to pass for 'planning', what actually happened was administrative chaos. When the Germans invaded the Soviet Union in 1941, the whole system was taken completely by surprise. Stalin had prepared the country for an offensive war, to be launched at a time of his own choosing, while the situation that actually occurred in 1941 required a defensive response to an invasion launched by Stalin's intended victim. All the mechanisms related to the Five-Year Plans were geared to an offensive and could not be readily adapted to a defensive role. The result was that the planning mechanism actually had to be relaxed to meet the new situation. Stalin was forced to allow for more localised responses, mobilisation and production. If anything, the Soviet Union was therefore saved not by the Five-Year Plans but by their abandonment.

Yet, while allowing for the continuities between Stalin and the earlier period, as well as for the structural weaknesses of the Five-Year Plans themselves, it is still possible to use the term 'turning point'. This, however, acquires more negative connotations since it is associated with a trend leading to the eventual collapse of the Soviet Union. Lenin had left the Soviet economy at the crossroads in 1924, without taking any final decision on its future direction. One possibility was the indefinite continuation of the NEP, thereby perpetuating the 'mixed economy'; the alternative was the immediate abandonment of the NEP and the introduction of a 'command' economy. Stalin's choice of the latter option was a turning point in that it determined the type of regime the Soviet Union would become. Instead of being flexible it became increasingly rigid, with a planning system centred on Gosplan and administered by an ever-expanding bureaucracy. This had administrative implications for both the state and the people. A system of coercion was established to enforce collectivisation (through dekulakisation squads) and industrial quotas. This, in turn, led to the Stalinist Terror and purges, the *Gulag* network being used to extend the labour force to ensure the completion of more difficult projects such as the Belamor Canal. Prioritising heavy industry had a deep impact on social conditions and made the state appear even more repressive. Agriculture was clearly a lower priority than industry, which meant the subordination of the interests of the peasantry. In turn, light industry gave way to heavy industry, so that the consumer suffered severely by comparison with civilians in almost all other industrialised states.

The system that Stalin created – both the economy and the regime – may well have enabled the Soviet Union to survive the war with Germany and to confront the Western powers in the Cold War after 1945. It could not, however, guarantee the longer-term prosperity of the Soviet people or the security of the Soviet regime. Stalin's policies – especially the subordination of agriculture to industry and the imbalance between heavy and light industry – meant that the Soviet economy fell far behind those of the West during the 1970s and 1980s. Its structural weaknesses were further damaged by the inflexibility of the planning system created by Stalin in the 1930s and revived during the 1940s and 1950s. Despite the assistance it received from the West during the 1970s through grain treaties and technology transfer, the Soviet economy eventually buckled under the weight of its own inefficiency. Stalin's command economy was therefore a 'turning point' in that it directed the Soviet Union towards short-term survival – but long-term implosion.

Questions

1. Who achieved more for Russia's industrialisation: Witte or Stalin?
2. Did Stalin merely carry on where Witte had left off?

ANALYSIS 3: COMPARE THE ECONOMIC PERFORMANCES OF THE LATE-TSARIST REGIME (1855–1917) AND THE SOVIET UNION (1917–91).

Criteria used in answering this question will include the relative success of agriculture and industry, the importance of investment and trade, the roles of private and public sectors, and the use of available technology. The approach will be through direct and indirect comparisons – the former between the regimes themselves, the latter between each regime and other comparable states of its era.

The three main areas of any economy in the nineteenth and twentieth centuries were industry, agriculture and the tertiary sector.

In heavy industry the Soviet achievement was – quantitatively speaking – greater than the Tsarist. Coal and steel production exemplify this. The periods of most rapid growth were the reign of Nicholas II (1894–1917) as a result of the economic reforms of Sergei Witte (1892–1903), and the administration of Stalin (1929–53). By the time that the Bolsheviks had established their regime, Russian industrial production had been badly affected by the impact of the Civil War, sinking well below late-Tsarist levels (35 million tons of coal in 1913 and 3 million tons of steel). As a result of Stalin's Five-Year Plans, however, production within key industries rapidly outstripped pre-1914 figures. Coal production was up to 100 million tons by 1935 and 150 million tons by 1940, while the figures for steel in the same years were 13 million and 18 million. There was also a significant improvement by comparison with other states. In 1914, for example, Russia's 35 million tons of coal ranked fifth among the main producers, compared with 517 million from the United States, Britain's 292 million, Germany's 190 million and France's 40 million. Russia's steel production ranked fourth, behind the United States (31.8 million), Germany (18.3 million) and Britain (7.8 million). By 1941, the Soviet Union was second only to the United States in both areas, having outstripped Britain and Germany.

Of course, heavy industry formed only part of the picture, both regimes being deficient in the promotion of light or consumer industries. The overall trend here is that Tsarist Russia was moving forward – but slowly because a largely impoverished population provided a much smaller demand than in Germany, Britain or the US. Until the 1950s the Soviet Union made no advances in this area, largely because of the low priority placed upon it by Stalin. Although Khrushchev (1953–64) and his successors tried to meet some of the expectations of a huge consumer population, there was an ever-widening gap between Russians and the populations of Western countries. During the late 1980s, Yeltsin several times repeated his view that, in terms of the actual consumption of goods, the Soviet Union was further behind the other major economies than Russia had been in 1913.[2] An index of consumption, produced in 1991, showed the USSR on 20 compared with the US on 100 and Germany on 70. And yet the index for industrial production as a whole showed the USSR (on 48) behind only the US (100) and Japan (72). The implication of this is clear. The Soviet economy was never able to break away from the total dominance of heavy industry. This may have been appropriate during the eras of Witte and Stalin; in the second half of the twentieth century, however, this became a straitjacket, preventing diversification. Instead of being able to compete with the seven most developed countries (US, Japan, Germany, France, Britain, Italy and Canada), the Soviet Union found itself among the next rank of economies – those developing heavy industry (China, Taiwan, South Korea and India).

In the agricultural sector neither the Tsarist nor the Soviet regime achieved any notable degree of success. There seems, however, to have been an overall difference in momentum. The Tsarist period saw long-term improvements that were slowed down by impediments. Soviet agriculture, by contrast, experienced long-term decline that was sometimes levelled off by remedial measures and concessions.

In part, these trends were influenced by changes in land ownership. The key theme of the late-Tsarist period was the gradual emergence of a viable alternative to serfdom in the form of an alternative basis for land tenure. At first this was slowed down by the authority of those village communes that practised repartitional tenure; since this involved the periodic redistribution of land it prevented the consolidation of holdings into more productive units. Russia was, however, on the way to developing a more efficient structure by the end of the Tsarist regime. Stolypin's reforms had removed the obstacles to consolidation, resulting in the emergence of the more productive and prosperous *kulaks* owning about 10 per cent of the peasants' land and extracting substantially higher yields from it. Stolypin had pinned his hope on the efficacy of private enterprise, in the process overcoming some resistance from traditionalists. This was a step towards bringing Russia into line with land ownership in central and western Europe, although it was, of course, interrupted by war and revolution. The reverse process occurred after 1917. The ultimate intention was always to remove private ownership and to substitute *kolkhozy* or collective farms; eventually most of these gave way to *sovkhozy* (state farms). The problem was that state control over agriculture never really worked. In a country the size of the Soviet Union there were too many variations in climate, local conditions and social customs for centralisation to be anything other than a disincentive to production. It is therefore not surprising that the only periods in which agriculture seemed to recover – briefly – from the general trend of decline were those in which concessions were made to private enterprise, as in Lenin's NEP or Khrushchev's policy allowing private cultivation under licence. Gorbachev tried more radical measures, including the end of fixed prices. But by the 1980s the culture of centralised control was too strong to achieve the transformation from inertia to drive. *Perestroika* might have worked as an alternative to collectivisation – but it could not coexist with it.

The issue of land ownership was connected with productivity and consumption. Again, there was a difference in the dynamics of the late-Tsarist and the Soviet periods. Before 1913 the overall trend of agricultural production had, allowing for periodic downturns, been moving slowly upwards. The grain harvest was a substantial 81.6 million tons in 1913 and, between 1909 and 1913, Russia exported 14 million tons of food per annum. The first half of the Soviet period saw violent oscillations – between agricultural disaster (as under War Communism 1918–21 or the early period of collectivisation 1928–36) and slow recovery (as during the NEP or the late 1930s). At its worst, grain production sank to 37.6 million tons in 1921 and, even though there had been some recovery by the mid-1920s and again by the late 1930s, the production figures of 1913 were never achieved again. The latter half of the Soviet period did see an increase in production, finally overtaking the 1913 figure in 1952 with a harvest of 92.2 million tons. But steady year-on-year increases could not be guaranteed: the 1953 figure, for example, was down again to 82.5 million and there were similar fluctuations in the Brezhnev era. The overall trend was stagnation tending towards decline rather than the interrupted improvement that was more characteristic of the period before 1914. Tellingly, there was no export trade in agricultural produce from the Soviet Union after 1950. Indeed, under Brezhnev, large quantities of grain were imported from North America as one of the concessions accompanying detente. Two figures show the extent of the problem reached by the last decade of the regime. In 1980, approximately 80 per cent of the potato crop rotted, either through inefficient harvesting or through inadequate storage and distribution; 10 years later, the index of per capita agricultural production in the USSR was 9 (compared with 100, 85 and 56 for the US, Canada and Britain respectively).

The third main area of the economy involved trade and investment. Here there was another fundamental contrast between the Tsarist and Soviet periods. The late-Tsarist period saw the rapid growth of contacts with the West, as Vyshnegradskii and Witte sought to develop Russian industry with injections of foreign capital. The main Soviet emphasis was on self-sufficiency, sometimes to the point of autarchy. Industrial development in the 1930s made far more intensive use of the country's own resources, whether through a tightly controlled and disciplined workforce or through the transfer of capital from agriculture into heavy industry – both of which occurred under Stalin. In one respect, this shows greater success by the Soviet leaders. Soviet sources could claim that the Soviet industrial achievement was self-made, while any advances before 1914 were beholden to the operation of capitalist dynamics through the leading banks; as a result 'tsarist Russia at the end of the 19th and beginning of the 20th centuries was already drawn into a system of world imperialism, occupying therein a subordinate position'.[3] The Soviet Union was also more resistant to the Great Depression of the 1930s, whereas Tsarist Russia succumbed to all the slumps that hit the rest of Europe during the 1880s and 1890s.

The alternative view is that it became increasingly difficult – and unwise – to try to withdraw from world economic trends. Although

Tsarist Russia's economic growth was far more dependent on Western investment, this had corresponding benefits in the form of increased trade. The Soviet Union could turn for its external contacts only to the satellite economies brought with its orbit in 1949 in the Council for Mutual Economic Assistance (Comecon); but these were limited in scope and increasingly resented the brake exerted by the Soviet Union on their own growth. By the 1970s, attempts were being made to return to the mainstream of world trade, only for the Soviet leaders to find that conditions were being attached by the West – based as much on the military and ideological criteria of detente as on economic factors. Overall it does seem that Tsarist Russia, with far less effort, was moving into a more positive position than the Soviet Union in international economic terms. But its capacity for competition and integration was wrecked by war, first with Japan, then with Germany. The Soviet Union, on the other hand, gradually lost the ability to integrate and compete because it developed a more insulated approach – which was actually intensified by war.

Affecting all three economic areas – industrial, agricultural and tertiary – was the role of state policy and private enterprise. Most countries have room enough for both. Russia found it more difficult than its rivals to set a balance, which partly explains the disparity, in both regimes, between periods of intensive activity on the one hand and lassitude on the other. The Tsarist period saw periodic attempts at kick-starting economic growth, whether in agriculture or industry. Policy was based on the realisation that the private sector was not strong enough to maintain economic growth and the state therefore had to step in to provide objectives and to secure foreign investment. The problem was that the state also tended to monopolise the benefits of any growth that did occur – especially in industry – by directing it into foreign policy and war. The Soviet Union, too, had an imbalance between state control and private enterprise – but approached the problem from the opposite direction. The aim was for the state sector to predominate in order to prevent the recurrence of capitalism in the future. It was therefore an ideological issue. Moves in the direction of private enterprise were seen only as temporary expedients to revitalise economic growth that had been rendered sluggish by excessive state involvement. The problem was that, unlike the Tsarist economy, there was no real indication that it was even beginning to move in the right direction. Belated remedies like *perestroika* actually killed the ailing patient. In Tsarist Russia, by contrast, a convalescing economy was overburdened with strenuous demands before it had gained sufficiently in strength.

One factor exercised a more decisive influence on the Soviet economy than on the Tsarist – technology. Tsarist Russia had always borrowed heavily from the West, a habit started during the reign of Peter the Great (1682–1725) and, by 1914, had more or less the same access as its rivals to technological advances. Technological disparities or relative backwardness therefore had no part to play in the collapse of the Tsarist regime. The Soviet experience was to be very different. Soviet leaders emphasised the technological creativity of their own system, whether in the form of industrial methods, nuclear weaponry or space research. But the second half of the twentieth century brought far more intensive change than the second half of the nineteenth. During the period of the Cold War, especially in the Brezhnev era, the Soviet Union fell into an increasingly difficult situation. In Western economies the technological revolution was carried out largely in the private sector, the state adapting selected changes for its own use. Soviet technology was generated entirely by the state sector, which therefore focused on projects involving national security or prestige. Inevitably it developed on a much more limited scale, a significant side effect being the very limited application of computers in any area outside administration or defence. This, in turn, made economic performance still more sluggish – at a time when the Western economies were able to sharpen their performance. Brezhnev was certainly aware of this, which is why Western technology transfer to the Soviet Union formed an important part of the detente process. One thing led to another as the United States and Britain stopped the transfer after the Soviet invasion of Afghanistan while, at the same time, President Reagan deliberately stepped up the pressure on the Soviet economy by vastly increasing US defence expenditure and presenting proposals for the highly complex Strategic Defence Initiative (SDI). This forced the Soviet Union into a series of economic measures, which, however, failed to save either the Soviet economy or the Soviet Union itself.

Might Gorbachev have pulled the Soviet economy round but for the pressure applied by Reagan? No answer can be given with certainty, just as the debate will continue about the viability of Tsarist Russia outside the context of the First World War. There is, however, one essential difference between the two cases. Tsarist Russia collapsed after the sharp reversal of a period of economic growth, whereas the Soviet Union's demise was the final part of a process of economic stagnation and decline. If the Tsarist economy experienced a sudden fatal blow, the Soviet economy suffered a final fatal straw. This suggests that the Tsarist system still had potential for change, whereas the Soviet economic process had run its course.

SOURCES

1. WITTE AND RUSSIAN INDUSTRY

Source 1: From Michael Lynch, *Reaction and Revolutions: Russia 1881–1921*, published in 1992.

There is no question that Witte's policies had a major effect on the growth of the Russian economy, but doubts have been expressed about whether that effect was wholly beneficial. Critics of Witte as an economic strategist have argued that he made Russia too dependent on foreign loans and investments, that in giving priority to heavy industry he neglected vital areas such as light engineering, and that he paid no attention to Russia's agricultural needs.

However, any criticism of Witte should be balanced by reference to the problems he faced. The inertia and resistance to change that characterised the court and the government severely restricted his freedom of action. In addition, military requirements often interfered with his plans for railway construction and the siting of industry. The main purpose of his economic policies was to protect tsardom against the disruptive elements in Russian society, but ironically he was mistrusted by the royal court. Witte was faced with the dilemma that confronted any minister who sought to modernise tsarist Russia; he was regarded with suspicion by the representatives of the very system he was trying to save.

The improvement of the Russian economy in the 1890s was not simply the result of the work of Witte. It was part of a worldwide industrial boom. However, by the turn of the century the boom had ended and a serious international trade recession had set in.

Source 2: From John F. Hutchinson, *Late Imperial Russia 1890–1917*, published in 1999.

Witte was once regarded as a figure of near-heroic proportions, a veritable Peter the Great, who almost single-handedly battled indifference and obscurantism to bring Russia into the modern age. More recent scholarship has questioned the components of his 'system', and consistently scaled down earlier evaluations of his personal responsibility for the economic boom that Russia enjoyed during the 1890s. Some stress his debt to earlier ministers of finance who had encouraged railroad development and attracted foreign investors by stabilizing the currency and producing export surpluses. The extremely high tariff of 1891, introduced by Vyshnegradskii, was a vital component of the industrial boom that lasted until the end of the decade. Whether the Trans-Siberian railway, the emblem of Witte's programme, helped to teach Russians anything about managerial capitalism has been questioned, as has the centrality of railroad development to the industrialization and modernization of Russia. Witte himself, after leaving the Finance Ministry, recognized and lamented the fact that a policy of state leadership seemed to have accustomed too many Russian businessmen to expect that the state would always lead. Both the weaknesses and the strengths of his economic programme derived from its ultimate political purpose, the salvation of the autocracy. Yet would the hesitant new emperor continue to support a programme that demanded so much from so many, and was therefore vulnerable to criticism from all sides?

Source 3: From *A History of the USSR*, published by Stalin's regime in 1948 and used as an official textbook in Soviet schools.

The tsarist government was obliged to foster the growth of capitalism in the country. Already in Alexander III's time a protective tariff was introduced (1881) establishing high customs duties on imports. This placed the home market under the exclusive control of Russian capitalists. Tsarism's policy, aimed at protecting the interests of the bourgeoisie, was prosecuted by Witte, the Minister of Finance, who succeeded in greatly stimulating the growth of capitalist industry and consolidating the state finances.

The development of capitalism in Russia was hampered by the instability of the currency. . . . The absence of a stable currency had a deleterious effect on trade and industry. Witte in 1897 carried out a reform of the currency. Banknotes were secured by a gold reserve and made exchangeable for gold at the rate of 66 kopeks per paper ruble.

Witte introduced a government monopoly for the sale of alcohol, which yielded huge profits to the treasury. Thanks to Witte's efforts the St Petersburg banks began to play an important role in the country's economic life.

All these reforms were implemented by the tsarist government with the aid of foreign loans. . . . The influx of foreign capital during the industrial boom of the nineties considerably increased. Attracted by prospects of earning large profits from the exploitation of cheap and abundant labour-power foreign capitalists readily exported their capital to Russia.

The nineties witnessed the beginning of monopolistic organizations in Russia and the fusion of industrial with bank capital. Eight big banks in 1899 owned more than half of the total bank capital. . . .

Tsarist Russia became the vast reserve of western imperialism. She provided free access for foreign capital which controlled such important branches of the national economy of Russia as the fuel and metallurgical industries.

Source 4: From Edward Acton, *Russia: The Tsarist and Soviet Legacy*, first published in 1986.

It was in a sense paradoxical that a regime for which the social repercussions accompanying industrial development in the West were anathema should have become actively committed to industrialization. Yet its motives are not difficult to see. In large measure it was responding to the rapid industrialization of Russia's Great Power rivals. Unless she could dispose of the same modern means of transport and production, the same machinery and armaments, Russia could not hope to uphold her political independence. The strategic necessity of railways, in particular, was becoming ever more pressing. Likewise, even conservative ministers felt the force of the argument, ably expounded by Witte, that the regime's domestic stability depended upon its financial strength – and this required sustained economic growth. In any case few statesmen grasped that there was a profound contradiction between the economic and the social policies being pursued by the government. This was in part because there was still no unified policy-making body, no cabinet. Each minister reported to the Tsar only about his particular field of responsibility, and the monarch's own gruelling routine of official audiences, requests, petitions, reports and ministerial visits minimized the chances that he would provide strategic coherence. The government, therefore, could pull in two opposite directions without fully realizing that it was doing so. While the Ministry of Finance energetically fostered industrialization, the other ministries still pursued conservative social policies which ignored or even impeded economic change.

Questions

1. Compare Sources 3 and 4 as evidence for the degree of cooperation between Witte and the Tsarist government. (20)
2. Using Sources 1 to 4, and your own knowledge, discuss the extent to which Witte's industrial policies affected Russia. (40)

Total (60)

2. STALIN AND SOVIET AGRICULTURE

Source 5: Stalin's explanation in 1929 of the need for the collectivisation of agriculture.

There are two solutions. There is the capitalist way, which is to enlarge the agricultural units by introducing capitalism in agriculture. This way brings the impoverishment of the peasantry and the development of capitalist enterprises in agriculture. . . . There is . . . the socialist way, which is to set up collective ('kolkhoz') and State farms. This way leads to the amalgamation of small peasant farms into large collective farms, technically and scientifically equipped, and to the squeezing out of the capitalist elements from agriculture.

Source 6: Levels of agricultural production 1928–35 (Soviet figures).

	1928	1929	1930	1931	1932	1933	1934	1935
Grain (million tons)	73.3	71.7	83.5	69.5	69.6	68.6	67.6	75.0
Cattle (million head)	70.5	67.1	52.5	47.9	40.7	38.4	42.4	49.3
Pigs (million head)	26.0	20.4	13.6	14.4	11.6	12.1	17.4	22.6
Sheep and goats (million head)	146.7	147.0	108.8	77.7	52.1	50.2	51.9	61.1

Source 7: From *A Short History of the Communist Party of the Soviet Union*, published under Brezhnev as an official record. Stalin is nowhere mentioned in the book.

The collective farms set up in 1930 operated smoothly and achieved outstanding successes. The state machine-and-tractor stations helped them to till the soil and harvest the crop. In the course of a single year former poor peasants found themselves prospering. They received more grain and other products than the middle peasants used to obtain from their farms. The division into poor and middle peasants disappeared in the collective farms. All enjoyed equality in the sense that the income of each depended on his work in the socialised economy. The fine example set by the first collective farms and their achievements provided convincing proof of the advantages of large-scale collective farming over small individual farming. The Party used these achievements further to promote the collective-farm movement. By the summer of 1931 a total of 13 million peasant households or more than half the number of peasant households in the country had joined the collective farms.

The consolidation of the collective-farm system was a *fundamental turning-point* in Soviet agriculture, a *most deep-going revolutionary change* which had been organised and directed by the Party and the Government.

Source 8: From Alec Nove, *An Economic History of the USSR*. Originally published in 1969, this edition was issued in 1986 and refers to information made available during the regime of Gorbachev since 1985.

In looking back at the impact of those years on agriculture and the peasants, critical comment is superfluous. The events described cast a deep shadow over the life of the countryside, of the whole country, for many years thereafter. Far too many works on the period say far too little about what occurred. Of course, much more evidence has recently become available. . . . It is very much to the credit of Soviet scholarship that so much has been made available, after so prolonged a silence (for which the scholars cannot be blamed) about what by common consent must be a painful period, of which many men in high places must feel ashamed in their hearts.

Questions

1. Explain the meaning of 'collective' and 'State' farms mentioned in Source 5. (10)
2. Compare Sources 6 and 7 as evidence for the effectiveness of collectivisation in the 1930s. (20)
3. Using Sources 5 to 8, and your own knowledge, comment on the view that 'Stalin introduced his policy of collectivisation for ideological rather than economic reasons'. (30)

Total (60)

8

THE SOCIAL CLASSES

ANALYSIS 1: EXAMINE THE DEVELOPMENT OF THE
PEASANTRY AND URBAN WORKERS BETWEEN 1855
AND 1991.

The rural proletariat (peasantry)

The peasantry, who comprised over 80 per cent of the population of
late-Tsarist Russia, were before 1861 either privately owned or state
serfs. Nicholas I (1825–55) considered that serfdom was problematic – but that 'to tamper with it now would be an evil still more
perilous'. No action was taken, therefore, until after the accession of
Alexander II, whose 1856 Manifesto declared that it would be 'better
to abolish serfdom from above than to wait until the serfs liberate
themselves from below'. Five years later his Edict of Emancipation
granted serfs legal freedom while making provision for them to buy
land from the nobility, repaying government loans through long-term
redemption payments.

This brought certain major advantages to the serfs. But there were
also significant knock-on reforms affecting the peasantry, including
the establishment of the *zemstva* (1864), the overhaul of the judicial
system (1864) and a modified form of military conscription (1874). At
the same time, there were obvious limitations, especially in the burden
imposed by the redemption payments and by authority of the village
communes to impose different and restrictive types of tenure such as
the repartitional rather than the more straightforward hereditary. In

many areas agricultural productivity actually fell after 1861, resulting in more widespread poverty. In these conditions Populist revolutionary movements like People's Will made considerable headway, creating a permanent barrier between the regime and the subjects with which it had tried to come to terms.

The terms of emancipation had, therefore, been too restrictive to allow for any real improvement in the conditions experienced by the peasantry. There were a few attempts over the longer term to remedy this. Alexander III, for example, ended in 1881 the period of 'temporary obligation', established a State peasant bank (1881) and abolished the poll tax (1887). Similarly, the reign of Nicholas II ended the responsibility of the communes for the redemption repayments (1903), reduced and then abolished the payments themselves between 1905 and 1907 and attempted to establish a stratum of wealthy peasants, or *kulaks*, to increase agricultural productivity and provide additional political support for the Tsarist regime. But these measures, carried out by Stolypin, were of little benefit to the large mass of the peasant population, who had become increasingly radical in their demands by 1917. Many used the overthrow of the Tsar in March, and the increasing difficulties faced by the Provisional Government by August, to seize the estates of the nobility and to establish their rights to individual ownership. Indeed, most recent historical interpretations suggest that the peasantry were both assertive in their demands and well organised at a local level.

The Bolshevik seizure of power in October 1917 was followed immediately by the Decree on Land, which fulfilled the promise of Lenin's *April Theses* to recognise the peasant takeover of noble estates. The position of the peasantry was, however, affected in different ways by Lenin's rule between 1918 and 1924. The Bolshevik regime sought, through the policy of War Communism (1918–21), to requisition the grain produced by the peasantry in order to guarantee food supplies to the cities and the Red Army. The backlash was severe, as agricultural production dropped and many peasants joined the widespread revolts affecting the rural areas between 1920 and 1921, prolonging the Civil War even after the White counter-revolutionaries had been driven back. In 1921 Lenin was forced to introduce the NEP, which confirmed the right of the peasantry to produce for private sale and profit, subject to the payment of a tax. This 'state capitalism' was a compromise that postponed into the future any form of collective ownership of land or of produce. It also prolonged the existence of the *kulaks*, who had become established during the late-Tsarist period.

The NEP opened up a debate on the whole future of the Soviet economy. This, in turn, became caught up in personal motives and ambitions as Stalin became involved, from 1924, in a struggle with Trotsky for the political succession to Lenin. The ideological division between the two took the form of 'Socialism in One Country' versus 'Permanent Revolution' (see Chapter 1). At first the agricultural component of this meant that Stalin supported the continuation of the NEP, while Trotsky preferred rapid collectivisation. But, as he out-manoeuvred his rival politically, Stalin began to take over Trotsky's economic policies. The turning point came with the procurement crisis of 1926, when the peasantry refused, because of low prices, to release sufficient grain to feed the cities. Stalin's response was a return in 1927 to the requisitioning policy of Lenin, followed in 1928 and 1929 by a broader plan for the collectivisation of all peasant land, either in collective farms (*kolkhozy*) or state farms (*sovkhozy*). This was rigidly enforced by Stalinist terror (see Chapter 4), in the form of the dekulakisation squads of the NKVD.

The impact of Stalin's measures on the peasantry was colossal. Collectivisation proceeded rapidly – too rapidly for administrative effi-ciency, as Stalin's reproof in *Pravda* (*Dizzy with Success*) attested in 1930. The suffering of the peasantry was on an unprecedented scale. Food consumption fell rapidly (from 250 kilos of bread per head in 1928 to 215 in 1932). Areas like the Ukraine experienced wide-spread famine and mass starvation. The suffering also showed itself in unprecedented upheavals caused to Russian society as peasants turned against each other, layer by layer. The main target were the *kulaks*, several million of whom were killed or deported by the regime. Yet the opposition of the peasantry was also considerable, especially during the early years of collectivisation. Between 1928 and 1932, there was widespread resistance to Stalin's proposals and, rather than agree to voluntary collectivisation, the peasantry slaughtered their livestock in huge numbers. The impact of all these developments on agricultural production was so serious that it created a permanent distortion in the Soviet economy.

Stalin relaxed some of his measures during the war period (1941–5) but reintroduced the full force of collective farming in 1945. Although the *kolkhozy* and *sovkhozy* remained official policy, Stalin's successors tried to alleviate their impact on the population. Khrushchev (1953–64) was often seen as a 'wise peasant' and genuinely tried to hand back part of the initiative to his own class by restoring a degree of private enterprise. He also reduced rural poverty by guaranteeing higher agricultural prices. The problem, however, was that any positive measures were undermined by the severe damaged inflicted by Stalin on the agricultural infrastructure. The peasantry may have been better off under Khrushchev – but they had still not developed the necessary entrepreneurial skills because state control was essentially unsuited to the decision-making process of agricultural production. For this the peasantry needed to be 'embourgeoised', as they had been elsewhere in Europe, and as Gorbachev later recognised with his policy of *perestroika*. This, however, came too late to save the Soviet system. Following the collapse of the USSR in 1991, the peasantry had to face another painful period of adjustment, this time to the market economics followed by Yeltsin and Putin in Russia and within the other successor states.

The urban proletariat (industrial workers)

In total contrast to the peasantry, the industrial proletariat was relatively small at the time of Alexander II (1855–81). This meant that the influence from the lower orders came disproportionately from the rural areas. Most of the reforms from above were focused on land and village rather than on factory and city, while the early revolutionary movements grew out of Populism rather than Marxism.

The first major changes began to appear during the reign of Alexander III (1881–94). Although there was certainly no official intention to develop the size and influence of the urban working class, this did begin to happen for two reasons. First, Alexander III's finance ministers, Vyshnegradskii and Witte accelerated the pace of Russia's industrialisation and their focus on heavy industry quickly boosted the number of factory workers in key cities such as St Petersburg. Second, the spread of Marxist movements and societies increased rapidly after 1885, providing for the urban proletariat the organisation and leadership that had so far been confined to the peasantry through Populism.

Under Nicholas II (1894–1917) the industrial workers assumed a position of critical importance. Witte's intensive industrialisation in the 1890s continued to enlarge and concentrate the workforce, adding new mining pockets in more rural areas. At the same time, the blanket ban imposed by the regime on any form of trade union activity provoked widespread radicalism, some of it associated with the new Marxist Social Democrats. The 1905 Revolution was, above all, an urban-based attempt to defy Tsarist authority: the St Petersburg Soviet had a majority of industrial workers and held out until the end of the year, even though the middle classes and peasantry had been bought off by the offer of concessions from the regime. After 1905, the position of the urban workers was more ambivalent. The government legalised trade unions and introduced a range of reforms, including social insurance schemes. At the same time, Nicholas II was personally resolute to limit the scope of the changes and, after the assassination of Stolypin in 1911, ordered a tightening up against any form of radicalism. This explains the bloodshed of 1912 when security forces shot over 1,000 striking miners at the Lena goldfields. The year 1913 saw Russia on the brink of a general strike and it was clear that, whatever the attitude of the peasantry, the urban proletariat had not been reconciled to the regime. Nor, it should be said, was it particularly impressed by the Bolsheviks at this stage.

The First World War acted as a major catalyst for the destruction of the Tsarist regime – and then the Provisional Government. Local committees of workers coordinated a series of strikes in 1916, before bringing the capital to a complete standstill in March 1917. Severe shortages precipitated food riots, which grew into industrial action by steel workers and, in turn, sympathetic strikes. As in 1905, the workers formed a majority in the Petrograd Soviet, which developed during the course of 1917 as an alternative source of authority to the Provisional Government. Yet there is little evidence to associate the workers at this stage with a permanent Marxist system. What turned the urban proletariat into Bolshevik supporters was the refusal of the Provisional Government to heed their demands for specific reforms. This meant that in October 1917 Lenin was able to claim (probably with some justification) that his seizure of power had the support of the majority of the urban workers.

Lenin's regime (1918–24) experienced a conflict between meeting the aspirations of the urban workers and those of the peasantry. The workers, above all, needed food. This, in Lenin's view, necessitated War Communism and, in particular, the requisitioning of peasant grain. While the peasantry suffered between 1918 and 1921, the urban workers therefore became better off. Conversely, the NEP, introduced in 1921, clearly benefited the peasantry at the expense of the industrial workers. Stalin, increasingly conscious of the disparity, reintroduced requisitioning in 1927 and enforced full collectivisation from 1929. Although hated by the peasantry, this was initially popular with the proletariat since it guaranteed a more regular flow of food to the cities. The focus of Stalin's Five-Year Plans on industry also ensured full employment and the cities became a magnet for impoverished peasants. The swelling of the urban workforce in turn created severe social problems, particularly overcrowded living conditions.

Stalin's focus on heavy industry also deprived the industrial workers of any possibility of consumer-based prosperity.

The post-Stalin era saw attempts to modify the harsh living conditions that had become as characteristic of the towns as of the countryside. Hence Khrushchev and Brezhnev extended pension benefits and medical assistance, tried to increase the range of consumer goods and continued to guarantee full employment. Life in the cities was no longer fraught with deprivation and danger – but it did become uniformly drab by comparison with the rapid growth of consumerism in the West. Marxism had promised the urban worker greater prosperity than could ever be achieved in a capitalist economy. Whatever else Marxism managed, this undertaking was an abysmal failure.

Questions

1. Who fared better under the Tsarist and Soviet regimes: the peasantry or industrial workers?
2. Which did more for the peasantry and industrial workers: the Tsarist or Soviet regime?

ANALYSIS 2: 'A SUBSTANTIAL DIFFERENCE BETWEEN THEORY AND PRACTICE'. HOW EFFECTIVELY DOES THIS DESCRIBE THE OFFICIAL VIEW OF SOCIAL CLASS *EITHER* BETWEEN 1855 AND 1917 *OR* BETWEEN 1918 AND 1991?

Each of the two regimes had an overall approach to class – and an implicit or explicit concept of the key class. In its official policies it sought to develop these approaches and enhance the roles of the *key* class. To some extent this worked; there were, however, some departures from the preferred approach, some of them indicating lack of consistency in, and some of them absence of control over, other influences.

Tsarist Russia, 1855–1917

To what extent was there an official view of class in late-Tsarist Russia? On the one hand, the evolution of a particular form of political authority based on a social hierarchy was given a retrospective cohesion and rationale by the theories of Pobedonostsev who, in turn, had a direct influence on Alexander III and Nicholas II. On the other hand, changing economic conditions redefined the relation-ships between classes in ways that sometimes challenged the offi-cial structure – or necessitated changes to that structure by the regime itself. This can be seen in the context of each of the main social classes.

The attitude of the regime to the nobility depended very much on the circumstances of each individual reign. All Tsars, however, considered them to be the key class in terms of wealth and social leadership. They underpinned the social hierarchy that was an integral part of the whole concept of political autocracy. Without this, the political system would be unable to operate effectively. Some of the nobility were involved in the governing process – but this was not their key importance. From the reign of Peter the Great (1682–1725) official positions were also allocated to non-nobles and the principle of an administrative 'meritocracy' took root. Even Pobedonostsev accepted this, arguing that the real significance of the nobility was not their actual part in government; in any case, he added, 'it is important in the highest degree that the landowning nobility remain on their estates within Russia and not crowd into the capitals'.[1] As in Prussia – and early Germany – the tacit understanding was that the nobility's social powers were enhanced in return for an *acceptance* of autocracy that did not essentially involve a contribution towards its exercise.

There is significant evidence of this continuing under Alexander III and Nicholas II. As a class, members of the nobility were afforded major concessions by the Tsar's edicts. Economically they were heavily favoured by the establishment in 1885 of a Noble Land Bank to provide low-interest loans. The issue of land and debt was con-sidered further by a ministerial conference in 1897. Meanwhile, in 1889, the post of Land Captain was introduced to exercise greater local control over peasantry; wherever possible, this was filled by members of the provincial nobility. In 1890 Alexander III also changed the election and functions of the *zemstva* to strengthen the nobility's unquestioned predominance over the other classes.

And yet there were significant departures from the official approach. In some respects Alexander III and Nicholas II were the exceptions rather the norm in their efforts to enhance the status and power of the nobility. Another trend had also been established – as an undeclared alternative – by Peter the Great; from time to time this was revived by some of his successors. During the late-Tsarist period, for example, Alexander II was determined to introduce emancipation of the serfs irrespective of the views of the nobility. In his 1856

Manifesto he declared that it was essential 'to liberate the serfs from above' rather than wait for the serfs 'to liberate themselves from below'. This was in part a warning that the nobility would have to cooperate with the regime or be forced to comply. His subsequent administrative and judicial reforms were recognition that the emancipation of the serfs had created a need at local levels that could only partially be met by the nobility.

In some cases the relative decline of the nobility in late-Tsarist Russia occurred despite the policy of the last three Tsars, reflecting not so much their inconsistency as the greater importance of other factors. One was the significant professionalisation of the civil service, to which the nobility did *not* contribute: by 1900 the proportion of the latter among the higher officials was down to 30 per cent. Another, more unexpected, trend was the decline in the proportion of land owned by the nobility: by 1905 this was down to only two-thirds of that held in 1862. Part of the problem was a series of economic influences undermining the measures of Alexander III and Nicholas II mentioned above. These included a major depression in the 1880s and early 1890s, low grain prices, increased costs of labour and the difficulty of making sufficient improvements to offset such disadvantages.

The middle class comprised a greater variety of sub-groups than the nobility, each of which was seen in different ways by the Tsars. In their case, official policy was not so much inconsistent as fractured. The commercial and industrial entrepreneurs, for example, had a long tradition of underpinning Russia's economic growth and their value continued to be recognised in the industrialisation drives of both Vyshnegradskii and Witte between 1892 and 1903. Yet the extent of this sector's involvement was limited by an official policy of state capitalism, as advised by Witte in a secret memorandum to Nicholas II in 1899. It might be argued that this showed inconsistency in that the regime depended on entrepreneurs on the one hand while restraining them on the other. It is, however, much more likely that the extent of state involvement was dictated less by an attempt to limit private capitalism than by the need to make up for its limitations: certainly this was the gist of Witte's analysis. Another layer of the bourgeoisie, the administrative, was also considered inherently useful and, as we have seen, had come to dominate the bureaucracy by 1900. There was comparatively little interference with this process. Any inconsistencies in Tsarist policy tended to occur within local administration. Alexander II spread the load of responsibility through the bourgeoisie as well as the nobility, especially in the urban *dumas*, while Alexander III and Nicholas II took measures to reinstate the influence of the nobility over the other classes.

The third level of the bourgeoisie might be described as 'professional', comprising lawyers, doctors, teachers in schools and universities, and journalists. The official attitude to these was always ambivalent – it recognised the usefulness of some of the professions in developing necessary skills but, at the same time, saw that their practitioners might have to be prevented from being involved in potentially subversive political activity. There was, for example, a recognised connection between the professions and the demand for constitutional reform, which explains the constraints placed by Alexander III and Nicholas II on the judicial system, the press and universities. This inevitably involved a clash between the Tsarist attempt to control and use the middle classes and the latter's attempt to find a way round the obstacle of Tsarist control. State capitalism and service in the bureaucracy were the Tsarist recipe for stability but these were not always sufficient to contain the more extensive demands for free-market capitalism and political constitutionalism. This meant that the regime felt it necessary to switch from preferred cooperation to selected repression.

The imperial regime had always accepted the subordination of the peasantry to the landed nobility, although the legal definition of this changed over the centuries. An originally free peasantry were enserfed during the course of the fifteenth century and then emancipated by Alexander II in 1861. There was therefore an underlying continuity in the place of the peasantry in the social hierarchy but the potential for change within the precise nature of their relationship with the nobility. Within this overall trend there were, however, marked differences in the application of government policy over the peasantry. These could indicate overall inconsistency between theory and practice. Or, more likely, they could be seen as the application of different strategies to defend an existing system. None of the last three Tsars ever considered moving towards a political system in which the peasantry were fully enfranchised within a new constitutional structure. Pobedonostsev's views on this (see Chapter 1) were uncompromisingly hostile. Nor was there any possibility of a major redistribution of land from the nobility to the peasantry. That said, there was a difference in the policies between, on the one hand, the reign of Alexander II and the latter half of Nicholas II's and, on the other, the reign of Alexander III and the first half of Nicholas II's.

The former periods (1855–81 and 1906–13) saw the introduction of measures intended to strengthen the role of the peasantry within the Russian economy and reduce the chances of their involvement in revolutionary action. Alexander II's contributions to this were the Edict of Emancipation (1861), which conferred personal freedom, and local government reforms, including the establishment of the *zemstva* in 1864. Nicholas II – or rather his premier, Stolypin – went further by removing redemption payments in 1906 and consciously aiming to produce a wealthy layer of peasants in the form of the *kulaks*. In both cases there is an apparent inconsistency with the inertia of previous periods – but this can be explained in terms of urgent necessity. Alexander II was introducing changes that would prevent Russia's defeat in the Crimean War becoming a catalyst for administrative collapse and mass revolt by the peasantry, while Stolypin (hardly renowned for progressive views) aimed to embourgeois part of the peasantry and thus cut the connection between the peasantry and the more radical urban workers.

How, then, can one explain the somewhat different attitudes shown to the peasantry between 1881 and 1905? During this period Alexander III and Nicholas II did whatever they could to slow the pace of rural change. In particular, they increased the powers of the rural nobility, expanding the power of provincial governors and reducing the influence of the peasantry within the *zemstva*. In the context of the time, however, the inconsistency can be explained. Alexander III and Nicholas II were reacting to the assassination of Alexander II by People's Will in 1881, deducing from this a corrective policy to counteract the side effects of the previous reforms. In a sense, the next period of reform after 1905 was caused by an altogether different problem – the outbreak of revolution. The alternation between caution and change therefore has an underlying consistency in its reactive nature. Change was reactive to the failure of a reactionary policy; reactionary policies were reactive to the apparent limitations of change.

The working class, or proletariat, was to the Tsarist regime the most unfamiliar of the social classes. This was because of its more recent origin within the context of Russia's industrialisation – especially in the last quarter of the nineteenth century. Official attitudes therefore ranged from ignorance, based on the misconception that the working class was merely an urbanised peasantry, to antipathy and a fundamental fear that it was receptive to radical and subversive ideas. The latter was behind most of the policies pursued until 1905, including a ban on trade unions and rigorous action against Marxist groups. The assumption seems to have been that an expanded workforce was needed to implement Witte's industrialisation programme

– but that economic development should not be accompanied by social or political change.

And yet there were signs of an alternative approach. At the turn of the century the *Okhrana*, then under Zubatov, were following a strategy of 'police socialism' (see Chapter 4) that encouraged selective concessions to workers' groups, while after 1905 a range of measures was introduced to the benefit of the working class. The latter included partial enfranchisement in 1906, the Law on Associations (1906) permitting trade unions, and the introduction of national insurance in 1912. The switch of direction can be explained as concessions made by a regime that was under particular threat from urban revolution, especially in 1905. It could also be said that the changes made for this sector of the population were less extensive than those for the peasantry; there was no equivalent attempt to create a new middle class. There was even continuity in the counter-measures of repression. The *Okhrana* actually increased its surveillance and arrests after 1905 and the Lena goldfields massacre provided the clearest indication that the regime had a very limited interpretation of its concessions on trade unions.

The collapse of the Tsarist regime in March 1917 had the complicity of sections of all the classes, indicating that the system had managed to antagonise increasingly widely. This could be seen as the response either to extreme inflexibility of government policy or to uncertain application of concessions. Or, most likely, it was an alternation between the two.

The Soviet Union, 1918–91

The official view of class in the Soviet Union was uncompromisingly clear, based as it was on the Marxist approach to dialectical materialism as adapted to the situation in Russia by Lenin.

Marxist theory (see Chapter 1) was summarised in the 1848 *Communist Manifesto*, the opening sentence of which proclaimed that the 'history of all hitherto existing societies is the history of class struggle'. This was inevitable since the foundation of any political or social system is its economic base. Exploitation by the nobility within the context of feudalism had given way in most of Europe to the rise of capitalism under the control of the bourgeoisie and the exploitation of a newly created urban proletariat. The inevitable outcome would eventually be the overthrow of capitalism and the establishment of a dictatorship of the proletariat; this, in turn, would evolve into a classless society. The process would occur first where capitalism –

and hence the proletariat – were most developed. As it stood, the Marxist theory of class struggle was only partly appropriate to the Russian situation. Lenin's adaptation to meet the situation in Russia involved a change of strategy. Russia was, in fact, well suited to revolution since feudalism was dying and capitalism had not yet become fully entrenched. Hence the chain of capitalism could be 'broken at its weakest link' rather than where it was strongest. This involved an acceleration of class conflict in order to achieve the necessary transition.

A particular problem that Lenin and his successors had to face was the relationship between the industrial proletariat and the peasantry, the two main classes recognised by the Soviet state. The industrial workers had been the key to earlier Marxist analysis, while the peasantry had hardly featured. This was largely because their ownership of land in western and central Europe placed many of them within the 'bourgeoisie'; only landless labourers could really be seen as 'workers'. The situation in Russia was somewhat different. The emancipation of the serfs in 1861 had involved the transfer of small plots to an entire class of peasants. Official theory in the Soviet state was based on a compromise articulated in several stages by Lenin. His pamphlet *To the Rural Poor* (1903) deliberately brought the peasantry into the revolutionary sector by establishing them as allies to the vanguard – or industrial proletariat. This meant that there were two revolutionary classes, joined together in pursuit of a common objective – the overthrow of capitalism in Russia. The wealthier peasants, or *kulaks*, were excluded from this relationship since, in enriching themselves, they had become embourgeoised. As for the issue of land ownership, Lenin argued in his *April Theses* (1917) for 'confiscation of all landed estates' from the nobility and for 'nationalisation of *all* lands in country, the land to be disposed of by the local Soviets of Agricultural Deputies of Poor Peasants'. The implication, therefore, was that collective ownership would be the future pattern.

Because of this unusual relationship between the two classes, official theory had to involve some compromises and the practical implementation of policies involving the industrial proletariat and the peasantry involved numerous changes between 1918 and 1991. Whether this meant inconsistency between theory and practice depends on the overall strategy involved: a change of direction can imply a new theory or, alternatively, another way of achieving the existing one.

Anomalies between theory and practice are apparent from the start of the Soviet regime. In his *The Immediate Tasks of the Soviet*

Government (1918), Lenin allowed for a period of transitional small-commodity production, as opposed to the private capitalist economy of the urban and rural bourgeoisie. The Bolshevik premise was that this was unacceptable in the long term but might have to be accepted in moderation for the time being. At first both the peasantry and the industrial workers were seen as occupational sectors cooperating within a mixed system, the former part of privately run businesses or trusts, the latter as individual landowners. This was, however, suddenly changed by the introduction of War Communism in 1918, which placed workers under state control and introduced state requisitioning of the peasants' grain. By 1921 the process had been partially reversed again and 'state capitalism' was restored in the form of the NEP. The regime explained the imposition – and then abandonment – of War Communism as an emergency measure designed to enable the peasantry to contribute most efficiently to the war effort by foregoing their own profits to feed the industrial workers and the Red Army, then engaged in a struggle for survival against the Whites; the end of the Civil War in 1921 enabled Lenin's original strategy of moderate change to be restored. This is not, however, entirely convincing. Under the NEP the peasants were given far more extensive concessions than the workers, probably because their resistance to War Communism had become more and more determined: many had joined the widespread revolts led by the Greens during the final phase of the war. It is more likely that Lenin's strategy held good for the industrial workers, whose jobs were now largely within the state sector, whereas he had to acknowledge that the peasantry were not yet ready for collective farming. In other words, his original estimate of the pace of change had been misjudged. There was also some unevenness in the apportionment of political rights: the 1918 Constitution had weighted the franchise for elections to the Supreme Soviet in favour of the urban workers, possibly in recognition of their more direct contribution to the development of socialism.

Stalin's solution to the unequal status of workers and peasants was to accelerate the pace of change. In some ways the process was more logical – but the way in which it was implemented threw up further contradictions between theory and practice.

There was certainly logic in Stalin's imposition of a command economy to increase state control over the economic process, at the same time necessitating a more disciplined workforce. The severity of the measures against both the industrial workers and the peasantry was justified in terms of the 'dictatorship of the proletariat', which was intended to bring the social structure more into line with a socialist economic system. This also meant that a more progressive constitution, introduced in 1936, could give equal measure to votes from the industrial workers and the peasantry, removing the weighted franchise and granting full political equality for the first time.

And yet there were still major inconsistencies. In the first place, there was a shift away from Lenin's emphasis on social change being a response to the gradual transformation of the economic infrastructure. Stalin's more radical policies inverted the whole concept of base and superstructure (see Chapter 1). Stalin also distorted the whole notion of equality within a classless system; the industrial proletariat rapidly diversified into mutually antagonistic groups as a direct result of Stalin's decision to abolish 'wage equalisation' and reintroduce differentials. He replaced the Marxist principle of 'from each according to his ability, to each according to his needs' with the more openly competitive 'from each according to his ability, to each according to his work'. This was bound to lead to new elites. The Stakhanovites, for example, were given higher wages and the best accommodation in specially constructed flats. The peasantry, it is true, were levelled by the end of individual land ownership and the elimination of the *kulaks*. But Stalin's policies maimed the whole agricultural sector and greatly reduced the peasant population. It does seem that Stalin had relegated the peasantry from their previous status – as allies of the proletariat – to expendable workhorses. If agriculture subsidised industrial growth, then the peasants experienced greater impoverishment than any urban or industrial equivalent. The NEP was not so much reversed as inverted – perhaps the least logical of all the options open to Stalin.

After Stalin's death there was a real effort to update the whole concept of classlessness and to deal with the issue of exploitation. Khrushchev picked up on a theme that had long been ignored – the material well-being of the Soviet people, whether collective farmers or industrial workers. Lenin and Stalin had always emphasised the commitment of the population to future improvements and growth. But the reason for this was always ascribed to the state, not to the individuals or groups within it. Official propaganda had shown prosperous collective farmers and eager industrial workers, but the fruits of their labour were actually very few. Khrushchev was more determined to meet the challenge of improving the actual standard of living. This was the next logical direction to take. After all, capitalism and class-based exploitation had been ended and it was now time to demonstrate that Communism could deliver greater material prosperity than capitalism. The measures Khrushchev took were all in line with this new perspective. He emphasised that the 'dictatorship of the proletariat' had been over for some time and that the Soviet Union was well on the way to achieving classlessness. Two new terms came into increasing use to emphasise this – 'New Soviet Person' and 'Developed Socialism'. The time had also come for the state to ensure improved living conditions. The peasantry were allowed to increase their levels of private production while, at the same time, agricultural prices were raised to guarantee a reasonable income from meeting state quotas. Industrial workers had more access to consumer goods and refrigerators, washing machines and television sets began to appear in many homes. Unfortunately, the economic policy that underlay this approach opened up a whole series of further contradictions. Greater prosperity and freedom of enterprise had to be imposed and decentralisation required increasing interference from the centre. Khrushchev may well have freed the Russian population from being potential *Gulag* victims – but he could not free the economic structure that had redefined the classes.

Brezhnev (1964–82) seemed at first to offer a more balanced approach. On the one hand, he maintained Khrushchev's concessions to the population, confirming that these were justified by the progress being made towards classlessness. He also continued with the theme of 'Developed Socialism', which was made the theoretical foundation for the 1977 Constitution. On the other hand, he aimed to avoid the unsuccessful political changes of Khrushchev by strengthening political controls and maintaining the 'stability of cadres'. Again, however, this proved highly problematic. In accepting the Stalinist rigidities of the economic planning system, he adopted the approach that improvements in living conditions were a benefit conferred from above rather than a right earned by the population through increased productivity. This meant that concessions became increasingly unbalanced. Under Brezhnev incomes crept up, especially on collective farms, while production actually declined. There was therefore a strange ambivalence about Brezhnev's approach. His partial return to Stalinism had damped down the free market but a more benevolent attitude to the working population prevented any revival of terror and exploitation. Trying to introduce any form of capitalism would be a step backwards from the classlessness that was implicit in 'Developed Socialism'.

This 'soft' version of Stalinism raised concerns about the longer-term prospects of the working people within an increasingly unstable economy. Gorbachev, in particular, reconnected society and politics with the Soviet Union's industrial base. Where was the logic of more prosperous peasants producing less food and more consumer-conscious workers being fed on grain imported from North America? The 'New Soviet Person', whether urban or rural, needed a more efficient economic system within which an improving lifestyle could be supported by greater productivity. *Perestroika* involved a decision to abandon Stalinism in any form, even at the risk of increasing differentials in pay and the emergence of a new underclass of unemployed. To moderates like Gorbachev and Shevardnadze, and radicals such as Yeltsin, this was part of the price that had to be paid to prevent economic collapse. Inevitably there was strong resistance from the more conservative elements within the party, including Kryuchkov, Pugo and Yaneyev, who saw *perestroika* as an ideological u-turn and a threat to the social harmony reputedly achieved during the Brezhnev era. Neo-Stalinists were, however, seen as pressing an outdated concept based on 'proletarian chauvinism'. A showdown between the two was inevitable.

The development of Russia's two main classes – peasants and industrial workers – seemed to follow a course that was inherently contradictory. On the one hand, Soviet leaders were always conscious that social classes were integral to the economic infrastructure. They therefore pursued policies that would eventually produce classlessness. On the other hand, emerging from the 'dictatorship of the proletariat' seemed to produce its own problem: the economic infrastructure was incapable of sustaining the 'New Soviet Person' and 'Developed Socialism'. The attempt through *perestroika* to redesign the infrastructure threatened to restore market mechanisms and hence restore class distinctions based on economic roles. The clash between this new future and the neo-Stalinist past accelerated the collapse of the Soviet Union in 1991.

Questions

1. Why did the Tsarist regime find the peasantry more acceptable than the urban proletariat as a social class?
2. How far did the Soviet Union manage to go along the road to the 'classless society'?

ANALYSIS 3: COMPARE THE RESPONSE OF THE DIFFERENT CLASSES TO THE LATE-TSARIST AND SOVIET REGIMES, 1855–1991.

There are, at the outset, certain problems in defining 'class'. The Tsarist understanding of the term was primarily social, while the Soviet emphasis was economic. The problem with both of these is that they are not fully comprehensive; both developed rigidities that took no account of transition and change. The Tsarist system officially had more classes than the Soviet regime since the latter was – officially at least – moving towards classlessness. There were, however, many parallels between the Tsarist and Soviet periods, which suggest that a broader approach to class is needed. This analysis therefore considers class also as an attribute of the regime itself, subject to political influences as well as to economic factors. It will also attempt to go beyond some of the more stereotypical views of class responses to the regime.

The aristocracy is a case in point. In the Tsarist period it was the social elite and is therefore easy to identify. Within the Soviet system it was officially banned and can, strictly speaking, be covered only within the first few years of the new regime. Yet the emergence of a new regime soon produced a new elite that rapidly assumed the characteristics of a new ruling class.

A stereotypical view of the Tsarist nobility is of a defensive elite desperately trying to hold on to its privileged status and preventing any broadening to include other social sectors. This would cover the landed nobility (which had to be forced by Alexander II into emancipating the serfs), leading ministers and army officers. Partly responsible for this is the official Soviet view that sees the Tsarist nobility as the feudal remnants of the old regime. The counterpart, in the Soviet period, is the violent reaction of the Whiteguards – the most extreme base of resistance to the Bolsheviks during the Civil War between 1918 and 1921. It is certainly true that the nobility had a large proportion of the diehards of the late-Tsarist and early Soviet periods; that most of the landed aristocracy did what they could to undermine the emancipation process; that the leading bureaucrats tried to keep closed the access to higher posts; and that military commanders such as Kolchak, Deniken and Wrangel actively sought the return of the old regime in 1918. This type of nobility *was* permanently eliminated.

But the situation is more complex and varied than this, both regimes experiencing a greater variety of responses from the nobility. Within Tsarist Russia there were significant numbers of progressive nobles. Many of the landed gentry – such as Count Leo Tolstoy – pressed hard for further reforms on behalf of the peasantry, while officials like Stolypin recognised the need to broaden the base of support for the regime by reducing the gap between the landed nobility and a new class of wealthy peasants. Part of the military leadership joined with other sections during the First World War to urge the Tsar to control the activities of Rasputin and to exercise more responsible government, even putting pressure on Nicholas II to abdicate in March 1917. There was a similar diversity during the early Soviet period. Apart from the more assertive Whiteguards, there were substantial numbers within the nobility who adapted to the new system. Not all nobles suddenly went into exile. Many remained, some reduced to bartering whatever private possessions had remained to them, others sinking to the status of peasants in the redistribution of land in November 1917. It is true that, by whatever means, the old nobility did disappear. But new elites emerged to take their place. An aristocracy is more than the social elite that results from the economic base of feudalism. It is also a form of power-sharing, based on the recognition that certain groups can inflict damage on the leadership unless given a special status. Historically, feudalism was an understanding, based on the allocation of land, between the monarchy and its potential rivals. Within the Soviet system there was clearly no economic parallel with the feudal structure. But the political apparatus was redolent with hierarchy, established privilege and layers of dependence. There were parallels between the relationship between the hierarchy and its ruler as Lenin and Stalin both assumed characteristics of 'red tsars'. At times there were even explicit comparisons between Tsarist and Soviet attempts to cut away the encrustations of such privilege. Stalin, for example, compared himself with Tsar Ivan the Terrible, seeing a direct parallel between Ivan's struggle to control the Boyars under Kurbsky and his own need to reduce the 'old Bolsheviks' under Trotsky.

The terms 'middle class' and 'bourgeoisie' provide another powerful stereotype, reinforced by both liberal and Marxist views of historical development. A positive approach is the emergence of a new economic force acting as an important impetus for commercial and financial growth and providing a key hope for Russia's future, with other sectors contributing to cultural, professional, educational and legal expertise. Yet the middle classes had ambivalent views about the regime itself. On the one hand, they depended upon it to prevent violent change that would destroy their own achievements. On the other, they were committed to creating a more constitutional monarchy – this was especially apparent with the Constitutional Democrats (Kadets). There is a strongly contrasting negative approach that forms part of the official Soviet view justifying the 1917 revolutions. The economic slant emphasises not only the bourgeois contribution to the growth of capitalism but also the consequent exploitation of labour – to the ultimate detriment of the growing proletariat. Similarly, the attitude of the bourgeoisie to the Tsarist regime was based on a desire to update feudalism by being included within the political structure: in this sense liberalising the regime simply meant politicising capitalist exploitation. The attitudes of the bourgeoisie to the new Soviet regime could also be seen in contrasting lights. A positive interpretation emphasises their justifiable grievance at the closure of the Constituent Assembly in January 1918, the introduction of War Communism and the elimination of all opposition parties. A negative angle, however, would be that the bourgeoisie were resisting the Bolsheviks' right to deprive them of the tools of their repression, including the divisive nature of their political parties, which were finally banned in 1921. On the one hand, the bourgeoisie are depicted as defending their own hard-won rights, and on the other as clinging on to powers enabling them to exploit others.

Again, these are oversimplifications of the roles of the middle class. The Tsarist period saw two main tendencies, which actually moved in opposite directions in their attitudes to the regime. One section became ever more closely reconciled with the Tsarist regime as a new nobility that comprised an increasing proportion of the officials in the state bureaucracy and that became increasingly possessive of their new-found power and influence. In a sense they depended on the system that was serving them so well and they had no desire to change it. The counterpart to the more progressive members of the nobility were therefore the more conservative members of the bourgeoisie. The alternative channel pursued by the bourgeoisie was the change of the power structure through constitutional development. This section had no vested interest in the existing system. On the contrary, it had every reason for wanting this system made more accessible.

Was there a Soviet equivalent to the middle class? Officially, of course, there was none, since the whole purpose of the new regime was to destroy the residual influence of the bourgeoisie wherever it manifested itself. The period of the Civil War eradicated the whole middle-class ethos and destroyed the notion of constitutionalism. Yet there were certain parallels with what might be termed as the rise of a 'new middle class' in the Soviet system. A new layer of responsibility and privilege developed, comprising official members of the Communist Party; these were more than workers' representatives, actually owing their status to the intervention of the authorities, especially Stalin. It is hardly surprising, therefore, that Party members and civil servants who operated the details of the planning system showed unquestioning loyalty to the regime, especially since their status could be removed as readily as it had been conferred. A new middle class also emerged unofficially and, because of its economic motive, was more hostile to the regime. This was the wealthier layer of the peasantry – or *kulaks* – who had benefited from the redistribution of land in November 1917 and from Lenin's NEP from 1921. Although Stalin's collectivisation destroyed the *kulaks* as a class, elements remained of a semi-capitalist ethos as Khrushchev reintroduced a degree of private enterprise. This accelerated during the Gorbachev period of *perestroika* and entered the industrial sector as well. There was even an element of 'middle classness' in the expression of unorthodox political opinions. After the Stalin era, increasing numbers of dissidents, generally the most educated group, were open to influences from the West. They experienced a greater struggle than had their equivalent in Tsarist Russia, but men like Sakharov became highly influential during the period of *glasnost* introduced in 1985 by Gorbachev. Indeed, the combination of *perestroika* and *glasnost* allowed this new middle class to break through the surface in the late 1980s, although the most immediate form it tended to take was national self-determination. Hence, the new post-Soviet states owed a great deal to the convergence of the three sections of the new middle class – state administrators, new entrepreneurs and critics of the Soviet regime.

Unlike the nobility and the bourgeoisie, the peasantry were integral to both the Tsarist and Soviet regimes without there being any need to redefine or stretch the word. But the attitudes of the peasantry have also been subject to stereotyping. Within the Tsarist system, for example, they are traditionally seen as conservative in outlook. Even after the emancipation of the serfs in 1861 they remained socially rigid, unlikely to respond to new ideas or influences and concerned mainly about the problem of subsistence on the land now allowed to them. The majority were also religious and, at least until 1905, likely to be loyal to the Tsar. Towards the end of the period a wealthier layer began to emerge, which looked to the regime to enhance its upwardly mobile status as large landowners. The revolution of 1917 saw the temporary survival of the two layers, until one of them – the *kulaks* – were brutally annihilated and the rest tried to resist enforced collectivisation before succumbing to the inevitable. The development of the two sections of the peasantry is also part of the Soviet analysis of that class, although there is a different slant. According to Lenin, the majority, or 'poor peasants', resented the impoverishment that emancipation had substituted for serfdom and therefore came into alliance with the more radical urban workers in opposition to a brutal regime. The minority, or *kulaks*, simply joined the oppressors as a newly established layer of the bourgeoisie: unlike the 'poor peasants', they were therefore bound to the Tsarist regime. The Soviet system, by contrast, fulfilled the aspirations of the majority of the peasantry, who overcame their initial reservations and accepted the advantages of collective farming from 1929 onwards.

All of these assumptions can be challenged. For one thing, the peasantry were far more mobile than has been suggested. The traditional notion of emancipated peasants being tied to the land almost as firmly as their serf ancestors is not entirely true. Many of the younger peasants were driven from the land by the rigours of the redemption payments and the land tenure scheme – especially repartitional tenure – operated by the village communes. The obvious draw was the new industrial areas, especially in the Ukraine, Moscow and St Petersburg. Their motive was clearly the opportunity to earn more from the mining, engineering, oil and textile industries. Similarly, significant numbers of peasants migrated during the Soviet period. This was partly through resentment of Lenin's War Communism (1918–21) and Stalin's collectivisation from 1929, and partly through the perception that urbanisation offered better living and employment prospects. If anything, the process accelerated after 1953, even though Khrushchev tried to stem the flow by allowing private cultivation for profit to coexist with collective farming. By the Gorbachev era (1984–91) the proportion of peasants to urban workers had shrunk to a fraction of that in 1921.

Not only were peasants more mobile than has been suggested; they could also be more radical. Revisionist historians have shown that far from being inert and unresponsive to revolutionary pressure, peasants provided the main impetus for early mass movements. There were numerous precedents – including the Pugachev Revolt in the reign of Catherine the Great (1762–96) and Populist movements such as Land and Liberty, People's Will and Black Partition during the reign of Alexander II (1855–81). Peasants migrating to the industrial areas were often at the forefront of politically conscious factory committees and there was also a steady flow among this sector from Populists to Marxists. A direct parallel to this is the extent to which members of the peasantry were willing to risk everything to challenge the Bolshevik regime. There was widespread resistance to War Communism, especially to the requisitioning of grain supplies, and extensive support for the Green armies during the Russian Civil War. These were anti-Bolshevik without being in active support of the

White counter-revolutionaries and, although they did not succeed in changing the political structure imposed by the Bolsheviks, they did manage to force a u-turn in Lenin's economic policy when War Communism was replaced in 1921 by the NEP. Opposition in the 1930s was even more spectacular. Stalin's brutal measures to enforce collectivisation provoked the most widespread opposition, mass disobedience and open defiance that any Soviet leader ever faced between 1918 and 1991, the majority of peasants being prepared to slaughter their animals rather than surrender them to collective ownership. Because of this, the number of livestock suffered a catastrophic decline between 1928 and 1934: cattle from 70 to 48 million, sheep and goats from 146 to 42 million and pigs from 26 to 9 million. Even the 'dekulakisation' squads of the NKVD received rough treatment from the peasants, often in contrast to the fear and respect shown towards the NKVD in the towns. Ironically, the peasantry as a whole were probably more resistant to new ideas in the Soviet Union – where these were officially sponsored – than in the late-Tsarist period – when they had been advanced by revolutionaries. This rather changes the more traditional perspective that the peasants were essentially conservative.

The other class that was fully integral to both regimes was the industrial proletariat. Traditionally seen as the sector least reconcilable to the Tsarist regime, they were drawn to the radical Marxist parties and became progressively alienated as a result of the brutal suppression of the final stages of the Moscow and St Petersburg uprisings in December 1905 and the Lena goldfields massacre in 1912. Here there is some overlap between traditional Western and official Soviet interpretations. Both maintain that an alienated working class were ready for influence by the Bolsheviks – either as a group that was manipulated by a strongly organised and ruthless revolutionary party or, according to the official Soviet view, by a movement representing their interests and offering a release from their exploitation. Within the Soviet system, the urban proletariat was always considered the key class. According to the traditional Western view they were increasingly exploited but were generally deprived of any effective means of articulating their suffering or grievances. The official Soviet view, by contrast, maintains that the regime met their aspirations and thrived on their support.

Again, there are challengeable assumptions here. In the first place, the proletariat needs to be seen as a diverse sector containing groups and individuals with differing aspirations. In Tsarist Russia some were won over by Tsarist measures, whether in the unofficial form of 'police socialism' practised by the *Okhrana*, or by the post-1905 reforms allowing trade unions, conceding a limited franchise and introducing national insurance. Of those who were not impressed by these changes, the majority preferred the non-violent and evolutionary strategy for change offered by the Mensheviks. The rest, it is true, did support the Bolsheviks – but these were in a minority until the summer of 1917. As for the Soviet regime, the automatic support of the urban proletariat could no more be guaranteed than that of the peasantry. Among the opponents of the Bolsheviks in the Civil War were some sections of the workforce who had seen their preferred party, the Mensheviks, denied the representation they had won in the Constituent Assembly. Similarly, the tactical retreat of the regime into the NEP had much to do with the Kronstadt Revolt of 1921 and by the open expression of discontent in the towns as well as the rural areas. During the 1930s there was extensive resentment shown towards the Stakhanovites, the official shock-workers, and the reintroduction of wage differentials by Stalin and his successors created different levels within the working class that viewed each other with mutual wariness and suspicion. During the period of the Terror, individuals and groups were even prepared to collaborate with the NKVD in denouncing each other. After 1953, when terror ceased to be a factor in policy, the focus of resentment switched to the standard of living. The attempts of Khrushchev, Brezhnev and Andropov to improve consumer goods was never fully successful, resulting in an urban population that hardly clamoured to save the Soviet Union from extinction in 1991. At the same time, Gorbachev's introduction of market principles through *perestroika* emphasised further the divisions with the working class, so that the increasing number of unemployed began to regret the passing of Communism and the emergence of the new economic methods of Yeltsin.

Another generalisation that can be challenged is that the proletariat were always led from above – whether by revolutionary parties during the Tsarist period or by the regime itself after 1917. Revisionist historians have shown that this was far from the case, and that the Bolsheviks were actually influenced as a revolutionary party by factory committees both before and during 1917. This argument could actually be taken further. One of the basic reasons for the introduction of War Communism in 1918 was to satisfy popular demands in the towns for increased workers' control over industrial enterprises and to force the peasantry to release the grain supplies they were hoarding in the expectation of receiving higher prices. War Communism was therefore propelled by an urban workforce that was becoming increasingly resentful of what they saw as the privileged status of their rural cousins.

The issue of class is therefore a complex one, involving different layers, attitudes and interpretations. In both regimes class was fundamentally an ideological issue, whether the purpose was to maintain it or eradicate it. At the same time, the economic and political structures of the regime were such that class provided the main channel for mobility and hence access to promotion and approval. In the Tsarist system this took place within an official class structure, and in the Soviet regime within one that gradually developed as a replacement. At the same time, both regimes were troubled by the impact of economic and political mobility on the official perception of class; the Tsars were concerned about the threat it seemed to pose to traditional hierarchies, while the Soviet leaders maintained their long-term commitment to revolutionary 'classlessness'. Unofficial mobility and ideological perceptions frequently interfered with each other and both regimes failed to realise that ideological perceptions were an obstacle to the economic advancement that they both craved.

Questions

1. Which regime experienced the greatest changes to class structures – Tsarist or Soviet?
2. 'What mattered most to people was the prospect of upward social mobility.' Did this apply as much in the Soviet Union as in Tsarist Russia?

SOURCES

1. ALEXANDER II AND THE ABOLITION OF SERFDOM

Source 1: Extracts from Alexander II's Edict of Emancipation, 1861.

We thus became convinced that the problem of improving the condition of serfs was a sacred inheritance bequeathed to Us by Our predecessors, a mission which, in the course of events, Divine Providence has called upon Us to fulfill.

We have begun this task by expressing Our confidence toward the Russian nobility, which has proven on so many occasions its devotion to the Throne, and its readiness to make sacrifices for the welfare of the country.

We have left to the nobles themselves, in accordance with their own wishes, the task of preparing proposals for the new organization of peasant life –

proposals that would limit their rights over the peasants, and the realization of which would inflict on them [the nobles] some material losses. ...

We also rely upon the zealous devotion of Our nobility, to whom We express Our gratitude and that of the entire country as well, for the unselfish support it has given to the realization of Our designs. Russia will not forget that the nobility, motivated by its respect for the dignity of man and its Christian love of its neighbour, has voluntarily renounced serfdom, and has laid the foundation of a new economic future for the peasants. ...

The examples of the generous concern of the nobles for the welfare of peasants, and the gratitude of the latter for that concern, give Us the hope that a mutual understanding will solve most of the difficulties, which in some cases will be inevitable during the application of general rules to the diverse conditions on some estates, and that thereby the transition from the old order to the new will be facilitated, and that in the future mutual confidence will be strengthened, and a good understanding and a unanimous tendency towards the general good will evolve.

To facilitate the realization of these agreements between the nobles and the peasants, by which the latter may acquire in full ownership their domicile and their land, the government will lend assistance, under special regulations, by means of loans or transfer of debts encumbering an estate. ...

And now We confidently expect that the freed serfs, on the eve of a new future which is opening to them, will appreciate and recognize the considerable sacrifices which the nobility has made on their behalf.

Source 2: Extract from *A History of the USSR*, published in 1948 during Stalin's regime and used as a textbook in Soviet schools and universities.

The abolition of serfdom was a turning point in Russia's history. The country's economy was becoming capitalistic. Industrial capitalism in Russia developed faster than it had before 1861, in spite of the existing vestiges of serfdom which retarded its progress. The state system of feudal tsarist Russia underwent a slow and steady process of bourgeois reformation. Herein lay the progressive significance of the reform of 1861. 'This was,' wrote Lenin, 'a step towards the transformation of Russia into a bourgeois monarchy.' But since the reform was carried cut by the serf-owners, they tried to retain as many of their privileges as possible. Robbed by the landlords, the peasants found themselves entangled in a new form of enslavement, that of economic thrall to the landlords.

Source 3: from M. S. Anderson, *The Ascendancy of Europe 1815–1914*, published in 1972.

The intricacies of the system by which, under the decree of 1861, the serf was to compensate his lord for the labour services and other rights lost by the latter, the areas of redemption payments which accumulated until they were written off after the 1905 revolutions, form the most labyrinthine social and administrative story of the nineteenth century. But with all its deep-seated weaknesses (above all the fact that over most of Russia the former serf had less land to till than he had had under the old agrarian regime) the grant of individual freedom and a minimum of civil rights to twenty million people previously in legal bondage was the greatest single liberating measure attempted in the whole modern history of Europe. It was unique. Russia's problems, in nature and in mere size, were quite unlike those of any other European state. But more than anything else done or attempted during the 1850s and 1860s it marks these decades as a period of constructive social change over much of the continent. Moreover it was followed in Russia by a series of new departures which came close to revolutionizing the national life, above all the reforms in local administration and the judicial system which followed in 1864 and the military reforms of a decade later. No European state during the nineteenth century attempted so much so quickly as Russia in these years. Though this great effort to enter fully the modern world was not sustained and in many ways a failure this should not blind us to its scope and to the force of its tragic drama.

Source 4: From Edward Acton, *Russia: The Tsarist and Soviet Legacy*, first published in 1986.

The Tsar's support for emancipation must be understood within the broader context of the State's role in a serf-based society. That role involved two primary and overriding responsibilities: to guarantee domestic and foreign security. The head of the Third Section had explicitly warned Nicholas that friction between serf and master constituted a time-bomb which threatened the whole Empire. Peasant disturbances grew ominously in number and intensity as each decade passed, and outbreaks were overwhelmingly concentrated on private estates. Confronted by noble resistance and alarmed by foreign upheaval, Nicholas had shelved the issue and committed himself to upholding the status quo at home and abroad. It was the catastrophe of the Crimean War which rendered this commitment untenable. Humiliated on her own doorstep, Russia's ability to influence Western affairs was sharply curtailed. The whole framework within which Nicholas had viewed the options before him broke down. Moreover, the war rudely brought home the military cost of social and economic backwardness. The Treasury had run up a huge deficit. Russian forces had been incomparably less well armed than those of Britain and France. Supply problems during the war made it seem madness to postpone further the steps necessary to improve communications and construct strategic railways. The correlation between serfdom and economic backwardness was now conventional wisdom, vague though the economic analysis on which it was based might be. The case for following the Western example of reducing the costly standing army by building a reserve of trained men became incontrovertible. Yet as long as serfdom remained, so did the objection that it was not safe to return hundreds of thousands of trained men to the countryside. Serfdom was becoming a dire threat to both domestic and/foreign security.

It is this conjuncture which explains why a State rooted in the social and economic dominance of the serf-owning nobility should have undertaken Emancipation. It also explains why the Tsar was able to secure the acquiescence of the nobility. The sense of urgency over the issue took time to spread. It was not at first shared by most serf-owners in the provinces, or indeed by most of the great landowners among senior officials. Individual noblemen had of course learned to their cost of both peasant fury and Russia's military decline. A minority, responding to a combination of moral conviction, economic incentive, frustration at the cost and difficulty of overcoming the inefficiency and petty insubordination of serf labour, and fear, might favour some form of Emancipation. But the vast majority preferred to live with the moral problem and forgo the reputed advantages of freely hired labour rather than contemplate the abolition of their traditional rights over their peasants. Yet should their own government, run by fellow noblemen and dedicated to their security, conclude that serfdom was too dangerous to perpetuate, they would bow to the inevitable. And it was this message which, haltingly, the Tsar and some of his ministers began to communicate.

Questions

1. Compare the views of Sources 1 and 2 on the role of the nobility in the emancipation of the serfs. (20)
2. Using all of Sources 1 to 4, and your own knowledge, comment on the view that the Alexander II's emancipation of the serfs was a 'turning point' in Russia's social development. (40)

Total (60)

2. THE MOTIVATION OF THE SOVIET WORKFORCE IN THE 1930S

Source 5: From Christopher Read, *The Making and Breaking of the Soviet System*, published in 2001.

Certainly there were enthusiasts for Soviet construction. Many, particularly younger, men and women were enlisted in its service. Every party initiative brought forth a flood of Komsomol volunteers. Among established workers, the picture has been controversial. Some scholars have detected extensive support for Stalinist objectives among workers from the time of the Five-Year Plan and have posited a kind of generational and class struggle within the working class between older, artisanal workers, often former Mensheviks, and trade unionists, who were sceptical of Bolshevik aims, and younger workers who had acquired the newer skilled and semi-skilled practices of mass, mechanised production in factories and mines. Others have portrayed a cowed and sceptical working class whose enthusiasm and support for Stalin were purely synthetic and tokenistic, the result of enforced obeisance to a resented system which they passively subverted through frequent job changes, absences and poor-quality workmanship. In this view, workers mainly tried to live out their lives as comfortably as possible against a background of planners' incompetence and lack of concern for individuals and for their personal lives. Even studies of the undoubted enthusiasts of the time – those who participated in the extraordinary Stakhanovite movement of massive norm-busting – are ambiguous. Genuine Stakhanovites seem to have been few and far between, and ordinary workers were more likely to hate them than to imitate them. By and large, material incentives (wages, bonuses, living standards) rather than moral incentives (socialist enthusiasm, patriotic construction) seem to have motivated most workers. One of the most detailed regional studies reveals a workforce at Magnitogorsk which showed only superficial support for regime goals and which lived its own life avoiding, as much as it could, the restrictions put on it by the authorities and ignoring its own contractual obligations.

Source 6: From an official Soviet publication produced by a committee of historians, *A Short History of Soviet Society*, published in 1971.

... the Communist Party, while organising the campaign for socialist emulation and encouraging millions of workers to participate in it, grew considerably when large numbers of the people's finest representatives decided to join. The building of socialism gathered momentum and many tasks which had once seemed quite unfeasible were now being accomplished.

Nowadays such bastions of industry as Magnitogorsk and Novokuznetsk, the industrial centres in the Urals and Siberia, are famous far beyond the confines of the Soviet Union. In 1929 there was not even a railway station at the site of present-day Magnitogorsk. All that stood there was an isolated railway coach, yet the name was familiar to people throughout the country. Posters telling the people that the Magnitogorsk construction project was awaiting them could be seen in countless towns and villages, and thousands of people responded to this challenge and set off to the Urals.

Yes, the beginnings were difficult, the bulk of the work had to be done by hand in the early stages. Tractors and lorries for construction work were few and far between. More often than not there was a shortage of ordinary horse-drawn carts, wheel-barrows and spades, padded jackets and tarpaulin mittens, and the construction workers had to live in temporary huts. ... Overfulfilment of norms, voluntary overtime and work on leisure days soon became firmly established traditions at this as at all the new construction sites.

The most conscientious and energetic workers infected even the most materially-minded of their fellows with their enthusiasm. When Party and Komsomol members used to get up in the middle of the night to help in some emergency, the others would follow their example. Indifference was impossible when those working at your side would go on to complete an urgent piece of work after an exhausting working day or spend their free time helping others to learn to read and write.

Source 7: From a detailed study by Sarah Davies on reactions within the Soviet Union to Stalin's rule, *Popular Opinion in Stalin's Russia; Terror, Propaganda and Dissent, 1934–1941*. Published in 1997, this shows that criticism of Stalin was widespread.

At the end of the 1920s, Stalin launched the Great Leap Forward, an economic revolution of unprecedented speed and magnitude. Although crash industrialisation brought workers certain benefits, such as virtually full employment, it also created enormous hardship. Despite a modest improvement in their living standards during the second five-year plan, the immediate priority for most workers in the 1930s was sheer survival. Unsurprisingly, economic questions featured more prominently than any other issue in popular opinion. ...

Workers were acutely aware of fluctuations in their standard of living, frequently comparing prices with wages. It was patently obvious to them whether their own economic situation was improving or deteriorating, and they were not deceived by official rhetoric about rising standards. The rhetoric simply highlighted the disparity between the fictitious 'good life' and their actual situation. Their personal experience of the Soviet economy, with its queues and deficits, led to criticism of the regime's refusal to address such issues publicly. Many of their comments reveal a belief that the state ought to be providing for workers as it claimed it was doing. Workers showed no hesitation in invoking the regime's own ideological claims: for example, they readily deployed the party's own rhetoric on workers' emancipation. When objections were voiced to Stakhanovism or to the labour decrees of 1938–40, it was often on the grounds that these measures were 'exploitative', and reminiscent of 'capitalism'.

Source 8: An extract from the official political account of the development of the USSR, *A Short History of the CPSU*, revised in 1970.

Soviet workers, like the Party, lived with one desire, that of fulfilling the five-year plan at all costs. The country was turned into a building site. Two mammoth metallurgical projects, the Magnitogorsk and Kuznetsk plants, were erected in the Urals and in Western Siberia. Coal-mines were built nearby. In the course of the five years these had to form another huge coal and metallurgical centre – in the East. There already was a base in the Donbas, in the South, where new factories were also built and the old ones modernised. A hydropower station, the world's largest at the time, was built on the Dnieper, in the Ukraine. The foundation of the first large-scale industries was laid in the Central Asian Soviet Republics that formerly had no factories at all.

The trade of builder became the most numerous and honourable in the country, and the foremost among the builders were Communists and members of the Komsomol. They went to uninhabited areas, carrying away with them hundreds of thousands of enthusiasts and creating and cementing collectives of young workers. The builders of the new projects were supported and provided with everything they needed by the entire people.

The Party foresaw difficulties in the mastering of new technologies and industries. Hundreds of higher and secondary technical schools were opened. To make it easier for workers to enter institutions of higher learning, special workers' faculties were opened at these institutions. ...

The breath-taking targets of the five-year plan released the energy of the masses. In Leningrad the workers advanced the slogan: "The five-year plan in four years!" The Party supported this patriotic initiative, and the emulation movement was joined by more than two-thirds of the workers of all the large factories in the country. It was emulation between teams, factory departments and enterprises. Communists set examples in labour. The socialist emulation movement was a new, unparalleled phenomenon.

Questions

1. Compare either Sources 5 and 6 or Sources 7 and 8 as evidence for the attitude of Soviet workers to the policy of industrialisation in the 1930s. (20)
2. 'The entire Soviet workforce considered that Stalin's Five-Year Plans were in their own best interest.' How far do Sources 5 to 8 and your own knowledge support this view? (40)

Total (60)

GLOSSARY OF TERMS

autocracy A style of rule based on the absolute power of the monarchy, claimed through hereditary lineage and untrammelled by limitations imposed by a legislature. It was claimed as the basis of their power by Alexander II, Alexander III and (although with more difficulty from 1906) Nicholas II. Autocracy was upheld as the only true form of government by Konstanin Pobedonostsev.

Bolsheviks Literally meaning 'majority', a section within the Social Democrats (RSDLP) who separated from the more moderate Mensheviks at the 1903 Congress held in Brussels and London. The dispute involved organisation and strategy, the Bolsheviks favouring limited party membership, centralised control and a conspiratorial strategy. Under the leadership of Lenin the Bolsheviks seized power in October 1917 and set up a Communist regime. The Bolsheviks were renamed the Communist Party of the Soviet Union (CPSU).

Cheka Extraordinary Commission for the Suppression of Counter Revolution, Speculation and Sabotage, this was established at the end of 1917 as a secret police force under the control of Felix Dzerzhinsky. It was ended in 1921 but later revived by Stalin in the form of the NKVD.

CIS Commonwealth of Independent States established in 1991 as a form of cooperation between the former republics of the USSR. It proved useful for the settlement of some disputes between the successor states but never became a real alternative to the Soviet Union.

classless society The final stage of economic and political development envisaged by Marx and Engels. All history was seen to be based on 'class conflict', which would eventually involve the overthrow of capitalism and the bourgeoisie. Following the revolution would be a temporary phase, the 'dictatorship of the proletariat', which would evolve into the 'classless society', the distinctive feature of which would be the withering of the coercive institutions of the state.

collectivisation A policy introduced by Stalin in 1928 to complete the abolition of private ownership of land. The new units were either *kolkhozy*, organised jointly by large groups of peasants, or *sovkhozy* (state farms), which were owned directly by the state.

Comecon The Council for Mutual Economic Assistance (also known as CMEA) was set up in 1949 by Stalin. This coordinated the economic planning of the eastern European states brought under Soviet control after 1945.

Constituent Assembly Promised by the Provisional Government but postponed because of Russia's involvement in the First World War, this was eventually convened by Lenin, who ordered elections in November 1917. When the Assembly was due to convene in January 1918 it was dissolved by Lenin. The stated reason was that the Constituent Assembly was inferior to the system of soviets that was also being established. The probable explanation, however, is that the Bolsheviks were in a minority as a result of the election, the largest single party being the Right SRs.

Constitutional Democrats (Kadets or Cadets) A party that was legalised in 1905–6 and adopted a programme based on liberal democracy. It aimed for full parliamentary sovereignty based on universal suffrage and full guarantees of civil rights. It played an important part in the 1917 Provisional Government but was eventually wiped out by the Bolsheviks between 1921 and 1922.

dekulakisation squads Detachments of the NKVD formed specifically to enforce the policy of collectivisation and to eliminate the *kulaks*, or wealthy peasantry.

'Developed Socialism' A term used by Brezhnev to denote an intermediate stage between the 'dictatorship of the proletariat' and the 'classless society'. It was a key theme in the 1977 Constitution of the USSR.

'dictatorship of the proletariat' A theoretical construction of Marx and Engels to describe the period immediately following the overthrow of capitalism. During this phase other classes would be eliminated in an economic sense, which would allow the eventual transition to a 'classless society'. The term was, however, taken literally by both Lenin and Stalin, who established a one-party system and institutions of coercion, such as the *Cheka* and NKVD.

Duma   Originally one of a series of elected town councils established by Alexander II in 1870. The term was also used for the elected chamber of the central legislature established by the Fundamental Laws in 1906.

GOKO   State Committee for Defence, this was the main institution of central government used by Stalin during the war with Nazi Germany (1941–5).

glasnost   Introduced by Gorbachev, it literally meant 'transparency' or 'openness'. It was a policy intended to allow greater criticism of officials and to loosen the hold of censorship. Gorbachev's belief was that greater freedom of thought and expression would help promote his economic objectives of *perestroika*.

Gosplan   State Planning Committee, which laid down the detailed targets to be achieved by the Five-Year Plans.

Greens   A term generally associated with those sections of the peasantry which resisted Bolshevik rule during the civil war 1919–21. It has also been used to describe the more specfiic opposition of non-Bolshevik revolutionary parties, especially the Socialist Revolutionaries.

Gulag   The administration for the labour camps in the Soviet Union, this was set up by Stalin during the purges and eventually abolished by Khrushchev.

KGB   The successor to Stalin's secret police (NKVD and NKGB), the KGB was set up in 1953. It was responsible for internal and external security, although stripped of some of the more extreme powers previously wielded by the NKVD. Some heads of the KGB were later heavily involved in politics: Andropov became Soviet leader in 1982, Kryuchkov was involved in the 1991 coup against Gorbachev, and Putin was elected President of the Russian Federation in 2000.

kolkhoz (plural *kolkhozy*)   Collective farms established by Stalin from 1928 onwards.

kulaks   Wealthier members of the Russian peasantry, who existed in both Tsarist Russia and the Soviet Union. The official policy of Stolypin had been to promote an upper layer of peasants who would be loyal to the Tsarist regime. During the Bolshevik period (1918–24) Lenin initially put pressure on the kulaks through a policy of War Communism, before reversing this from 1921 in his NEP. During the first half of the 1920s the *kulaks* therefore experienced a second period of relative prosperity. Stalin, however, saw them as 'class enemies' and they became the main target of the dekulakisation squads set up to enforce collective farming. Hundreds of thousands of *kulaks* were killed.

Left SRs A minority splinter-group within the SRs who went over to the Bolsheviks in 1917 and 1918.

Marxism-Leninism Eventually known as Communism, this was the means by which Lenin converted a theory that was initially aimed more at the developed industrial economies of western and central Europe to the conditions prevailing in late-Tsarist Russia. This is covered in detail in Chapter 1.

Marxists Followers of the ideas of Marx and Engels. The basic components of Marxism are an approach to history based on class conflict; a belief in the necessity to end capitalism; and a view of the future that involved moving, via the 'dictatorship of the proletariat', to the 'classless society'. Since Marx did not produce a practical strategy for achieving these changes, different approaches developed in Europe. These usually involved rivalry between evolutionary and revolutionary strategies. In Russia, for example, the original Marxist party was the Social Democrats or RSDLP. This split in 1903 between the moderate Mensheviks and the more radical Bolsheviks, who adapted Marxism to Russian conditions in the form of Marxism-Leninism.

Menshevik Internationalists A minority group within the Mensheviks who were more radical, emphasising the priority of international revolution. A key figure was Trotsky, who took a number of like-minded party members over to the Bolsheviks in 1917 and played an important part in the October Revolution. The Menshevik Internationalists eventually merged with the Bolsheviks.

Mensheviks The moderate group within the RSDLP, which believed in the gradual replacement of capitalism rather than its forcible overthrow. From 1903 onwards they followed a different strategy to the Bolsheviks, preferring evolution and open membership to revolution and conspiracy. In 1917 they collaborated with the Provisional Government and, for the most part, opposed the Bolshevik seizure of power in October 1917, the closure of the Constituent Assembly in January 1918 and the policy of War Communism. The Mensheviks had been eliminated by 1922.

NEP New Economic Policy, introduced by the Bolsheviks in 1921 to end the previous policy of War Communism. The NEP allowed the return of many industries to private ownership and trusts and enabled the peasantry to sell their produce subject to state licence. After Lenin's death in 1924 there was a major controversy over its future, which ended in Stalin's decision to introduce Five-Year Plans and collectivisation.

NKVD People's Commissariat for Internal Affairs – Stalin's secret police force, which was largely responsible for implementing the Terror and for the running of the *Gulag* system.

October Manifesto Issued by Nicholas II in October 1905, this promised basic liberties and the summoning of a representative assembly.

Octobrists A moderate conservative party that took its stand on the principles of the October Manifesto. At first it strongly supported the Tsar but, from 1915, some Octobrists joined the Progressive Bloc in the Duma to protest against the exercise of arbitrary despotism.

perestroika Meaning 'reform' or 'reconstruction', this was introduced by Gorbachev in 1985 to restructure the Soviet economy after two decades of stagnation. Based on the principles of greater competition and private enterprise, *perestroika* was a direct challenge to the bureaucracy of the Stalin and Brezhnev eras. It was accompanied by *glasnost*, which allowed for more explicit criticism of government policies – especially of earlier periods.

'Permanent Revolution' The programme followed by Trotsky after Lenin's death and opposed to 'Socialism in One Country'. It emphasised the need to (1) spread revolution to other countries and (2) end the NEP, collectivise agriculture and accelerate industrialisation.

pogroms Violent persecutions, especially of Jews in Tsarist Russia.

Politburo Political Bureau, set up within the Central Committee of the Communist Party in 1919. It consisted of the top ten Bolsheviks. Stalin tended to bypass it in favour of smaller groups and the GOKO. Between 1942 and 1964 it was known as the Presidium, but Khrushchev's successors reverted to the original name.

Populists One of the two main branches of Russian revolutionaries, the other being Marxist. The Populists were supported mainly by the peasantry and followed a programme based on rural socialism. They divided into different groups that included moderate organisations such as Black Partition and radicals such as *Narodnaya Volya* (People's Will). In 1900 the Populist groups united to form the SRs.

Presidium   see Politburo

Procurator General of the Holy Synod   The Russian government minister responsible for the Russian Orthodox Church, the clerical head being the patriarch. This could be a highly influential post in the hands of a man with strong conservative views and a determination to control the country's progressive influences. Pobedonostsev, who served as procurator general under Alexander III and Nicholas II, was just such a person.

Progressive Bloc   A group of members in the Duma comprising mainly Constitutional Democrats and Octobrists who, from 1915, tried to put pressure on the Tsar to consult the Duma and abandon his attempted return to autocratic rule under the impetus of the First World War. From the Progressive Bloc eventually emerged those who put pressure on the Tsar to abdicate in March 1917 and who set up the Provisional Government in his place.

Provisional Government   Established by the Provisional Committee of the Duma to replace the Tsar after his enforced abdication on 15 March, 1917. Initially a coalition under Prince Lvov, its political base narrowed under Kerensky and it was overthrown in October 1917 in the Bolshevik revolution.

radical   In its political context, a term meaning extreme – either on the left or on the right. Hence communists usually started as radical socialists or Marxists.

reaction   In political terms, a strong resistance to progressive change. In the period of this book, reactionary policies were most common in Tsarist Russia, especially under Alexander III (1881–94).

reactive   Frequently confused with 'reaction' but actually quite different, 'reactive' means responding to a situation and hence being influenced by it. An example of a 'reactive' measure was the October Manifesto, issued by Nicholas II to try to end the 1905 Revolution.

Red Guard   see Reds

Reds   (Bolsheviks)   The term 'Reds' was used most frequently during the Russian Civil War to distinguish the Bolsheviks from the counter-revolutionary Whites. The Revolutionary Military Committee, which seized power in October 1917, organised the Red Guard, which, in turn was expanded into the Red Army. Red is, of course, the colour of both revolution and the working class.

RSFSR   The Russian Soviet Federated Socialist Republic set up by Lenin's 1918 Constitution, it was intended to be a federal system representing the different regions of Russia. The later constitutions of 1924 and 1936 added the USSR to include the other, non-Russian, parts of the former Russian Empire. The RSFSR (or Russia) therefore came to exist as one of the republics of the USSR (or Soviet Union). After the break-up of the USSR in 1991, the RSFSR separated from the other republics and became the Russian Federation.

Russification   The imposition of Russian influence on the national and ethnic minorities within both the Russian Empire and the USSR. Examples included the attempts to destroy the autonomy of Poland after the 1863 Polish Revolt, and to eradicate the Ukrainian language and culture. Soviet Russification occurred primarily under Stalin as a means of ensuring central political and cultural control from Moscow; Russification tended in practice to cancel out the theoretical concessions provided by federalism.

Social Democrats   The Russian Social Democratic Labour Party was formed in 1898 as an amalgamation of various Marxist groups. Its early leaders were Lenin, Martov and Plekhanov (formerly a Populist). The Social Democrats effectively split into Bolsheviks and Mensheviks in 1903, although the name remained until the final division at the Prague Congress in 1912.

'Socialism in One Country'   The strategy pursued after 1924 by the Stalin faction – in opposition to Trotsky's focus on 'Permanent Revolution'.

'Socialist Realism'   Stalin's official approach to cultural themes, this emphasised the need for art, literature and music to serve the 'higher' objectives of the Communist ideology and the Soviet state. It was also an integral part of his personality cult, as much of the work of the period resorted to his glorification.

Socialist Revolutionaries (SRs)   The unification of the various Populist groups in Russia in 1900. The SRs were the main revolutionary alternative to the Marxists and, because their main support came from the peasantry, they were more widely popular than either the Bolsheviks or the Mensheviks. In 1917 the Right SRs (for example, Kerensky) supported the Provisional Government, while the Left SRs broke away and collaborated with the Bolsheviks. The Right SRs formed the main revolutionary opposition to the Bolsheviks in 1919. They won the election to the Constituent Assembly and, when Lenin closed the Assembly in January 1918, the SRs established their own government to the east of the area controlled by the Bolsheviks. The Right SRs were eventually eliminated by the Bolsheviks in 1921 and 1922.

soviets Workers' and soldiers' councils, first established during the 1905 Revolution and revived in March 1917. They were eventually seen by the Bolsheviks as an alternative to Western liberal representative institutions and, following the dissolution of the Constituent Assembly by Lenin in January 1918, the soviets became the sole representative legislatures. They existed at many levels and were reformed in the constitutions of 1918, 1924 and 1936.

SSR Soviet Socialist Republic, a title given to a full member of the Union of Soviet Socialist Republics (USSR). An example was the Ukrainian SSR.

Stakhanovites 'Shock-workers' in Stalinist Russia who were renowned for exceeding their production quotas and were therefore made an official model for the rest of the workforce. Needless to say, they were not popular.

totalitarian A style of dictatorship that aimed at establishing total control over the population by activating the masses through propaganda and indoctrination. It was based on a one-party system and a head of state who was usually the focus of a personality cult. The overall system was based on an ideology.

USSR Union of Soviet Socialist Republics, established by treaty between the republics in 1922 and based on the Constitution of 1924. It was steadily expanded to include 15 SSRs – the RSFSR, Estonia, Latvia, Lithuania, Belarus, Moldova, Ukraine, Georgia, Azerbaijan, Armenia, Uzbekistan, Kazakhstan, Tajikistan, Kirgistan and Turkmenistan. The USSR eventually collapsed in 1991, each of the republics becoming fully independent. An attempt to replace the USSR with a looser CIS failed.

ukaze Imperial edict issued by the Tsar without reference to any legislature.

War Communism An attempt by Lenin's regime in 1918 to accelerate the growth of state control over industry and to requisition the grain of the peasantry. It resulted in starvation and widespread opposition, in the face of which the Bolsheviks had to backtrack into the NEP in 1921.

Whites Opposition to the Reds in the Russian Civil War. They aimed to overthrow the regime established in the October Revolution, although they were not agreed on what should replace it.

zemstvo (plural *zemstva*) Elected local government set up by Alexander II in 1864.

NOTES

1. IDEOLOGIES AND REGIMES

1 Quoted by R. F. Byrnes, 'Russian Conservative Thought Before the Revolution', in T. G. Stavrou (ed.), *Russia Under the Last Tsar* (Minneapolis, 1969), p. 49.

2 B. Dmytryshyn (ed.), *Imperial Russia. A Source Book, 1700–1917* (Hinsdale, Illinois, 1974), p. 339.

3 Dmytryshyn, p. 341.

4 Dmytryshyn, p. 347.

5 V. I. Lenin, *Karl Marx* (London, 1914).

6 F. Engels, *Anti-Duhring*, extract in C. Wright Mills, *The Marxists* (Harmondsworth, 1963).

7 Marx and Engels, *Manifesto of the Communist Party* (Moscow, 1848), I.

8 V. I. Lenin: *Karl Marx* (London, 1914).

9 *V.I. Lenin: A Short Biography*, trans. B. Isaacs (Moscow, 1968), p. 50.

10 Trotsky: 'The Permanent Revolution', extract in C. Wright Mills.

11 Khrushchev, Speech to the Twentieth Congress, 25 February 1956, extract in C. Wright Mills.

12 Quoted in A. E. Adams: 'Pobedonostsev: Preserve the Autocratic System and its Institutions', in A. E. Adams (ed.), *Imperial Russia after 1861* (Boston, 1965), p. 46.

13 Extracts from Stalin's 1951 writings on language, quoted in T. H. Rigby (ed.), *Stalin* (Englewood Cliffs, New Jersey, 1966).

14 Adams, p. 44.

Source 1: Quoted in A. E. Adams: 'Pobedonostsev: Preserve the Autocratic System and its Institutions', in A. E. Adams (ed.), *Imperial Russia after 1861* (Heath, Boston, 1965), p. 44.

Source 2: Alexander Blok, *Revenge*, details unknown.

Source 3: B. Dmytryshyn (ed.), *Imperial Russia. A Source Book, 1700–1917* (Dryden Press, Hinsdale, Illinois, 1974), Document 14: The Fundamental Laws of Imperial Russia.

Source 4: Quoted in M. T. Florinsky, *The End of the Russian Empire* (Collier, New York, 1961), pp. 63 and 68.

Source 5: Quoted in R. Kowalski (ed.), *The Russian Revolution 1917–21* (London, Routledge, 1997), pp. 25–6.

Source 6: Marx and Engels, *Manifesto of the Communist Party* (Moscow, 1848), p. 51.

Source 7: *V.I. Lenin: A Short Biography*, trans. B. Isaacs (Progress Publishers, Moscow, 1968), p. 50.

Source 8: T. H. Rigby (ed.), *Stalin* (Englewood Cliffs, New Jersey, 1966)

Source 9: Rigby, pp. 118–25

2. CONSTITUTIONAL DEVELOPMENT

1 Quoted in A. Ascher (ed.), *The Mensheviks in the Russian Revolution* (London, 1976), Introduction.

2 A. Mendel, 'On Interpreting the Fate of Imperial Russia', in T. G. Stavrou (ed.), *Russia under the Last Tsar* (Minneapolis, 1969).

3 B. Dmytryshyn (ed.), *Imperial Russia: A Source Book, 1700–1917* (Hinsdale, Illinois, 1974), Source 49, p. 387.

4 Dmytryshyn, p. 367.

5 Dmytryshyn, p. 388.

6 Dmytryshyn, p. 387.

7 R. Kowalski (ed.), *The Russian Revolution 1917–21* (London, 1997), Document 7.7, p. 109.

8 R. Sakwa, *The Rise and Fall of the Soviet Union 1917–1991* (London, 1999), Document 5.22, p. 208.

9 S. N. Silverman (ed.) *Lenin* (New York, 1966), ch. 2.

10 J. L. H. Keep (ed.), *The Debate on Soviet Power: Minutes of the All-Russian Central Executive Committee of Soviets* (Oxford, 1979), Introduction.

11 Kowalski, p. 109.

12 Dmytryshyn, pp. 387–8.

13 M. T. Florinsky, *Russia: A Short History* (London, 1969), pp. 487–8.

Source 1: B. Dmytryshyn (ed.), *Imperial Russia: A Source Book, 1700–1917* (Dryden Press, Hinsdale, Illinois, 1974), Source 49.

Source 2: *A Short History of the Communist Party of the Soviet Union* (Progress Publishers, Moscow, 1970), pp. 61, 65.

Source 3: A. Chubarov, *The Fragile Empire* (Continuum, New York and London, 2001), p. 153.

Source 4: M. T. Florinsky, *The End of the Russian Empire* (Collier, New York, 1961), p.18.

Source 5: V. I. Lenin, *Collected Works* (Progress Publishers, Moscow, 1960–70), vol. 25, p. 88.

Source 6: R. Sakwa, *The Rise and Fall of the Soviet Union 1917–1991* (Routledge, London, 1999), Document 3.2.

Source 7: Sakwa, Document 9.5.

Source 8: Sakwa, Document 10.19.

Source 9: Sakwa, Document 10.21.

3. POLITICAL PARTIES

1 *A Short History of the Communist Party of the Soviet Union* (Moscow, 1957), p. 238.

2 *A Short History of the CPSU*, p. 239.

3 *A Short History of the CPSU*, p. 245.

4 *A Short History of the CPSU*, p. 248.

5 *A Short History of the CPSU*, p. 252.

Source 1: B. Dmytryshyn (ed.), *Imperial Russia: A Source Book, 1700–1917* (Dryden Press, Hinsdale, Illinois, 1974), Source 50, p. 396.

Source 2: Dmytryshyn, Source 50, pp. 406–7.

Source 3: Dmytryshyn, Source 50, p. 412.

Source 4: M. McCauley, *Octobrists to Bolsheviks: Imperial Russia 1905–1917* (Arnold, London, 1984), pp. 71–2.

Source 5: *A Short History of the Communist Party of the Soviet Union* (Progress Publishers, Moscow, 1970), pp. 230–71.

Source 6: *The Anti-Stalin Campaign and International Communism. A Selection of Documents* (ed.) by the Russian Institute, Columbia University (New York, 1956), extracts from pp. 9–85.

Source 7: D. Volkogonov, *The Rise and Fall of the Soviet Empire* (HarperCollins, London, 1999), p. 84.

Source 8: G. Gill, *Stalinism* (Macmillan, Basingstoke, 1998), p. 42.

4. REPRESSION AND TERROR

1 C. Andrew and O. Gordievsky, *KGB. The Inside Story* (New York, 1990), p. 19.

2 O. Figes, *A People's Tragedy. The Russian Revolution 1891–1924* (London, 1996), p. 646.

3 R. Hingley, *The Russian Secret Police* (London, 1970), p. 102.

4 H. Rogger, *Russia in the Age of Modernisation and Revolution*, p. 55. Quoted in Hingley, p. 87.

6 J. Daly, 'The Security Police and Politics in Late Imperial Russia', in A. Geifman (ed.), *Russia under the Last Tsar. Opposition and Subversion 1894–1917* (Oxford, 1999), p. 226.

7 E. Acton, *Russia: The Tsarist and Soviet Legacy* (Harlow, 1995), p. 96.

8 R. Conquest, *The Great Terror* (London, 1990 edition), p. 79.

9 J. Arch Getty, 'The Politics of Stalinism' in A. Nove (ed.), *The Stalin Phenomenon* (London, 1993), p. 132.

10 R. G. Suny, 'Stalin and His Stalinism: Power and Authority in the Soviet Union, 1930–1953', in I. Kershaw and M. Lewin (eds), *Stalinism and Nazism: Dictatorships in Comparison* (Cambridge, 1997).

11 S. Tormey, *Making Sense of Tyranny: Interpretations of Totalitarianism* (Manchester, 1995).

Source 1: Quoted in L. I. Strakhovsky, 'Stolypin: To Save the Crown Suppress Revolutionaries and Create Individual Peasant Landowners', in A. E. Adams (ed.) *Imperial Russia After 1861: Peaceful Modernization or Revolution?* (Heath, Boston, 1965), p. 60.

Source 2: Quoted in L. I. Strakhovsky, p. 46.

Source 3: O. Figes, *A People's Tragedy. The Russian Revolution 1891–1924* (Jonathan Cape, London, 1996), p. 174.

Source 4: S. Phillips, *Lenin and the Russian Revolution* (Heinemann, Oxford, 2000), p. 45.

Source 5: *The Anti-Stalin Campaign and International Communism. A Selection of Documents* (ed.) by the Russian Institute, Columbia University (New York, 1956), extracts from pp. 9–85.

Source 6: R. C. Tucker, *The Soviet Political Mind: Studies in Stalinism and Post-Stalin Change*, originally published in

1957, quoted in T. H. Rigby (ed.) *Stalin* (Englewood Cliffs, New Jersey, 1966), from pp. 153–64. (Frederick A. Praeger, New York)

Source 7: J. Arch Getty and Roberta T. Manning, 'Introduction', in J. Arch Getty and Roberta T. Manning (eds) *Stalinist Terror: New Perspectives* (Cambridge University Press, Cambridge, 1993), p. 1.

Source 8: R. W. Thurston, *Life and Terror in Stalin's Russia* (New Haven, Connecticut, and London, 1996), p. 227.

5. THE NATIONALITIES

1 G. Hosking, *Russia: People and Empire 1552–1917* (Cambridge, Massachusetts, 1997), p. 375.

2 D. Lane, *Politics and Society in the USSR* (London, 1970), p. 396.

3 V. Lelchuk, Y. Polyakov and A. Protopopov (eds), *A Short History of Soviet Society* (Moscow, 1971), p. 116.

4 B. Dmytryshyn (ed.), *Imperial Russia: A Source Book, 1700–1917* (Hinsdale, Illinois, 1974), Source 49.

5 A. L. Unger, *Constitutional Development in the USSR: A Guide to the Soviet Constitutions* (London, 1981).

6 R. Sakwa, *The Rise and Fall of the Soviet Union 1917–1991* (London, 1999), Document 5.22, p. 208.

7 Dmytryshyn, Source 49.

8 See D. Lieven, 'Russia as Empire' in G. Hosking and R. Service (eds) *Reinterpreting Russia* (London, 1999).

9 Lane, p. 429.

Source 1: Adapted from R. Kowalski (ed.), *The Russian Revolution 1917–21* (Routledge, London, 1997), Document 11.1, p. 167.

Source 2: M. Lynch, *Reaction and Revolutions: Russia 1881–1924* (Hodder & Stoughton, London, 1994), p. 19.

Source 3: R. G. Suny 'Nationality Policies' in E. Acton, V. Cherniaev and W. G. Rosenberg (eds) *Critical Companion to the Russian Revolution* (Arnold, London, 1997), p. 660.

Source 4a: *A Short History of the Communist Party of the Soviet Union* (Progress Publishers, Moscow, 1970).

Source 4b: V. Lelchuk, Y. Polyakov and A. Protopopov (eds), *A Short History of Soviet Society* (Progress Publishers, Moscow, 1971), p. 116.

Source 5a: E. Acton, *Russia: The Tsarist and Soviet Legacy* (Longman, Harlow, 1995), p. 106.

Source 5b: Acton, pp. 194–5.

Source 6: S. Fitzpatrick, 'Constructing Stalinism: Changing Western and Soviet Perspectives', in A. Nave (ed.) *The Stalin Phenomenon* (Weidenfeld and Nicholson, London, 1993) p. 93.

6. THE IMPACT OF WAR

1 T. H. Rigby (ed.), *Stalin* (Englewood Cliffs, New Jersey, 1966), p. 48.

Source 1: R. Kowalski, *The Russian Revolution 1917–1921* (Routledge, London, 1917), p. 18.

Source 2: Leon Trotsky, *My Life* (1971). Extracts quoted in N. Rothnie, *Documents and Debates: The Russian Revolution* (Macmillan, London, 1990), p. 25.

Source 3: A. F. Kerensky, *The Road to the Tragedy* (Hutchinson, London, 1935), pp. 61–3.

Source 4: Michael Karpovich, *Imperial Russia 1801–1917* (Holt, Rinehart, and Winston, New York, 1932).

Source 5: E. Acton, *Rethinking the Russian Revolution* (Arnold, London, 1990), p. 82.

Source 6: N. A. Voznesensky, *The Economy of the USSR During World War II* (Public Affairs Press, Washington, 1948).

Source 7: V. Lelchuk, Y. Polyakov and A. Protopopov (eds), *A Short History of Soviet Society* (Progress Publishers, Moscow, 1971), p. 306.

Source 8: *The Memoirs of the R. Hon. Sir Anthony Eden K.G., P.C., M.C.: Full Circle* (Cassell and Company Ltd, London, 1960), p. 50.

Source 9: M. Lynch, *Stalin and Khrushchev: The USSR, 1924–64* (Hodder & Stoughton, London, 1990), p. 46.

Source 10: C. Ward, *Stalin's Russia* (Arnold, London, 1993), pp. 187–8.

7. AGRICULTURE AND INDUSTRY

1 R. Hutchings, *Soviet Economic Development* (Oxford, 1967), Ch. 6.

2 R. Sakwa, *The Rise and Fall of the Soviet Union 1917–1991* (London, 1999), p. 427.

3 A. M. Pankratova (ed.), *A History of the USSR* (Moscow, 1948), vol. II, p. 249.

Source 1: Michael Lynch, *Reaction and Revolutions: Russia 1881–1921* (Hodder & Stoughton, London, 1992) p. 24.

Source 2: John F. Hutchinson, *Late Imperial Russia 1890–1917* (Longman, Harlow, 1999), p. 21.

Source 3: A. M. Pankratova (ed.), *A History of the USSR* (Foreign Languages Publishing House, Moscow, 1948), vol. II, pp. 277–8.

Source 4: Edward Acton, *Russia: The Tsarist and Soviet Legacy* (Longman, Harlow, 1986), p. 94.

Source 5: Quoted in Robert Wolfson, *Years of Change* (Arnold, London, 1978), p. 346.

Source 6: Wolfson, p. 347.

Source 7: V. Lelchuk, Y. Polyakov, A. Protopopov (eds), *A Short History of the Communist Party of the Soviet Union* (Progress Publishers, Moscow, 1970), p. 215.

Source 8: Alec Nove, *An Economic History of the USSR* (Penguin, Harmondsworth, 1986), p.187.

8. SOCIAL CLASSES

1 R. F. Byrnes, *Russian Conservative Thought Before the Revolution* in T. G. Stavrov (ed.), *Russia Under the Last Tsar* (Minneapolis, 1969), p. 64.

Source 1: B. Dmytryshyn (ed.), *Imperial Russia: A Source Book, 1700–1917* (Dryden Press, Hinsdale, Illinois, 1974), Source 33.

Source 2: *A History of the USSR* (Foreign Languages Publishing House, Moscow, 1948), pp. 217–18.

Source 3: M. S. Anderson, *The Ascendancy of Europe 1815–1914* (Longman, London, 1972), p.119.

Source 4: E. Acton, *Russia: The Tsarist and Soviet Legacy* (Longman, Harlow, 1995), pp. 68–9.

Source 5: Christopher Read, *The Making and Breaking of the Soviet System* (Palgrave, Houndmills, 2001), p. 112.

Source 6: V. Lelchuk, Y. Polyakov, A. Protopopov (eds), *A Short History of Soviet Society* (Progress Publishers, Moscow, 1971), pp. 156–8.

Source 7: Sarah Davies, *Popular Opinion in Stalin's Russia; Terror, Propaganda and Dissent, 1934–1941* (Cambridge University Press, Cambridge, 1997), p. 23.

Source 8: B. N. Ponamarev and others: *A Short History of the Communist Party of the Soviet Union* (Progress Publishers, Moscow, 1970).

SELECT BIBLIOGRAPHY

A book of this nature could well recommend a vast range of sources. But this would undermine its purpose, which is to provide a synoptic view of an extended period. This means that the bibliography is particularly 'select'.

PRIMARY SOURCES

Recommended individual works are: V. I. Lenin, *Collected Works* (Moscow, 1960–70); and A. F. Kerensky, *The Road to the Tragedy* (London, 1935). Selections of primary sources can be found in J. Laver (ed.), *The USSR 1945–1990* (London, 1991); B. Dmytryshyn (ed.), *Imperial Russia. A Source Book, 1700–1917* (Hinsdale, Illinois, 1974); S. Phillips, *Lenin and the Russian Revolution* (Oxford, 2000); R. Kowalski, *The Russian Revolution 1917–1921* (London, 1997); N. Rothnie, *Documents and Debates: The Russian Revolution* (London, 1990); and R. Sakwa, *The Rise and Fall of the Soviet Union 1917–1991* (London, 1999).

GENERAL HISTORIES OF RUSSIA, COVERING BOTH PERIODS

A particularly useful synoptic survey is Edward Acton: *Tsarist and Soviet Legacy* (Harlow, 2nd edn, 1995). More conventional surveys of the extended period include M. T. Florinsky, *Russia – A Short History* (London, 1969).

HISTORIES OF TSARIST RUSSIA

A straightforward introduction is provided by M. Lynch, *Reaction and Revolutions: Russia 1881–1924* (London, 1994). More advanced works include Michael Karpovich, *Imperial Russia 1801–1917* (London, 1932); N. V. Riasanovsky, *A History of Russia* (Oxford, 1984); R. Pipes, *Russia Under the Old Regime* (New York, 1974); M. T. Florinsky, *The End of the Russian Empire* (New York, 1961); J. F. Hutchinson, *Late Imperial Russia 1890–1917* (Harlow, 1999); O. Figes, *A People's Tragedy. The Russian Revolution 1891–1924* (London, 1996); P. Waldrom, *The End of Imperial Russia 1855–1917* (Basingstoke, 1997); D. Offord, *Nineteenth-Century Russia – Opposition to Autocracy* (Harlow, 1999); and M. McCauley, *Octobrists to Bolsheviks: Imperial Russia 1905–1917* (London, 1984). The Tsarist secret police are covered in J. Daly: 'The Security Police and Politics in Late Imperial Russia', in A. Geifman (ed.), *Russia under the Last Tsar. Opposition and Subversion 1894–1917* (Oxford, 1999). An economic focus is provided by H. Rogger, *Russia in the Age of Modernisation and Revolution* (London, 1983); O. Crisp, *Studies in the Russian Economy before 1914* (London, 1976); and P. Gatrell, *The Tsarist Economy 1850–1917* (London, 1986), in A. E. Adams (ed.), *Imperial Russia After 1861: Peaceful Modernization or Revolution?* (Englewood Cliffs, New Jersey, 1965).

HISTORIES OF SOVIET RUSSIA AND THE SOVIET UNION

M. Lynch, *Reaction and Revolutions: Russia 1881–1924* (London, 1994) provides a brief introduction, continued by M. Lynch, *Stalin and Khrushchev: The USSR, 1924–64* (London, 1990). More interpretative is C. Read, *The Making and Breaking of the Soviet System* (Basingstoke, 2001). Specific aspects of Soviet history are covered in A. L. Unger, *Constitutional Development in the USSR: A Guide to the Soviet Constitutions* (London, 1981); T. H. Rigby (ed.), *Stalin* (Englewood Cliffs, New Jersey, 1966); C. Andrew and O. Gordievsky, *KGB. The Inside Story* (New York, 1990); R. Hingley, *The Russian Secret Police* (London, 1970); and R. Conquest, *The Great Terror* (London, 1990 edition). Soviet perspectives on the period are provided by V. Lelchuk, Y. Polyakov and A. Protopopov (eds), *A Short History of Soviet Society* (Moscow, 1971); *V.I. Lenin: A Short Biography*, trans. B. Isaacs (Moscow, 1968); *A Short History of the Communist Party of the Soviet Union* (Moscow, 1970); and *A History of the USSR* (Moscow, 1948).

REINTERPRETATIONS

Major reappraisals are given in G. Hosking and R. Service (eds), *Reinterpreting Russia* (London, 1999); A. Chubarov, *The Fragile Empire* (New York and London, 2001); E. Acton, *Rethinking the Russian Revolution* (London, 1990); C. Ward, *Stalin's Russia* (London, 1983); D. Volkogonov, *The Rise and Fall of the Soviet Empire* (London, 1999); G. Gill, *Stalinism* (Basingstoke, 1998); I. Kershaw and M. Lewin (eds), *Stalinism and Nazism: Dictatorships in Comparison* (Cambridge, 1997); and R. W. Thurston, *Life and Terror in Stalin's Russia* (New Haven, Connecticut, and London, 1996).

INDEX

Florinsky, M.T. (historian) 47
  The End of the Russian Empire
  44
France 39, 57, 109, 110, 119, 131,
  132, 140, 150, 185
Franco 137
Franco-Russian alliance 132
French Revolution 2
1906 Fundamental Laws xvi, xix, 11,
  16, 17, 19, 22, 27, 28, 31, 32,
  37, 38, 40, **42**, 43, 47, 58, 63,
  64, 72, 106, 126, 192

Genghis Khan 110
Georgia xix, xx, 93, 94, 97, 98, 102,
  103, 104, 108, 109, 110, 112,
  113, 114, 197
Germany 6, 7, 8, 39, 54, 57, 69, 80,
  82, 94, 95, 105, 109, 110,
  113, 119, 121, 122, 123, 128,
  130, 131, 132, 133, 134, 140,
  142, 144, 145, 146, 147, 148,
  150, 153, 166, 192
Gestapo 80
Gill, G (historian)
  Stalinism 70
glasnost 14, 29, 35, 38, 40, 55,
  76, 85, 95, 122, 179, 192,
  194
GOKO *see State Committee for
  Defence*
Gorbachev xiv, xv, xviii, xix, xxii, 9,
  14, 27, 29, 35, 36, 38, 40, 41,
  55, 56, 65, 76, 85, 95, 98,
  107, 109, 122, 128, 142, 151,
  154, 163, 174, 175, 179, 182,
  192, 194
Goremykin 31, 72
Gosplan 34, 82, 122, 147, 148
GPU *see State Political
  Administration*
Great Depression 152
Great Leap Forward 188
Great Patriotic War xx, xxi, 61, 69,
  109, 132, 133, 136
Greens 60, 103, 122, 172, 180
GTU *see Main Prison
  Administration*
Gulag system xviii, 74, 76, 80,
  81, 82, 142, 148, 174, 192,
  194

Hingley, R (historian) 77
A History of the USSR 156, 184
Hitler 121, 131, 132
Hungary xx, 8, 128, 129
Hutchings, R (historian) 147
Hutchinson, J.F. (historian)
  Late Imperial Russia 1890–1917
  155

Ignatiev 106
India 150
industrialisation 82, 110, 133, 140,
  141, 143, 144, 145, 147, 157,
  169
Industrialists 52,
intelligentsia 49, 80, 89
Iron Curtain 128
Italy 57, 128
Ivan the Terrible xviii, 2, 13, 71, 75,
  86, 87, 90, 109, 177

Japan 3, 89, 150, 153
Jews 87, 99, 101–102, 105, 106,
  113, 115, 194

Kadets *see Constitutional
  Democrats*
Kamenev xvi, 13, 55, 60, 63, 74
Karakozov 99
Karpovich, M (historian)
  Imperial Russia 1801–1917 135
Katkov 101
Kazakhstan xx, 34, 93, 95, 96, 97,
  98, 103, 104, 107, 110, 112,
  197
Kerensky xiv, 33, 73, 120, 195, 196
KGB *see Committee for State
  Security*
Kirghizia xx, 93, 95, 96, 97, 104
Kirgistan xx, 97, 98, 107, 110, 113,
  197
Kokovtsev 31
kolkhozy 151, 158, 162, 191, 192
Kolyma 82
Korea 105, 150
Kornilov 103
Kosygin 63
Kronstadt Revolt 77, 85, 182
Krushchev xiv, xvii, 8, 9, 13, 18, 24,
  29, 35, 40, 41, 55, 60, 61, 63,
  69, 76, 80, 85, 87, 89, 95,